Microsoft® SQL Server® 2008 MDX Step by Step

Bryan C. Smith

C. Ryan Clay, Hitachi Consulting

Published with the authorization of Microsoft Corporation by:
O'Reilly Media, Inc.
1005 Gravenstein Highway North
Sebastopol, California 95472

Library of Congress Control Number: 2008940528

Printed and bound in the United States of America.

1 2 3 4 5 6 7 8 9 LSI 4 3 2 1 0 9

Distributed in Canada by H.B. Fenn and Company Ltd.

A CIP catalogue record for this book is available from the British Library.

Microsoft Press books are available through booksellers and distributors worldwide. For further information about international editions, contact your local Microsoft Corporation office or contact Microsoft Press International directly at fax (425) 936-7329. Visit our Web site at *www.microsoft.com/mspress*. Send comments to *mspinput@microsoft.com*.

Microsoft, Microsoft Press, Excel, SQL Server, Visual Basic, Visual Studio, Windows, and Windows Vista are either registered trademarks or trademarks of the Microsoft group of companies. Other product and company names mentioned herein may be the trademarks of their respective owners.

The example companies, organizations, products, domain names, e-mail addresses, logos, people, places, and events depicted herein are fictitious. No association with any real company, organization, product, domain name, e-mail address, logo, person, place, or event is intended or should be inferred.

This book expresses the author's views and opinions. The information contained in this book is provided without any express, statutory, or implied warranties. Neither the authors, Microsoft Corporation, nor its resellers, or distributors will be held liable for any damages caused or alleged to be caused either directly or indirectly by this book.

Acquisitions Editor: Ken Jones
Developmental Editor: Sally Stickney
Project Editor: Maureen Zimmerman
Editorial Production: S4Carlisle Publishing Services
Technical Reviewer: Todd Meister; Technical Review services provided by Content Master, a member of CM Group, Ltd.
Cover: Tom Draper Design

Body Part No. X14-72187
ISBN: 978-0-735-62618-8
[LSI]

[2012-03-16]

To my wife, Haruka, for her love, support,
and—above all else—patience

—Bryan C. Smith

To the three most important women in my life,
who have shaped who I am today:
my mother, Phyllis; my wife, Donna;
and my daughter, Emma Kay

—C. Ryan Clay

Contents at a Glance

List of Figures

List of Tables

Table of Contents

What do you think of this book? We want to hear from you!

Microsoft is interested in hearing your feedback so we can continually improve our books and learning resources for you. To participate in a brief online survey, please visit:

www.microsoft.com/learning/booksurvey/

What do you think of this book? We want to hear from you!

Microsoft is interested in hearing your feedback so we can continually improve our books and learning resources for you. To participate in a brief online survey, please visit:

www.microsoft.com/learning/booksurvey/

Acknowledgements

The book you hold in your hands represents the thought, time, and energy of so many more people than those listed on the front cover. We owe all these folks our gratitude for their support without which this book would not be possible.

To identify just a few of these people, we'd like to thank the folks at Microsoft Press for the opportunity to work with them to address what we both perceive as an important need in the Microsoft Business Intelligence community. To Maureen Zimmerman and her team, thank you for your help in crafting this book and keeping things on track. To Ken Jones, thank you for championing us at all the right times.

Thanks also goes out to the Microsoft SQL Server Analysis Services product team for serving as a sounding board early on in the development process. Your encouragement helped us find our voice.

At Hitachi Consulting, we're grateful for the support of Lance Baldwin and Paul Turley who helped us get the ball rolling on this effort and provided continued support throughout the development process. To Eric Winton, Ryan Trout, and Drew Naukam, thank you for your patience while we focused our energy in this direction. To Hilary Feier and Scott Cameron, thank you for your support at critical junctures in this process. To Eric Noack, Reggie Nitcher, Jon Moore, Andrew Alexander, and Bryan Martin, thank you for your feedback and encouragement on the critical chapters of this book. Finally, a big thank you goes out to Reed Jacobson, whose MDX course provided the inspiration for this book and whose feedback was critical in shaping our content.

Last, but by no means least, we'd like to thank our families who have quietly sacrificed alongside us as this book was brought into being. We could not have done this without you and promise we will not do this again (for a little while, at least).

Bryan C. Smith

C. Ryan Clay

Introduction

Microsoft SQL Server Analysis Services is a powerful tool for Business Intelligence. Many organizations, both large and small, have adopted it to provide secure, high-performance access to complex analytics.

MDX is the language used by Analysis Services for data access. Proficiency with this language is essential to the realization of your Analysis Services databases' full potential. The innovative and elegant model underlying the MDX language makes it a very powerful but at the same time challenging tool for data analysis. In this book, we address this model head-on and then guide you through various functions and applications of the MDX language.

Who This Book Is For

This book has been written based on our own experiences as well as those of numerous clients and students. From these, we believe there are a few prerequisites to effectively learning the MDX language.

First, you must have basic familiarity with the concepts of dimensional modeling and data warehousing. If you do not have this knowledge, the overall purpose of Analysis Services and the MDX language will be lost.

Second, you must have basic familiarity with Analysis Services. You do not necessarily have to be a cube designer, but it does help to have worked with Analysis Services enough to be comfortable with its objects and terminology. If you are relatively new to Analysis Services, we recommend that you review *Microsoft SQL Server 2008 Analysis Services Step by Step* by Scott Cameron (Microsoft Press, 2009) before proceeding with this book.

Finally, you must be able put aside the traditional notions of data access you may have become familiar with. Some of the folks whom we've seen struggle the most with MDX have been some of the most talented users of more traditional languages such as SQL. MDX requires you to think about data very differently.

What This Book Is About

This book is about the core concepts and basic applications of MDX; it is not an exhaustive text. Instead, it is intended as a primer for those relatively new to the language. Through the discussions and exercises presented in each chapter you will be introduced to core concepts and applications. This will provide you with a solid foundation for continued learning in real-world scenarios.

This book is divided into three sections, each building on the one before it. We strongly encourage you to read these sections in sequence to ensure that you fully grasp later concepts and techniques.

Part I, "MDX Fundamentals," teaches you the fundamentals of the MDX language and the primary query development tool you use throughout this book.

Chapter 1, "Welcome to MDX," presents MDX as a means to deliver business value. This chapter is critical to establishing the concepts and vocabulary we employ throughout this book.

Chapter 2, "Using the MDX Query Editor," introduces you to the practical aspects of constructing and executing an MDX query using the MDX Query Editor.

Chapter 3, "Understanding Tuples," presents the concept of tuples. Understanding tuples is key to the successful use of the MDX language.

Chapter 4, "Working with Sets," expands the concept of tuples to include sets. With knowledge of tuples and sets, the MDX *SELECT* statement is explored.

Chapter 5, "Working with Expressions," introduces MDX expressions. Using calculated members, you explore expressions as a means for deriving values through Analysis Services.

Part II, "MDX Functions," builds upon the foundation established in Part I to explore the more frequently used MDX functions.

Chapter 6, "Building Complex Sets," guides you through the assembly of complex sets using a variety of MDX functions. Building just the right set is critical to retrieving the data you need from your cubes.

Chapter 7, "Performing Aggregation," explains the appropriate use of the MDX aggregation functions. Thoughtful application of these functions provides access to insightful metrics.

Chapter 8, "Navigating Hierarchies," explores the positioning of members in hierarchies and how this can be exploited using the navigation functions.

Chapter 9, "Working with Time," introduces you to the time-based MDX functions, through which critical business metrics can be derived.

Part III, "MDX Applications," uses concepts and functions explored in Parts I and II to implement three basic applications of the MDX language.

Chapter 10, "Enhancing the Cube," explores the enhancement of the MDX script through which calculated members and named sets can be incorporated into the definition of a cube.

Chapter 11, "Implementing Dynamic Security," presents a few approaches to implementing identity-driven, dynamic dimension data and cell-level security in your cube.

Chapter 12, "Building Reports," guides you through the process of developing MDX-driven reports in Reporting Services, Microsoft's enterprise reporting solution.

Conventions and Features in This Book

This book uses conventions designed to make information easily accessible. Before you start, read the following list, which explains conventions and helpful features within the book.

Conventions

- Each chapter contains multiple exercises demonstrating concepts and functionality. Each is presented as a series of numbered steps (1, 2, and so on) which you should follow in sequence to complete the exercise.

- Notes labeled "Note" provide additional information or alternative methods for completing a step successfully.

- Notes labeled "Important" alert you to information you need to be aware of before continuing.

- Most exercises demonstrate concepts of the MDX language through the use of an MDX *SELECT* statement. As steps progress, the *SELECT* statement introduced in previous steps may be altered. These changes appear in **bold**.

Other Features

- Sidebars are used throughout the book to provide important information related to an exercise or a topic. Sidebars might contain background information, supplemental content, or design tips or alternatives. Sidebars are also used to introduce topics supporting exercises.

- Each chapter ends with a Quick Reference section. The Quick Reference section contains quick reminders of how to perform the tasks you learned in the chapter.

System Requirements

You'll need a computer with the following hardware and software to complete the exercises in this book:

- Microsoft Windows Vista Home Premium edition, Windows Vista Business edition, Windows Vista Enterprise edition, or Windows Vista Ultimate edition

- Microsoft SQL Server 2008 Developer edition or Microsoft SQL Server 2008 Evaluation edition with Analysis Services, Database Engine Services (including Full-Text Search), Business Intelligence Development Studio, Client Tools Connectivity, and Management Tools installed

- CD-ROM or DVD-ROM drive to read the companion CD

- 150 MB free space for sample databases and companion content

In addition to these requirements, you should be able to log on directly to this computer with administrative rights. In addition to operation-level administrative rights, you should have full administrative rights in the SQL Server Database Engine and Analysis Services instances. Without these rights, you will not be able to install the sample databases or complete exercises in some chapters.

Samples

This book's companion CD contains database samples against which you will perform the chapters' exercises. MDX, SQL, and project code samples are also provided for you to verify your work. Instructions provided in the following sections will guide you through the installation of the companion CD's content to a local drive on your computer. This content is placed under the following path:

> *<Drive>:\Microsoft Press\MDX SBS*

The MDX, SQL, and project code samples are provided under the Samples subfolder whereas database samples are provided under the Setup subfolder. Additional instructions are provided to make the sample databases operational.

Before attempting to complete the provided instructions, please verify your computer meets the hardware and software requirements and you have the required access described in the preceding section, "System Requirements."

> **Digital Content for Digital Book Readers:** If you bought a digital-only edition of this book, you can enjoy select content from the print edition's companion CD.
> Visit **http://go.microsoft.com/fwlink/?LinkId=139491** to get your downloadable content. This content is always up-to-date and available to all readers.

Installing the Samples

Install the companion CD content

1. Insert the book's companion CD in your computer's CD-ROM drive. A menu screen will appear. If AutoPlay is not enabled, run StartCD.exe at the root of the CD to display a start menu.

2. From the start menu, click Install Samples.

3. Follow the instructions that appear, selecting the drive to which the samples will be installed. These are installed to the following location on that drive:

   <Drive>:\Microsoft Press\MDX SBS

Attach the SQL Server database

1. On the Microsoft Windows task bar, click the Start button.

2. From the Start Menu, select All Programs and then Microsoft SQL Server 2008 to expose the SQL Server Management Studio shortcut.

3. Click the SQL Server Management Studio shortcut to launch the application.

   If this is the first time you have run Management Studio, you may see a dialog box indicating the application is being configured for its first use. This process may take a few minutes to complete before the application is then fully launched.

   Once fully launched, Management Studio presents the Connect To Server dialog box. If you are launching Management Studio for the first time on your machine, the dialog appears as shown below. If this is not the first time, selections and entries may differ.

4. In the Server Type field, verify Database Engine is selected.

5. In the Server Name field, type the name of your SQL Server instance. If you are connecting to a local default instance, you can simply enter **LOCALHOST** for the instance name.

6. Click Connect to establish a connection to SQL Server.

7. Once connected, use the File menu to select Open and then File, launching the Open File dialog box.

8. Using the Open File dialog box, navigate to the following folder installed in previous steps:

   <Drive>:\Microsoft Press\MDX SBS\Setup\SQL Server

9. Select the attach_db.sql file and click OK to open it.

10. If needed, modify the drive letter assigned to the sample database's .mdf file in the script. By default, the script assumes this file is on the C: drive in the following location:

    C:\Microsoft Press\MDX SBS\Setup\SQL Server\MdxStepByStep.mdf

11. With the drive letter modified as needed, select Execute from the Query menu to execute the script.

12. Review the messages provided to confirm the database was successfully attached to SQL Server.

13. From the File menu, select Close to close Management Studio. Select either Yes or No if prompted to save changes to the attach_db.sql file.

Restore the Analysis Services database

1. Launch SQL Server Management Studio as you did in the previous steps.

2. In the Connect To Server dialog box, select Analysis Services for the Server Type field and enter the name of your Analysis Services instance in the Server Name field. If you are connecting to a local default instance, you can simply enter **LOCALHOST** for the instance name.

3. Click Connect to establish a connection to Analysis Services.

4. Once connected, use the File menu to select Open and then File, launching the Open File dialog box.

5. Using the Open File dialog box, navigate to the following folder installed in previous steps:

   <Drive>:\Microsoft Press\MDX SBS\Setup\Analysis Services

6. Select the restore_db.xmla file and click OK to open it.

7. If needed, modify the drive letter assigned to the sample database's .abf file in the script. By default, the script assumes this file is on the C: drive in the following location:

   C:\Microsoft Press\MDX SBS\Setup\Analysis Services\MdxStepByStep.abf

8. With the drive letter modified as needed, select Execute from the Query menu to execute the script.

9. Review the messages provided to confirm the database was successfully attached to Analysis Services.

10. From the File menu, select Close to close Management Studio. Select either Yes or No if prompted to save changes to the restore_db.xmla.

Uninstalling the Samples

Drop the Analysis Services database

1. Launch SQL Server Management Studio and connect to Analysis Services as described in the steps for restoring the Analysis Services database.

2. Once connected, select Open and then File from the File menu.

3. Using the Open File dialog box, navigate to the following folder installed in previous steps:

    <Drive>:\Microsoft Press\MDX SBS\Setup\Analysis Services

4. Select the drop_db.xmla file and click OK to open it.

5. Select Execute from the Query menu to execute the script.

6. Review the messages provided to confirm the database was successfully dropped from Analysis Services.

7. From the File menu, select Close to close Management Studio.

Detach the SQL Server database

1. Launch SQL Server Management Studio and connect to SQL Server as described in the steps for attaching the SQL Server database.

2. Once connected, select Open and then File from the File menu.

3. Using the Open File dialog box, navigate to the following folder installed in previous steps:

    <Drive>:\Microsoft Press\MDX SBS\Setup\SQL Server

4. Select the detach_db.sql file and click OK to open it.

5. Select Execute from the Query menu to execute the script.

6. Review the messages provided to confirm the database was successfully detached from SQL Server.

7. From the File menu, select Close to close Management Studio.

Remove the companion CD content

1. From your computer's Control Panel, open Add or Remove Programs.

2. From the list of Currently Installed Programs, select Microsoft SQL Server 2008 MDX Step by Step.

3. Click Remove.

 Important If you have not detached or dropped the sample SQL Server database, you may be prevented from completing these steps.

4. Follow the instructions that appear to remove the samples.

Find Additional Content Online

As new or updated material becomes available that complements your book, it will be posted online on the Microsoft Press Online Developer Tools Web site. The type of material you might find includes updates to book content, articles, links to companion content, errata, sample chapters, and more. This Web site is available at *http://www.microsoft.com/learning/books/online/developer,* and is updated periodically.

Support for This Book

Every effort has been made to ensure the accuracy of this book and the contents of the companion CD. As corrections or changes are collected, they will be added to a Microsoft Knowledge Base article.

Microsoft Press provides support for books and companion CDs at the following Web site:

http://www.microsoft.com/learning/support/books/

Questions and Comments

If you have comments, questions, or ideas regarding the book or the companion CD, or questions that are not answered by visiting the preceding site, please send them to Microsoft Press via e-mail to:

mspinput@microsoft.com

Or via postal mail to:

Microsoft Press
Attn: *Microsoft SQL Server 2008 MDX Step by Step* Editor
One Microsoft Way
Redmond, WA 98052-6399

Please note that Microsoft software product support is not offered through the above addresses.

Part I
MDX Fundamentals

Chapter 1
Welcome to MDX

After completing this chapter, you will be able to:

- Explain the role of Analysis Services within the business intelligence landscape
- Explain the role of MDX within Analysis Services

MDX is the language used to interact with data in Microsoft SQL Server Analysis Services cubes. It is a versatile and powerful language but one that requires you to approach data in a whole new way. This is the primary challenge to the successful use of the MDX language, one we assist you in addressing in Part I of this book.

This chapter serves as a relatively gentle introduction to the MDX language and familiarizes you with its role in the Microsoft business intelligence landscape. This chapter also serves as a check for you, the reader, to determine whether you have the familiarity with Analysis Services needed to successfully explore the concepts in this book. If the material presented in this chapter is largely unfamiliar to you, you are strongly encouraged to pick up a copy of *Microsoft SQL Server 2008 Analysis Services Step by Step* by Scott Cameron (Microsoft Press, 2009) before continuing.

The Business Intelligence Landscape

A business's data is one of its most critical assets. Transactions are recorded with data. Events are triggered and activities proceed, each leaving data in its wake. Data surrounds and flows from all aspects of a business's operations.

Access to a business's data can provide incredible insight into its operations. Through data analysis, problems can be detected and new opportunities can be identified. The potential value obtained through analysis is immeasurable.

However, this value can only be realized when data is made accessible in a form conducive to analysis. And although that exact form is debatable, many businesses have moved toward the use of data warehouses to meet their analytical needs.

The data warehouse exists as a layer in a larger system, referred to here as the business intelligence environment. A conceptual illustration of a business intelligence environment is provided in Figure 1-1.

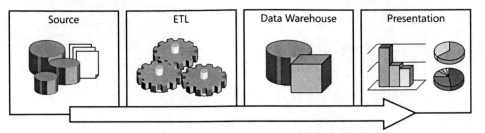

FIGURE 1-1 A conceptual illustration of a business intelligence environment

The business intelligence environment is divided into four discrete layers:

- **The Source layer** consists of the operational data sources and any supplementary data sources containing data of interest for the purposes of analysis.

- **The Extraction, Transformation, and Loading or ETL layer** is responsible for extracting, cleansing, and integrating data from the Source layer before it is published to the Data Warehouse layer.

- **The Data Warehouse layer** serves as the persistent, secured store of data ready for business analysis.

- **The Presentation layer** provides users interfaces for interacting with data in the Data Warehouse layer. The Presentation layer is often not monolithic but instead consists of a variety of tools, each supporting the different needs of the varied end-user population.

Welcome to Adventure Works Cycles!

To help demonstrate concepts and features within the Microsoft SQL Server product suite, Microsoft makes use of a series of sample databases and applications centered on the fictional company Adventure Works Cycles.

Adventure Works Cycles, or Adventure Works for short, is a multinational manufacturer of bicycles and related components, clothing, and accessories. Operational and data warehouse databases for Adventure Works are available for download from the Codeplex Web site at *http://www.codeplex.com* (search term: AdventureWorks). You are strongly encouraged to obtain copies of these databases for the exploration of various topics related to the SQL Server product suite.

For the purposes of this book, you will make use of databases derived from the Adventure Works DW (data warehouse) samples. These databases, the ones provided with this book, are employed to ensure that the results presented here match those returned to your screen when you perform the exercises. These databases also greatly simplify the structure of the Adventure Works DW database samples so that you can more easily focus on critical concepts. Instructions for the installation of the book's sample databases are provided in the book's Introduction.

The Dimensional Model

The Data Warehouse layer is the heart of the business intelligence environment. In this layer, data from across the enterprise is presented as a unified whole and in a manner focused more on business processes and less on the source systems from which the data originates. The dimensional model has been widely embraced as the data model of choice within the Data Warehouse layer.

Within the dimensional model, business processes and events are presented as *facts*. Measurements associated with these facts, known as *fact measures*, provide a means of evaluating the represented business process or event.

To illustrate this concept, consider the fictional company Adventure Works Cycles, described in the sidebar "Welcome to Adventure Works Cycles!" One critical business event within this company is the sale of products to resellers, which are the businesses focused on selling various products to customers like you and me.

In the dimensional model for this business, there is a Reseller Sales fact. This fact contains various fact measures allowing the analyst to evaluate sales. These facts include sales amount and order quantity in addition to many other sales-related measurements, as illustrated in Figure 1-2.

FIGURE 1-2 The Reseller Sales fact

Facts and their fact measures are of little value without their associated descriptive details. These details, referred to as *attributes*, provide the means by which facts are *sliced* (filtered) and *diced* (grouped). Attributes are organized in dimensions with closely related attributes residing in the same dimension.

Continuing with our example, attributes related to the Reseller Sales fact include the product sold, the product subcategory and category with which those products are related, the reseller to whom the product was sold, the date the product was sold, the employee credited with the sale, and many, many others. Those attributes related to the product sold form the Product dimension. Similarly, those attributes related to the order date form the Order Date dimension. These two dimensions are illustrated in Figure 1-3. Still other attributes form other dimensions in the dimensional model.

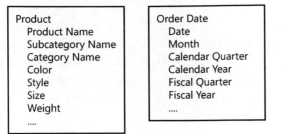

FIGURE 1-3 The Product and Date dimensions

Drawing a fact and its related dimensions produces a star-like diagram. This is illustrated in Figure 1-4 for the Reseller Sales fact and its related dimensions, a few of which we've just described. Because of this pattern, many people refer to dimensional models as *star-schemas* with the combination of a fact table with its associated dimensions referred to as *stars*.

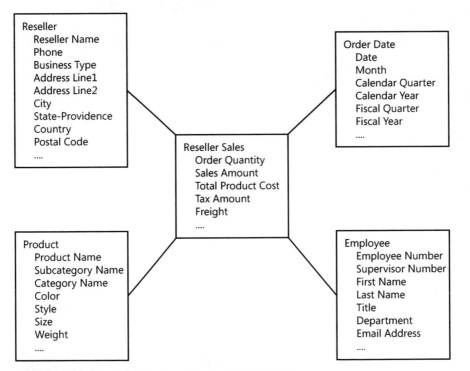

FIGURE 1-4 The Reseller Sales fact and associated dimensions

Stars, facts, and their associated dimensions, do not exist in isolation within the dimensional model. Just as various processes and events are interconnected within the business, so are facts in the dimensional model. Shared, or *conforming*, dimensions provide the linkage between facts and enable cross-fact analysis.

To illustrate this, consider another critical business event: the setting of quarterly sales quotas for various employees. These target values are captured in a Sales Quota fact with a single fact measure, Sales Quota. Associated with this fact are the dimensions Employee and Date, though the relationship to the Date dimension is at the quarterly level.

The Date and Employee dimensions in this model are conforming dimensions, as illustrated in Figure 1-5. By exploiting these shared dimensions, we can calculate cross-fact values such as actual-to-target sales ratios.

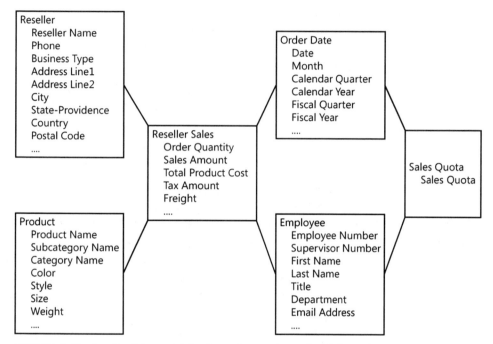

FIGURE 1-5 The Reseller Sales and Sales Quota facts and associated dimensions

> **Note** This has been a very high-level overview of dimensional modeling. If you are not familiar with these concepts, you are strongly encouraged to seek out additional materials on this topic.

Implementing the Dimensional Model

The dimensional model, as described in the preceding section, is a logical model. To house data, the logical model must be physically implemented. This is done using both relational and multidimensional database technologies.

The Relational Data Warehouse

Using a relational database platform, such as Microsoft SQL Server 2008 Database Engine Services, the dimensional model is implemented as a collection of tables. Dimensions are translated into *dimension tables* with columns housing attribute values. Likewise, facts are implemented as *fact tables* with columns housing fact measure values. Foreign keys within the fact tables record the relationships between facts and dimensions. Collectively, these objects form the *relational data warehouse*.

The relational data warehouse is ideally suited for the storage of data at the lowest level of granularity. The availability of such fine-grained data supports data maintenance, validation, and the flexible combination of data for specific forms of analysis. The relational data warehouse is a critical component of the Data Warehouse layer.

That said, the relational data warehouse is not ideal for every form of analysis. Although relational database technologies are perfectly capable of performing aggregations, aggregate values must be calculated in real time from individual fact table records. Modifications to the model to support the storage of precalculated aggregate values can minimize the performance impact but add complexity that impacts the model's accessibility.

Furthermore, semi-additive and non-additive aggregations may be challenging to support within a relational database. Consider a fact table recording daily exchange rates, as might be required in the data warehouse for a multinational company such as Adventure Works Cycles. You may wish to take the last published exchange rate or an average of exchange rates for a given period but require these values be determined over periods of varying duration. These values, the last exchange rate or the average exchange rate, can certainly be calculated in a relational database, but not as easily as more traditional, additive aggregations such as summations and counts.

Finally, dimensions contain related attributes. Though dimension tables keep related attributes in close proximity to one another, the exact nature of the relationships between the attributes of a dimension—such as the roll-up of product subcategories into categories—is not explicitly recorded in the star-schema (without implementing what is known as a snowflake schema, which is typically discouraged). The lack of explicit relationships between the attributes of a dimension creates an opportunity for the inappropriate combination of attribute values, which can be detrimental to effective analysis.

The Multidimensional Data Warehouse

Multidimensional database technologies, such as Microsoft SQL Server 2008 Analysis Services, are designed to address these issues through the transparent storage of preaggregated values, native support for complex aggregations, and the maintenance of relationship metadata.

Within Analysis Services, the dimensional model is presented as an object referred to as a *cube*. Within the cube, facts are translated into *measure groups*. Measure groups contain one or more *measures*, corresponding to fact measures in the dimensional model.

Through the cube, dimensions are presented as *cube dimensions*. Relationships between the measure groups and cube dimensions are maintained as metadata within the cube and are automatically employed as users interact with it.

> **Note** Starting with the next chapter, cube dimensions will simply be referred to as *dimensions*. Although the distinction between cube dimensions and (database-level) dimensions in Analysis Services is critical in the context of cube design, the distinction is typically not an issue in MDX development. With all data access through the cube, MDX developers interact almost exclusively with cube dimensions.

Within a cube dimension, attributes are presented as either *attribute-hierarchies* or *properties*. An attribute is presented as an attribute-hierarchy when the attribute is intended to be used to slice and dice the data. When an attribute is intended to provide supplemental information or to be used for simply filtering other attributes, it is best employed as a property.

An attribute-hierarchy is typically implemented as a two-level hierarchy. The bottom (*leaf*) level of the hierarchy contains a distinct listing of the individual values (members) of the attribute. The top level of the hierarchy contains a single member, the *(All) member*, which represents the combination of all the members in the level below it. Figure 1-6 illustrates this concept for the Category attribute-hierarchy for the product category attribute described in the logical dimensional model.

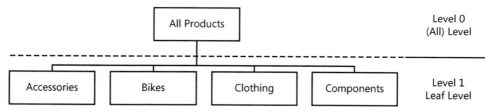

FIGURE 1-6 The members of the Category attribute-hierarchy

Relationships between attributes within a dimension are explicitly defined. As with the relationships between measure groups and cube dimensions, this information is maintained within the multidimensional database and automatically employed as users interact with the cube. The key benefit is to prevent the invalid association of members from related attributes. This is critical because users frequently wish to see a value associated with the members of one attribute broken down by the members of another, related attribute in what is referred to as a *drill-down* operation. A good example is the drill-down of a Category member (Bikes, for example) into its related Subcategory members (Mountain Bikes, Road Bikes, and Touring Bikes, for example).

This practice is so commonplace that Analysis Services allows a predefined collection of attribute-hierarchies (from within a given dimension) to be presented as a multilevel hierarchy referred to as a *user-hierarchy*.

Each attribute-hierarchy associated with a user-hierarchy is assigned to a level. Relationships between the attribute-hierarchies, as previously discussed, preserve the integrity of the data, allowing users to drill down from a parent member of one level into its related child members on another even though the levels derive from different attribute-hierarchies within a dimension.

To further illustrate this concept, consider the Product Categories user-hierarchy depicted in Figure 1-7. This user-hierarchy defines a drill-down path from Category to Subcategory and then to Product at the leaf level. With the exception of the (All) level, each of these levels is derived from the leaf-levels of different attribute-hierarchies in the dimension. For example, the Category level represents the leaf-level of the Category attribute-hierarchy. Relationships between these attribute-hierarchies, defined within the dimension, ensure that as a user drills-down from the Category level member Bikes he or she is presented with only the related Subcategory members Mountain Bikes, Road Bikes, and Touring Bikes.

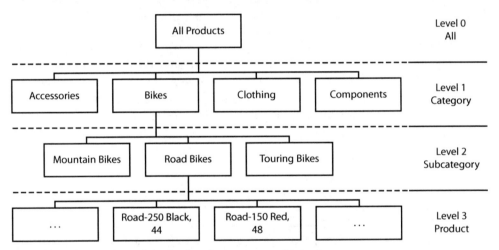

FIGURE 1-7 The members of the Product Categories user-hierarchy

It is critical to keep in mind that although user-hierarchies, such as the preceding one, are presented as separate objects within a cube dimension, they are nothing more than logical structures. References to members in user-hierarchies are ultimately resolved to attribute-hierarchy members.

With all these incredible features within the multidimensional database, it is easy to lose sight of the relationship between the multidimensional and relational data warehouses. Although the multidimensional data warehouse addresses many of the shortcomings of the relational data warehouse, it is dependent upon the relational data warehouse as the source of its data.

In addition, the added functionality of the multidimensional data warehouse comes at the price of additional complexity in accessing data. This is due to the use of a radically different data storage and retrieval mechanism within the multidimensional database. The multidimensional and relational data warehouses are best viewed as complementary implementations of the logical dimensional model, each serving different end-user needs.

The MDX Language

As mentioned earlier, Analysis Services employs a very different data storage and retrieval mechanism from that of a relational database technology. This mechanism is based on the concept of an n-dimensional space. In a relational database, such as SQL Server Database Engine Services, data storage and retrieval is based on set theory.

This fundamental difference between the two technologies requires you to handle interaction with the data in very different ways. With relational databases, the SQL language is used to assemble sets of data. With Analysis Services, the MDX language is used to assemble tuples identifying points of data within an n-dimensional space.

> **Note** You will explore the concept of tuples and n-dimensional space in detail in Chapter 3, "Understanding Tuples."

MDX stands for multidimensional expressions. As the name suggests, expressions are a critical part of the language. *Expressions* are units of MDX code that can be evaluated to return a value or object reference and are a critical part of various object properties and MDX statements. Expressions are covered in detail in Chapter 5, "Working with Expressions."

> **Note** Although the MDX language originated with the Microsoft product, MDX is not exclusive to Analysis Services. Instead, it is part of a vendor-neutral specification known as *XML for Analysis* (*XMLA*). As a result, you will find some flavor of MDX implemented within a number of other products, including SAP Netweaver BI, Hyperion Essbase, and SAS OLAP Server.

The MDX language also supports a number of statements. Of all the MDX statements, the *SELECT* statement, used to retrieve data from a cube, is the most useful for the purposes of learning MDX.

> **Note** We will focus on the *SELECT* statement throughout much of this book. However, unless you are a report or application developer, you will seldom need to construct a *SELECT* statement for purposes other than testing. Most presentation layer tools for interacting with cubes assemble *SELECT* statements for you behind the scenes, shielding you from the details.

To understand the *SELECT* statement, it is critical to understand a number of concepts, such as tuples (mentioned at the beginning of this section). The remainder of Part I gradually introduces you to these concepts and shows how they are exercised through the MDX *SELECT* statement to access data. Along the way, you will gain greater familiarity with the statement.

That said, it's important that you take a quick look at an MDX *SELECT* statement now, if for no other reason than to avoid a common trap encountered by individuals new to MDX.

The MDX *SELECT* statement in Listing 1-1 executes against the Step-by-Step cube in the multidimensional database accompanying this book. It returns combined Internet and reseller sales amounts for the calendar year 2004 for the top 10 products of calendar year 2003 based on combined sales during that year.

LISTING 1-1 MDX *SELECT* statement returning combined sales in calendar year 2004 for the top 10 products of 2003 based on combined sales in that year

```
WITH
MEMBER [Measures].[Total Sales Amount] AS
    ([Measures].[Internet Sales Amount]) + ([Measures].[Reseller Sales Amount])
SET [Top 10 Products of 2003] AS
    TOPCOUNT(
        {[Product].[Product]. [Product].Members},
        10,
        ([Measures].[Total Sales Amount], [Date].[Calendar Year].[CY 2003])
        )
SELECT
    {([Measures].[Total Sales Amount])} ON COLUMNS,
    {[Top 10 Products of 2003]} ON ROWS
FROM [Step-by-Step]
WHERE ([Date].[Calendar Year].[CY 2004])
```

In Listing 1-2, a SQL *SELECT* statement returning the same set of data from the relational database accompanying this book is presented.

LISTING 1-2 SQL *SELECT* statement returning combined sales in calendar year 2004 for the top 10 products of 2003 based on combined sales in that year

```
SELECT
    m.EnglishProductName, o.TotalSalesAmount
FROM dbo.DimProduct m
INNER JOIN ( -- TOP 10 PRODUCTS OF 2003
    SELECT TOP 10
        a.ProductKey, SUM(a.SalesAmount) AS TotalSalesAmount
    FROM (
        SELECT
            x.productkey, x.salesamount
        FROM dbo.FactInternetSales x
        INNER JOIN dbo.DimDate y
            ON x.OrderDateKey=y.DateKey
        WHERE y.CalendarYear=2003
        UNION ALL
        SELECT
            x.productkey, x.salesamount
        FROM dbo.FactResellerSales x
        INNER JOIN dbo.DimDate y
            ON x.OrderDateKey=y.DateKey
        WHERE y.CalendarYear=2003
    ) a
```

```
      GROUP BY a.ProductKey
      ORDER BY TotalSalesAmount DESC
      ) n
      ON m.ProductKey=n.ProductKey
  LEFT OUTER JOIN ( --PRODUCT SALES IN 2004
      SELECT
          a.ProductKey, SUM(a.SalesAmount) AS TotalSalesAmount
      FROM (
          SELECT
              x.productkey, x.salesamount
          FROM dbo.FactInternetSales x
          INNER JOIN dbo.DimDate y
              ON x.OrderDateKey=y.DateKey
          WHERE y.CalendarYear=2004
          UNION ALL
          SELECT
              x.productkey, x.salesamount
          FROM dbo.FactResellerSales x
          INNER JOIN dbo.DimDate y
              ON x.OrderDateKey=y.DateKey
          WHERE y.CalendarYear=2004
          ) a
      GROUP BY a.ProductKey
      ) o
      ON m.ProductKey=o.productkey
  ORDER BY n.TotalSalesAmount DESC
```

At this point it is not critical that you understand either of these queries. Instead, observe some of the similarities between the two statements. Both statements have a *SELECT* clause, a *FROM* clause, and a *WHERE* clause. And though it is not demonstrated, both return the same data.

Still, the sheer size difference between the two statements should impress upon you how differently each approaches data access. Look a little closer and you see even more differences, making it harder to believe that the two have any meaningful technical relationship.

The similarities between the MDX and SQL *SELECT* statements are completely superficial. Attempting to understand the MDX *SELECT* statement in the context of the SQL *SELECT* statement as you learn MDX will cause you to unnecessarily struggle with the language. We say this from our own experience and the experience of many others around us. For now, we strongly advise you to work under the notion that the MDX *SELECT* and the SQL *SELECT* statements are two means of accessing data associated with a dimensional model but beyond that share no meaningful similarities.

Chapter 1 Quick Reference

This	Means this
Dimensional model	The logical data model used within the Data Warehouse layer, which is focused more on business processes and less on the source systems from which the data originates. The dimensional model contains both dimension and fact information.
Dimension	Represents a set of related attributes that can be used to analyze data in the dimensional model. For example, the Adventure Works model contains a Product dimension, which enables analysis of data by product attributes.
Attribute	A descriptive characteristic included in a dimension. For example, in the Adventure Works model the Product dimension contains Product, Category, and Subcategory attributes.
Fact	Representation of a business process or event in the dimensional model. For example, the Adventure Works model contains the Reseller Sales fact, which represents the business process of product sales to resellers.
Fact measure	The measurement of a business process or event, which is typically numeric and additive by nature. For example, in the Adventure Works model the Reseller Sales Amount is the measurement of sales dollars to resellers.
Cube	Representation of the dimensional model in Analysis Services.
Attribute-hierarchy	A typically two-level representation of the data associated with an attribute with the top-level member, the (All) member representing all attribute values. For example, the (product) Category attribute in the Adventure Works model would be represented as a two-level attribute-hierarchy with the All Products member in the top-level representing all attribute members.
Property (Member Property)	Representation of an attribute in Analysis Services that is intended to provide supplemental information. For example, a product's List Price attribute may be presented as a property as this is not an attribute by which data would typically be sliced-and-diced.
User-hierarchy	A predefined collection of attribute-hierarchies from within a given dimension presented as a multilevel hierarchy. For example, the Product dimension's Category, Subcategory, and Product attributes might be organized into a single, multi-level user-hierarchy called Product Categories.
Member	The individual value that comprises a specific item in an attribute-hierarchy. For example, Bikes is a member of the Product dimension's Category attribute-hierarchy.
Measure group	Representation of a fact in Analysis Services.
Measure	Representation of a fact measure in Analysis Services.
Slice and dice	Process by which measures are filtered (sliced) and grouped (diced) by members of an attribute-hierarchy.
MDX (multidimensional expressions)	Tuple-based language used to interact with data in Analysis Services.

Chapter 2
Using the MDX Query Editor

After completing this chapter, you will be able to:

- Connect to Analysis Services using Microsoft SQL Server Management Studio
- Construct and execute an MDX query using the MDX Query Editor

The last chapter provided an overview of the business intelligence landscape and the role of Analysis Services. The MDX language was introduced as the language for accessing data from Analysis Services. In this chapter, you learn the practical aspects of constructing and executing an MDX query using the MDX Query Editor. With this information, you will be prepared for the subsequent chapters of this book.

The MDX Query Editor is a fairly simple tool for connecting to an Analysis Services database, browsing its cubes' contents, and assembling MDX queries. This tool is only accessible through the SQL Server Management Studio application.

For the purposes of this and subsequent chapters, it is expected that you have installed the sample database provided on this book's companion CD. If you have not already done so, please return to this book's Introduction for instructions on how to install this.

SQL Server Management Studio

SQL Server Management Studio, or Management Studio for short, is SQL Server's primary administrative console. Through this tool, you can connect to instances of SQL Server services—including Analysis Services—on both local and remote systems. Once connected, you can use Object Explorer to browse the objects in an Analysis Services instance.

Connect to an Analysis Services instance using SQL Server Management Studio

1. On the Microsoft Windows task bar, click the Start button.
2. From the Start Menu, select All Programs and then select Microsoft SQL Server 2008 to expose the SQL Server Management Studio shortcut.
3. Click the SQL Server Management Studio shortcut to launch the application.

   If this is the first time you have run Management Studio, you may see a dialog box indicating that the application is being configured for its first use. This process may take a few minutes to complete before the application is fully launched.

   Once fully launched, Management Studio presents the Connect To Server dialog box. If you are launching Management Studio for the first time on your computer, the dialog box appears as shown in the following screenshot. If this is not the first time, your screen will differ.

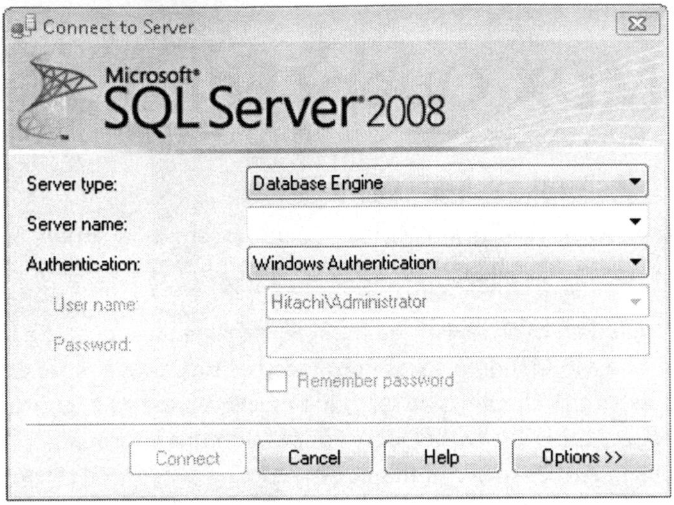

4. Use the Server Type drop-down list to select the Analysis Services server type.

5. In the Server Name field, type the name of the Analysis Services instance to which you installed the sample database accompanying this book.

   The Connect To Server dialog box should now look similar to what is shown in the following screenshot. In this image, a connection is being established to a default instance of Analysis Services on the local system. You can use the keyword *LOCALHOST* (or a simple period) to connect to this instance from Management Studio. If you are connecting to another instance, be certain to enter the appropriate information.

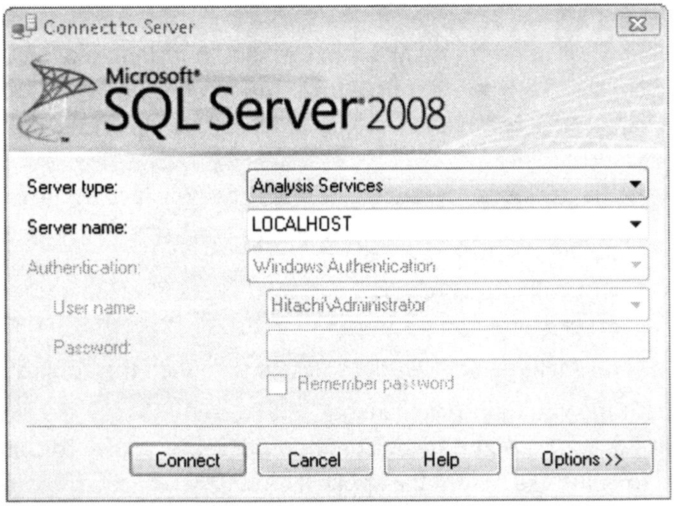

6. Click Connect to establish a connection to Analysis Services.

   SQL Server Management Studio starts and you are connected to Analysis Services, as illustrated in Figure 2-1.

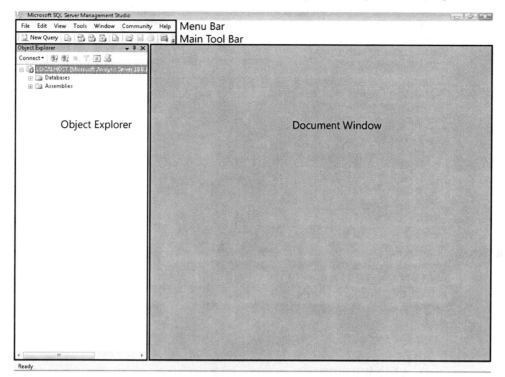

FIGURE 2-1 SQL Server Management Studio and its various sections

The default layout of Management Studio is divided into a number of distinct sections. The sections important for our purposes are the menu bar, the main toolbar, Object Explorer, and the document workspace:

- **The Menu Bar**   The menu bar is located at the top of the screen and provides access to various Management Studio features. If you have used other Microsoft products, you are probably already familiar with the concept of the menu bar.

- **The Main Toolbar**   The main toolbar is located just below the menu bar and provides quick access to frequently used features otherwise available through menus. Other toolbars associated with interfaces such as Object Explorer or the MDX Query Editor appear separately within Management Studio.

- **Object Explorer**   The Object Explorer window provides a tree view of the SQL Server product instances with which you have established connections. Subfolders below these top-level objects provide access to other objects maintained by particular instances.

- **The Document Workspace**   The document workspace is the largest portion of the Management Studio interface. This space is where browsers and query editors, such as the MDX Query Editor appear. On its own, the document workspace itself supports very little interactivity.

Browse the objects within an Analysis Services instance

1. With a connection to the Analysis Services instance housing this book's sample database established as described earlier in the chapter, navigate to Object Explorer.

2. Within the Object Explorer window, select the Analysis Services instance.

Notice that the instance is identified by a cube-like icon indicating this is an Analysis Services instance as opposed to an instance of the SQL Server (relational) Database Engine, Reporting Services, or Integration Services.

3. Click the plus sign (+) next to the instance's Databases subfolder to expand its contents. Notice that once expanded, the plus sign becomes a minus sign (–).

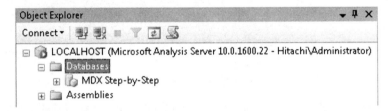

In the preceding screenshot, only the MDX Step-by-Step database is displayed. If you have installed this book's samples to an Analysis Services instance containing other databases, these may also be displayed on your screen.

4. Click the plus sign (+) next to the MDX Step-by-Step database to expand its contents.

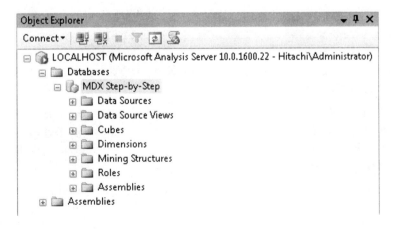

The Object Explorer window now displays the different types of objects contained within the Analysis Services database. Each folder can be expanded to reveal the actual objects associated with the MDX Step-by-Step database. In Chapter 11, "Implementing Dynamic Security," you interact with the Roles folder to create database-roles employing MDX-driven, dynamic security.

5. Click the minus sign (–) next to the MDX Step-by-Step database to collapse the display of its contents.

The MDX Query Editor

The MDX Query Editor is a basic tool for the construction and execution of MDX statements against Analysis Services databases. It is launched through SQL Server Management Studio and presented within the Management Studio document workspace. Like Management Studio itself, the MDX Query Editor is divided into several sections, each of which you explore in the following exercise.

Open the MDX Query Editor

1. With SQL Server Management Studio open, as described in the previous exercise, right-click the MDX Step-by-Step database, select New Query, and then select MDX from the shortcut menu.

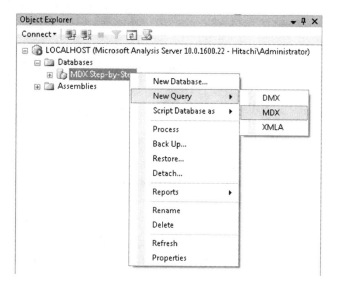

2. Verify the MDX Query Editor launches as displayed here:

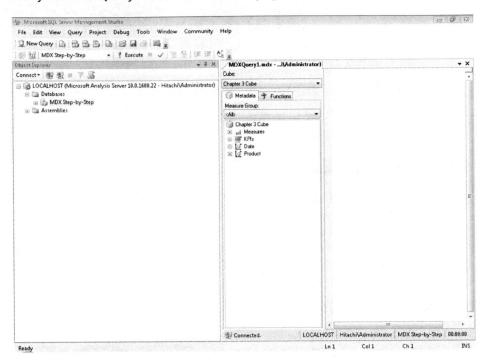

You should now see the MDX Query Editor within Management Studio's document workspace. Depending on the size and resolution of your screen, you may find this space to be a bit confined. To free up space, you can hide Object Explorer by simply unpinning it.

3. Click the pin icon in the upper right-hand corner of Object Explorer to hide (unpin) this browser window.

Releasing your mouse causes Object Explorer to slide to the side of the Management Studio interface. A small tab labeled Object Explorer remains on the edge of the Management Studio interface, as shown in Figure 2-2.

> **Note** If you need to access Object Explorer once it has been hidden, you can place your mouse just over the tab labeled Object Explorer and it will slide back to its original position. Moving your mouse away from Object Explorer will then cause it to slide back to the side of Management Studio. To fix Object Explorer in its original position, click the pin icon pinning it back into place.

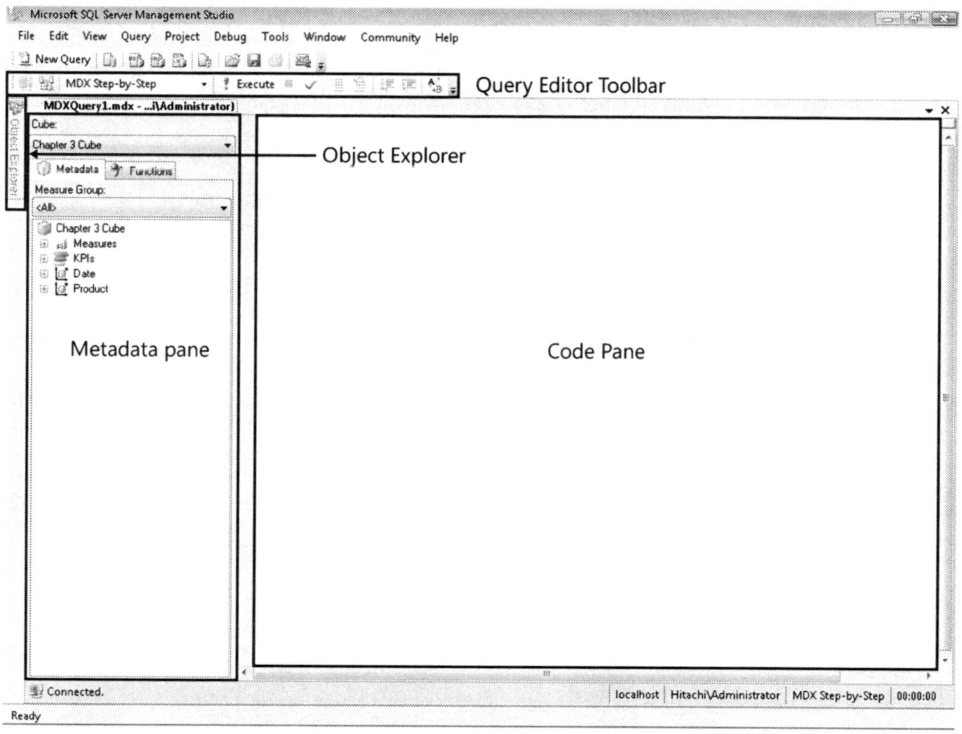

FIGURE 2-2 The MDX Query Editor and its various sections

With the MDX Query Editor now a bit easier to view, take a few moments to review its components. It is presented within Management Studio so you have access to the same menu bar and main toolbar as before. Just below these, the MDX Query Editor introduces the query editor toolbar.

The Query Editor toolbar provides access to features frequently used with the MDX Query Editor. The most frequently used of these features are identified in Figure 2-3 and described in the following list.

Available Databases   Execute   Parse

FIGURE 2-3 Key features of the Query Editor toolbar

- **Available Databases**   The Available Databases drop-down list presents a list of databases that are available to you within the instance of Analysis Services. The currently selected database is the one against which statements are to be submitted.

- **Execute**   The Execute button submits statements to Analysis Services for execution.

- **Parse**   The Parse button submits statements to Analysis Services for validation. This is useful at various stages of query development.

> **Note**   These features of the Query Editor toolbar are demonstrated in the next section of this chapter.

Just below the Query Editor toolbar, on the left-hand side of the document workspace, is the metadata pane. It contains the Available Cubes drop-down list and two tabs: Metadata and Functions.

- **Available Cubes**   The Available Cubes drop-down list provides a list of all cubes (and perspectives) associated with the database selected in the Available Databases drop-down list that you are authorized to access. The contents of the currently selected cube are reflected in the Metadata tab.

- **Metadata Tab**   The Metadata tab displays the structure of the cube identified in the Available Cubes drop-down list. By expanding the various measure groups and dimensions associated with the identified cube, similar to how you expanded objects in Object Browser, you can review a cube's contents.

- **Functions Tab**   The Functions tab displays an organized list of MDX functions. This tab is very helpful when assembling complex queries.

To the right of the metadata pane is the code pane, also known as the *Query Editor Window*. In the code pane, MDX statements are assembled. Clicking the Execute (or Parse) button on the Query Editor toolbar submits the statement in the code pane against the Analysis Services database selected in the Available Databases drop-down list. When statements in the code pane are highlighted (as demonstrated in the next section) and the Execute (or Parse) button is clicked, only the selected text is submitted.

After a statement is executed, one or two additional panes appear just below the MDX Query Editor's code pane. The messages pane presents informative text including warnings and errors associated with statements submitted to Analysis Services. The results pane presents query results if no errors preventing query execution occur. You explore these and the other critical features of the MDX Query Editor and Management Studio in the remaining sections of this chapter.

Building a Simple MDX Query

Now that you have been introduced to the MDX Query Editor, it's time to put it to use. Through the exercise that follows, you become familiar with those features critical to building and executing a simple MDX query.

Build a simple MDX query in the MDX Query Editor

1. If you have not already done so, open the MDX Query Editor, as described in previous exercises.

2. Verify that the MDX Step-by-Step database is selected within the Query Editor toolbar.

> **Note** To avoid redundancy, the act of opening the MDX Query Editor and setting the database within the Query Editor toolbar are treated as a single step for the remainder of this book. In subsequent exercises, you are instructed to open the MDX Query Editor to the MDX Step-by-Step database, which implies the preceding steps.

3. In the metadata pane, use the Available Cubes drop-down list to select the Step-by-Step cube.

Cube:

Step-by-Step ▼

🗐 Metadata   🐦 Functions

Measure Group:

<All> ▼

🗐 Step-by-Step
 ⊞ ▫▮ Measures
 ⊞ ▨ KPIs
 ⊞ 🗐 Account
 ⊞ 🗐 Customer
 ⊞ 🗐 Date
 ⊞ 🗐 Delivery Date
 ⊞ 🗐 Department
 ⊞ 🗐 Destination Currency
 ⊞ 🗐 Employee
 ⊞ 🗐 Geography

4. In the code pane, type in the following code. Be certain to place a space after the keyword *FROM*:

```
SELECT
FROM
```

5. From the Metadata tab of the metadata pane, drag the Step-by-Step cube object just to the right of the keyword *FROM* in the code pane. This should produce the statement illustrated here:

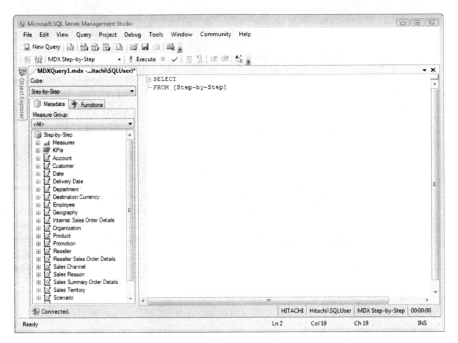

6. With no text selected in the code pane, click Parse on the Query Editor toolbar to validate the MDX query. Review the messages pane presented just below the code pane after you click the Parse button.

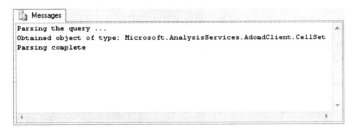

As explained in the previous section, clicking the Parse button submits the contents of the code pane to Analysis Services for validation. The results of the validation are displayed in the messages pane for review. If no error messages are returned, the code is valid.

7. Click Execute on the Query Editor toolbar to execute the query. In addition to the messages pane, notice that the results pane is now presented.

8. Review the data returned within the results pane.

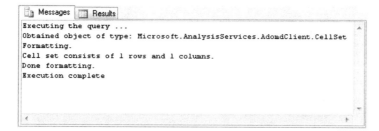

9. Select the messages tab and review the information presented. Pay particular attention to the number of columns and rows returned. Compare these to the data in the results pane.

```
Executing the query ...
Obtained object of type: Microsoft.AnalysisServices.AdomdClient.CellSet
Formatting.
Cell set consists of 1 rows and 1 columns.
Done formatting.
Execution complete
```

Congratulations! You have just successfully assembled and executed a simple MDX query using the MDX Query Editor. The results of this query are presented in the results pane with informational messages presented in the messages pane. You may be curious what exactly this query returned and how what appears to be an incomplete query could return any result. This becomes clear in the next chapter, "Understanding Tuples."

Exploring the Step-by-Step Cube

In the last exercise, you used the MDX Query Editor's metadata pane to interact with the Step-by-Step cube in a very limited manner. In the following exercise, you use the metadata pane to more fully explore the contents of the cube.

The Step-by-Step cube serves as the focal point of the exercises in this book. The exceptions to this are the exercises in Chapter 3, which focus on a greatly simplified version of the Step-by-Step cube.

Use the metadata pane to explore the contents of the Step-by-Step cube

1. If you have not already done so, open the MDX Query Editor to the MDX Step-by-Step database.

2. Use the Available Cubes drop-down list to select the Step-by-Step cube.

3. On the Metadata tab of the metadata pane, expand the Measures folder and note the many measure groups represented as subfolders.

4. Expand the Reseller Sales measure group and review its measures.

```
Step-by-Step
Measures
   Exchange Rates
   Financial Reporting
   Internet Customers
   Internet Orders
   Internet Sales
   Reseller Orders
   Reseller Sales
      Discount Amount
      Discount Percentage
      Reseller Average Sales Amount
      Reseller Average Unit Price
      Reseller Extended Amount
      Reseller Freight Cost
      Reseller Gross Profit
      Reseller Gross Profit Margin
      Reseller Order Quantity
      Reseller Ratio to All Products
      Reseller Ratio to Parent Product
      Reseller Sales Amount
      Reseller Standard Product Cost
      Reseller Tax Amount
      Reseller Total Product Cost
      Reseller Transaction Count
      Squared Reseller Sales Amount
   Sales Orders
   Sales Summary
   Sales Targets
KPIs
Account
Customer
Date
Delivery Date
Department
Destination Currency
Employee
Geography
Internet Sales Order Details
```

The Reseller Sales measure group contains a number of measures related to the sale of products to resellers. The Reseller Sales Amount measure represents the revenue associated with a transaction, whereas the Reseller Order Quantity measure represents the number of units of a given product sold. These are two of the more frequently employed measures in this measure group.

5. Expand the Reseller Orders measure group and review its measures.

The Reseller Orders measure group contains a single measure, Reseller Order Count. This measure represents a distinct count of the individual orders placed by resellers. (The Reseller Transaction Count measure in the Reseller Sales measure group is similar but provides a simple count of the individual line items associated with these orders.)

6. Expand the Internet Sales and Internet Orders measure groups and review their measures.

The Internet Sales and Internet Orders measure groups closely mirror the Reseller Sales and Reseller Orders measure groups, respectively. Where the Reseller Sales and Reseller Orders measure groups reflect orders placed by resellers, the Internet Sales and Internet Orders measure groups reflect orders placed directly by customers over the Internet. The Internet Sales Amount, Internet Order Quantity, Internet Order Count, and Internet Transaction Count measures within these two Internet-focused measure groups are corollaries of their reseller counterparts.

7. Collapse the Measures folder and locate the Date dimension.

    In the Step-by-Step cube, the Date dimension represents the date an order was placed. Sales targets are defined and finances are recorded against this dimension.

8. Expand the Date dimension and observe the attribute- and user-hierarchies associated with it. Attribute-hierarchies are denoted by a two-by-three stack of blue boxes while user-hierarchies are denoted by an expanding stack of blue boxes.

Notice that the Date dimension contains two folders, Calendar and Fiscal. Within the Calendar folder are hierarchies organizing dates around the standard calendar year. Within the Fiscal folder are hierarchies organizing dates around the company's fiscal calendar, which runs from July 1 to June 30 for a given year.

9. Expand the Calendar folder to reveal the Calendar user-hierarchy.

    The Calendar user-hierarchy provides a convenient means to navigate calendar years, calendar semesters (half years), calendar quarters, months, and individual dates.

10. Expand the Calendar user-hierarchy to reveal its Members folder and hierarchy levels.

Through the Members folder, you can explore the members of a hierarchy. Members are organized per their relationships to each other so that you can expand a parent member to reveal its children. Navigating members, as displayed in the Members folder of the metadata pane, can help you understand the relationship between members in a hierarchy.

Along with the Members folder, each level of the hierarchy is presented as a separate item. You can expand each level item to reveal its members.

11. Navigate the Members folder and levels associated with the Calendar user-hierarchy to familiarize yourself with the hierarchy's contents.

Once you are comfortable with the Calendar hierarchy, you should explore other hierarchies in the Date and other dimensions. A list of additional hierarchies you are suggested to explore is found in Table 2-1.

TABLE 2-1 Additional Hierarchies in the Step-by-Step Cube to Explore

Dimension	Hierarchy	Description
Date	Calendar Year	An attribute-hierarchy presenting calendar years associated with data in the data warehouse. This hierarchy is located within the Date dimension and is not presented within a folder.
Product	Product Categories	A user-hierarchy supporting the drilldown from categories to subcategories to individual products. This hierarchy is located within the Product dimension and is not presented within a folder.

TABLE 2-1 Additional Hierarchies in the Step-by-Step Cube to Explore

Dimension	Hierarchy	Description
Product	Category	An attribute-hierarchy presenting categories to which various product subcategories are assigned. This hierarchy is located within the Product dimension and is not presented within a folder.
Product	Subcategory	An attribute-hierarchy presenting subcategories to which various products are assigned. This hierarchy is located within the Product dimension and is not presented within a folder.
Product	Product	An attribute-hierarchy presenting products sold by the Adventure Works Cycles company. This hierarchy is located within the Product dimension and is not presented within a folder.
Product	Color	An attribute-hierarchy presenting colors assigned to various products. This hierarchy is located within the Stocking folder of the Product dimension.
Employee	Employees	A parent-child hierarchy presenting employees of the Adventure Works Cycles company in relation to their supervisors. This hierarchy is based on the hidden Employee attribute-hierarchy.
Geography	Country	An attribute-hierarchy presenting countries within which products are sold. This hierarchy is located within the Geography dimension and is not presented within a folder.

Building a More Complex Query

With a simple query under your belt and greater familiarity with the metadata pane, you can now assemble a slightly more complex query. In this exercise, do not be overly concerned with the query's logic but instead focus on the use of the MDX Query Editor to assemble and execute it.

As with previous exercises, this exercise assumes you are building knowledge regarding the use of the MDX Query Editor. The level of detail provided with each step diminishes as you proceed until a level of detail consistent with exercises in the remaining chapters of this book is achieved. In future exercises, you may employ the techniques demonstrated here to assemble your queries or you may manually enter the required MDX statements.

The MDX query constructed in this section is assembled over a series of several mini-exercises, each focusing on a different portion of the overall query. Because each exercise builds on the previous one, you should complete the exercises in this section in order.

Use the metadata pane to add a member to a query

1. If you have not already done so, open the MDX Query Editor to the MDX Step-by-Step database.

2. Configure the metadata pane to display the contents of the Step-by-Step cube.

3. In the code pane, enter the following query:

```
SELECT
FROM [Step-by-Step]
```

4. Parse the query to verify its syntax. Correct any problems identified.

5. Add a third line to the query containing the keyword *WHERE* followed by a single space:

```
SELECT
FROM [Step-by-Step]
WHERE
```

6. In the metadata pane, locate and expand the Date dimension.

7. Locate the CY 2004 member in the Date dimension's Calendar Year attribute-hierarchy. You can hover over the CY 2004 member to display its tool tip. Notice that each member item presents the member's name while the tool tip lists both the member's key and name.

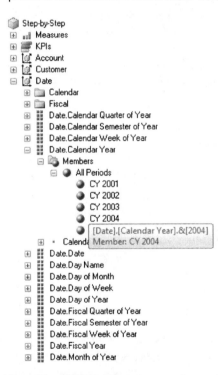

8. Drag the CY 2004 member to the code pane to the right of the keyword *WHERE*:

```
SELECT
FROM [Step-by-Step]
WHERE [Date].[Calendar Year].&[2004]
```

Notice that dragging a member from the metadata pane to the code pane causes a member key reference to be placed in the code. If you're a little fuzzy on the concepts of member keys and names, this is re-introduced in Chapter 3.

9. Execute the query and review the results.

Use the metadata pane to add a measure to a query

1. Ensure that you begin with the MDX query completed in the previous exercise:

```
SELECT
FROM [Step-by-Step]
WHERE [Date].[Calendar Year].&[2004]
```

2. In the metadata pane, locate and expand the Reseller Sales measure group.

3. Drag the Reseller Sales Amount measure from the metadata pane to the right of the keyword *SELECT*:

```
SELECT [Measures].[Reseller Sales Amount]
FROM [Step-by-Step]
WHERE [Date].[Calendar Year].&[2004]
```

4. To the right of the first line, type the phrase *ON COLUMNS*:

```
SELECT [Measures].[Reseller Sales Amount] ON COLUMNS
FROM [Step-by-Step]
WHERE [Date].[Calendar Year].&[2004]
```

5. Execute the query and review the results.

Reseller Sales Amount
$16,038,062.60

Use the metadata pane to add a function to a query

1. Ensure that you begin with the MDX query completed in the previous exercise:

```
SELECT [Measures].[Reseller Sales Amount] ON COLUMNS
FROM [Step-by-Step]
WHERE [Date].[Calendar Year].&[2004]
```

2. Insert a comma at the end of the first line, just after the phrase *ON COLUMNS*. Press Enter to create a new line following this:

```
SELECT [Measures].[Reseller Sales Amount] ON COLUMNS,

FROM [Step-by-Step]
WHERE [Date].[Calendar Year].&[2004]
```

3. Using the metadata pane, drag the Product dimension's Category attribute-hierarchy to the blank line just above the line starting with the *FROM* keyword:

```
SELECT [Measures].[Reseller Sales Amount] ON COLUMNS,
[Product].[Category]
FROM [Step-by-Step]
WHERE [Date].[Calendar Year].&[2004]
```

4. In the metadata pane, switch to the Functions tab.

5. Expand the Set folder and locate the first *Members* function item.

> **Note** The (All) folder presents a list of all available MDX functions. If you cannot locate a function under a specific folder, you may find it easier to locate it in the alphabetical listing under the (All) folder.

6. Hover over the *Members* function item to display its tool tip. Notice that functions display their syntax and a brief definition in their tool tips.

7. Drag the *Members* function item to the right of the *[Product].[Category]* phrase to assemble the following statement:

```
SELECT [Measures].[Reseller Sales Amount] ON COLUMNS,
[Product].[Category]«Hierarchy».MEMBERS
FROM [Step-by-Step]
WHERE [Date].[Calendar Year].&[2004]
```

8. Remove the *«Hierarchy»* placeholder, making certain to leave no spaces between *[Product].[Category]* and *.Members*:

```
SELECT [Measures].[Reseller Sales Amount] ON COLUMNS,
[Product].[Category].MEMBERS
FROM [Step-by-Step]
WHERE [Date].[Calendar Year].&[2004]
```

9. Complete the second line by appending *ON ROWS* to it:

```
SELECT [Measures].[Reseller Sales Amount] ON COLUMNS,
[Product].[Category].MEMBERS ON ROWS
FROM [Step-by-Step]
WHERE [Date].[Calendar Year].&[2004]
```

10. Execute the query and note the values returned.

	Reseller Sales Amount
All Products	$16,038,062.60
Accessories	$161,794.33
Bikes	$13,399,243.18
Clothing	$386,013.16
Components	$2,091,011.92

Execute a portion of a query

1. Ensure that you begin with the MDX query completed in the previous exercise.

```
SELECT [Measures].[Reseller Sales Amount] ON COLUMNS,
[Product].[Category].MEMBERS ON ROWS
FROM [Step-by-Step]
WHERE [Date].[Calendar Year].&[2004]
```

2. Highlight the first three lines of the query.

```
SELECT [Measures].[Reseller Sales Amount] ON COLUMNS,
[Product].[Category].MEMBERS ON ROWS
FROM [Step-by-Step]
WHERE [Date].[Calendar Year].&[2004]
```

3. Execute the query again. Notice the change in values.

	Reseller Sales Amount
All Products	$80,450,596.98
Accessories	$571,297.93
Bikes	$66,302,381.56
Clothing	$1,777,840.84
Components	$11,799,076.66

The last step of this exercise highlights a critical feature of the code pane. If text is highlighted in the pane, clicking the Execute or Parse button causes only the highlighted text to be submitted. If the highlighted text represents a valid statement, it is parsed or executed as requested. If the highlighted text does not represent a valid statement, an error is returned to the messages pane.

Saving and Restoring Queries

The construction of the query in the previous exercise involved a large number of steps. When assembling a large query, you may wish to save your progress and return to its construction at a later time. Once you complete the query, you may wish to preserve it for later use. You can easily do this with Management Studio.

To save an existing query in the MDX Query Editor, select File on the menu bar, and then select Save MDXQuery1.mdx As to display the Save File As dialog box.

> **Note** The default name of the file may vary in your display.

The Save File As dialog box should be familiar to any user of Windows applications. Save the file using an appropriate name to a location of your choice. The file is saved with an .mdx extension, which associates it with the SQL Server Management Studio application.

To open this file at a later date, simply connect to Analysis Services using Management Studio, select File on the menu bar, point to Open, and then click File. Locate and select the MDX file and it opens in a new MDX Query Editor window. You may be prompted to connect to an Analysis Services instance as the file is opened.

If you have created a new query or modified a query from a file and have not saved the new or modified code to file, closing the MDX Query Editor prompts you to save your work. The choice to save is up to you. With this book, exercises within a chapter may build upon one another, so you may wish to save your work until a particular chapter is completed. Between chapters, exercises do not build upon one another.

Chapter 2 Quick Reference

To	Do this
Connect to Analysis Services using Management Studio	Start Management Studio. In the Connect To Server dialog box, select Analysis Services in the Server Type field, type the name of your Analysis Services instance in the Server Name field, and then click Connect.
Open the MDX Query Editor	In Object Explorer, right-click your instance of Analysis Services, point to New Query, and then click MDX.
Change the target database for the MDX Query Editor	From the Query Editor toolbar, select the desired database in the Available Databases drop-down list.
Parse an MDX statement	While working in the MDX Query Editor, click Parse on the Query Editor toolbar. OR While working in the MDX Query Editor, select the portion of the statement you want to parse, and then click Parse on the Query Editor toolbar.
Execute an MDX statement	While working in the MDX Query Editor, click Execute on the Query Editor toolbar. OR While working in the MDX Query Editor, select the portion of the statement you want to execute, and then click Execute on the Query Editor toolbar.

Chapter 3
Understanding Tuples

After completing this chapter, you will be able to:

- Explain the concept of cube space

- Retrieve data from a cube using tuples

- Reference hierarchy members using a variety of syntax

For the purpose of data access, Analysis Services presents cubes as n-dimensional spaces referred to as cube spaces. Within a *cube space*, data are made accessible through *cells*, each uniquely identified by a *tuple*.

In this chapter, you learn how to assemble tuples to access individual cells. This is foundational to your success with MDX.

N-dimensional Space

To understand the concept of cube space, picture a simple number line. As you may remember from your school days, a number line is a line marked at regular intervals by integer (whole-number) values. Figure 3-1 provides an illustration of such a line.

FIGURE 3-1 A number line with a point at (3)

In this illustration, a point resides along the line at the position indicated by the number 3. This number, 3, is the point's *coordinate*. When you wrap the coordinate in parentheses like so

(3)

you have a simple system for expressing the point's position along the line.

Now consider the introduction of another number line perpendicular to the one above. These two lines define a two-dimensional space, as illustrated in Figure 3-2.

Traditionally, the horizontal line in this two-dimensional space is referred to as the x-axis and the vertical line is referred to as the y-axis. Points within this space are identified by their position relative to these two axes. (*Axes* is the plural of axis.)

To express the position of a point, the x-coordinate and y-coordinate of the point is presented in a comma-delimited list. In this list, the x-coordinate precedes the y-coordinate, and the entire list is wrapped in parentheses. This double coordinate system is generically described using the form (x, y).

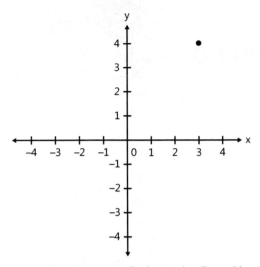

FIGURE 3-2 Two perpendicular number lines with a point at (3, 4)

To illustrate this, consider the point in Figure 3-2. It resides at the intersection of the value 3 along the x-axis and 4 along the y-axis. It is therefore identified using the double coordinate (3, 4).

Taking this one step further, consider the addition of a third line perpendicular to both the x and y axes. Keeping with tradition, the newly introduced third axis is referred to as the z-axis. The space formed by these three axes is illustrated in Figure 3-3. Together with the x and y axes, the z-axis forms a three-dimensional space. Points within this space are represented using a triple-coordinate system, (x, y, z). While challenging to see on paper, a point is presented in Figure 3-3 at the position identified by the triple coordinate (3, 4, 2).

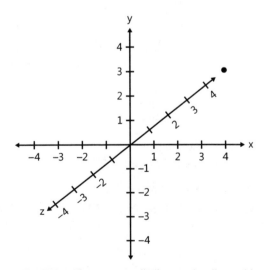

FIGURE 3-3 Three perpendicular number lines with a point at (3, 4, 2)

Now add a fourth axis. The four-dimensional space created can no longer be easily visualized. Still, points within this space can be located using a quadruple-coordinate system.

To describe the form of the quadruple-coordinate system, it's helpful to re-label the axes with the letter a and a numerical subscript. Using this approach, the x-axis becomes axis a_1, the y-axis becomes axis a_2, the z-axis becomes axis a_3, and the newly introduced fourth axis becomes axis a_4. Points within this space are then located using a quadruple-coordinate system of the form (a_1, a_2, a_3, a_4).

Adding a fifth axis makes the space even more complex, but points within this space are easily addressed using a quintuple-coordinate system of the form $(a_1, a_2, a_3, a_4, a_5)$. A sixth axis leads to a sextuple-coordinate system $(a_1, a_2, a_3, a_4, a_5, a_6)$; a seventh axis leads to a septuple-coordinate system $(a_1, a_2, a_3, a_4, a_5, a_6, a_7)$; and an eighth axis leads to an octuple-coordinate system $(a_1, a_2, a_3, a_4, a_5, a_6, a_7, a_8)$.

You could go on like this forever, and while imagining spaces such as these is a bit mind-blowing, locating a point within any of them is a simple matter of employing an appropriately sized coordinate system.

Generically, these spaces are referred to as *n-dimensional spaces*. These spaces have n number of axes, and points within them are located using coordinate systems of the form $(a_1, a_2,...,a_n)$. These coordinate systems are generically referred to as *tuples*.

> **Note** The question of how to properly pronounce the word *tuple* always seems to come up. Some folks pronounce it with a *u* like the one in *cup*. Others pronounce it like with a *u* like the one in *dude*. We aren't really sure which way is right and use both forms ourselves.

Cube Space

In Analysis Services, a cube is presented as an n-dimensional space referred to as a cube space. Each attribute-hierarchy within the dimensions of the cube forms an axis. Along each axis, each member of the associated attribute-hierarchy, including the (All) member, occupies a position. This translation of an attribute-hierarchy to a cube space axis is illustrated in Figure 3-4 for the Product dimension's Category attribute-hierarchy, first described in Chapter 1, "Welcome to MDX."

Measures are also assigned an axis. Although handled differently during cube design, for the purposes of defining a cube space, a cube's measures are simply members of an attribute-hierarchy called Measures, which belongs to the Measures dimension. One thing that differentiates the Measures attribute-hierarchy from other attribute-hierarchies is that it does not (and cannot) have an (All) member.

With each traditional attribute-hierarchy and the measures of a cube translated into axes, the cube space is defined. Points within the cube space can then be referenced using a tuple. Unlike tuples in the n-dimensional spaces formed by number lines, tuples in cube spaces use member references for coordinate values.

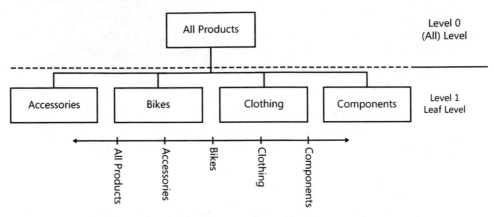

FIGURE 3-4 The representation of the Category attribute-hierarchy as a cube space axis

Basic Member References

You can reference a member within an attribute-hierarchy in a number of ways. The basic member reference identifies the member along with its associated attribute-hierarchy and dimension using the following form:

`[Dimension].[Hierarchy].[Member].`

Each of the dimension, attribute-hierarchy, and member object identifiers within the member reference are encapsulated in square brackets. These are separated from each other by periods.

The square brackets around a particular object identifier are optional as long as the object identifier:

1. Is not one of 200+ reserved words identified in SQL Server Books Online

2. Does not start with a character other than a letter or underscore

3. Does not otherwise contain any characters other than letters, numbers, or underscores

Instead of keeping up with all this, you might find it easier to just consistently wrap each identifier in square brackets. This is a standard used throughout this book.

Object names are used as the identifiers for dimensions and attribute-hierarchies. Members are a bit more complex in that they can be identified by either name or key.

A member's name is its user-friendly label. This is what is usually presented in result sets and browsers such as the MDX Query Editor. The following example demonstrates a name-based reference to the member Bikes of the Product dimension's Category attribute-hierarchy:

`[Product].[Category].[Bikes]`

Member names suffer one key drawback: They are not guaranteed to be unique within an attribute-hierarchy. This is problematic if more than one member within a hierarchy shares the same name (which is quite common in some dimensional models). Using key-based references resolves this problem.

A member's key is its unique identifier within its associated attribute-hierarchy. Because of its guaranteed uniqueness, a key is the most precise means of identifying a member within an attribute-hierarchy. When identifying a member by key, the identifier is preceded by the ampersand character (&). The previous Bikes reference is demonstrated using its key-based reference:

```
[Product].[Category].&[1]
```

This example illustrates a common issue with key-based references. If you are not aware that the member named Bikes employs a key-value of 1, the key-based reference may be difficult to interpret. This leaves you in the position of using name-based references that may be ambiguous or key-based references that may be difficult to interpret. In this book, we make use of named-based references for interpretability unless a particular concept or ambiguity dictates we use keys. The right choice in your applications depends on the structure of your data.

Accessing Data with Tuples

The MDX Step-by-Step sample database accompanying this book contains a highly simplified cube named Chapter 3 Cube. The cube consists of two dimensions—Product and Date—and a single measure, Reseller Sales Amount. Figure 3-5 presents the structure of this cube.

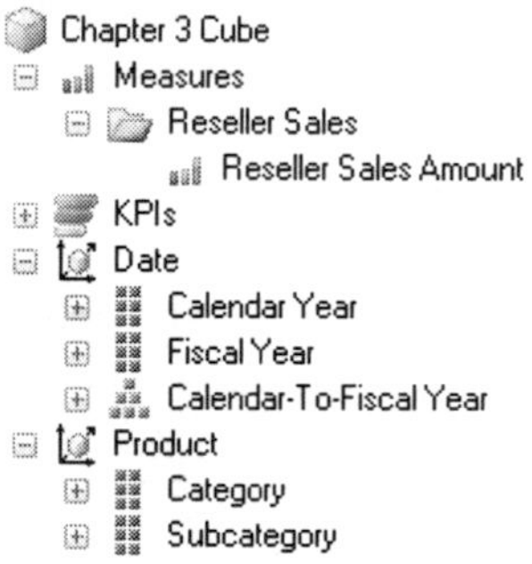

```
Chapter 3 Cube
├─ Measures
│  └─ Reseller Sales
│        Reseller Sales Amount
├─ KPIs
├─ Date
│  ├─ Calendar Year
│  ├─ Fiscal Year
│  └─ Calendar-To-Fiscal Year
└─ Product
   ├─ Category
   └─ Subcategory
```

FIGURE 3-5 The structure of the Chapter 3 Cube cube

Within the Product dimension are two attribute-hierarchies, Subcategory and Category. The Date dimension also contains two attribute-hierarchies, Fiscal Year and Calendar Year, which together form the levels of the user-hierarchy Calendar-To-Fiscal Year.

> **Note** The Calendar-To-Fiscal Year user-hierarchy is provided in this cube for no other purpose than to illustrate a few critical concepts while sidestepping a few issues addressed later on. The Calendar-To-Fiscal Year user-hierarchy is not found in the Step-by-Step cube, and such a user-hierarchy combining fiscal year and calendar year attributes is rarely found in the real world. Please consider this hierarchy nothing more than an educational construct.

With four traditional attribute-hierarchies plus the Measures attribute-hierarchy discussed earlier in this chapter, the cube space formed by this cube contains a total of five axes. Points within this cube space are therefore located using a five-part tuple.

For example, the point located at the intersection of the Category member Bikes, the Subcategory member Mountain Bikes, the Calendar Year and Fiscal Year members All Periods, and the Measures member Reseller Sales Amount is identified with the following five-part tuple:

```
(
    [Date].[Calendar Year].[All Periods],
    [Date].[Fiscal Year].[All Periods],
    [Product].[Category].[Bikes],
    [Product].[Subcategory].[Mountain Bikes],
    [Measures].[Measures].[Reseller Sales Amount]
)
```

The use of this tuple to retrieve data is demonstrated in the following exercise.

Use a tuple to access a point in a cube space

1. Open the MDX Query Editor to the MDX Step-by-Step database. If you need assistance with this task, refer to Chapter 2, "Using the MDX Query Editor."

2. In the code pane, enter the following query:

```
SELECT
FROM [Chapter 3 Cube]
WHERE (
    [Date].[Calendar Year].[All Periods],
    [Date].[Fiscal Year].[All Periods],
    [Product].[Category].[Bikes],
    [Product].[Subcategory].[Mountain Bikes],
    [Measures].[Measures].[Reseller Sales Amount]
    )
```

> **Note** The line breaks and indentions used with this tuple are purely for readability.

3. Execute the query.

> Messages   Results
>
> $26,492,684.38

The tuple is employed in the *SELECT* statement to retrieve data from a single point within the cube space formed by the Chapter 3 Cube. Like tuples associated with number lines, this tuple used here consists of a parentheses-enclosed, comma-delimited list of coordinate values. Each of these values consists of a basic member reference identifying a member (by name) and its associated attribute-hierarchy and dimension.

Since an attribute-hierarchy represents an axis in the cube space and a member reference identifies the attribute-hierarchy, the member reference identifies the axis with which it is associated. In other words, member references are self-describing. Therefore, you don't need to rely on the position of a member reference (coordinate value) in the tuple to determine which axis it is associated with. This allows member references to be placed in any order within a tuple without impacting the point identified.

4. Move the *[Product].[Subcategory].[Mountain Bikes]* member reference to the top of the tuple:

```
SELECT
FROM [Chapter 3 Cube]
WHERE (
    [Product].[Subcategory].[Mountain Bikes],
    [Date].[Calendar Year].[All Periods],
    [Date].[Fiscal Year].[All Periods],
    [Product].[Category].[Bikes],
    [Measures].[Measures].[Reseller Sales Amount]
    )
```

5. Execute the query and verify the same value as before is returned.

> Messages   Results
>
> $26,492,684.38

Try moving around other member references within the tuple. Notice that so long as the tuple is properly formed, the same point within the cube space is identified.

Understanding Cells

In the previous exercise, you used a tuple to locate a point within a cube space. On the surface, it appeared that a simple value is recorded at this point, which is what is returned by the *SELECT* statement. The reality is a bit more complex.

Points within cube spaces are occupied by cells. Cells are objects and as such have a number of properties. When cells are accessed, various properties are returned. The default properties returned are *VALUE* and *FORMATTED_VALUE*.

The *VALUE* property contains an aggregated measure value. That value is based on the measure aggregated against all the other attribute-hierarchy members associated with the cell. For example, the *VALUE* property of the cell associated with the previously employed tuple, repeated here for clarity, contains the aggregated value for the Reseller Sales Amount measure limited to the Calendar Year and Fiscal Year attribute-hierarchies' All Periods members, the Category attribute-hierarchy's Bikes member, and the Subcategory attribute-hierarchy's Mountain Bikes member:

```
(
    [Date].[Calendar Year].[All Periods],
    [Date].[Fiscal Year].[All Periods],
    [Product].[Category].[Bikes],
    [Product].[Subcategory].[Mountain Bikes],
    [Measures].[Measures].[Reseller Sales Amount]
)
```

The *FORMATTED_VALUE* property contains the string representation of the *VALUE* property, formatted per instructions associated with the cell at design time. The *FORMATED_VALUE* is what is displayed in the results pane of the MDX Query Editor. A bit more information on assigning formats is provided in Chapter 5, "Working with Expressions."

A number of other properties can be returned with a cell. Within a *SELECT* statement, these are accessed using the *CELL PROPERTIES* keyword as demonstrated in the following exercise.

Access cell properties

1. If you have not already done so, open the MDX Query Editor to the MDX Step-by-Step database.

2. In the code pane, re-enter the last query from the previous exercise:

```
SELECT
FROM [Chapter 3 Cube]
WHERE (
    [Product].[Subcategory].[Mountain Bikes],
    [Date].[Calendar Year].[All Periods],
    [Date].[Fiscal Year].[All Periods],
    [Product].[Category].[Bikes],
    [Measures].[Measures].[Reseller Sales Amount]
    )
```

3. Execute the query to retrieve the results.

4. Double-click the cell returned in the Results pane to open the Cell Properties dialog box.

The default properties *VALUE* and *FORMATTED_VALUE* are returned with the cell. The *CELL_ORDINAL* property, displayed as CellOrdinal, is also returned to indicate the position of the returned cell in the query's cell set. Cell sets are discussed in Chapter 4, "Working with Sets."

You can retrieve additional properties by including the *CELL PROPERTIES* keyword in your query. If you use the *CELL PROPERTIES* keyword, the *VALUE* and *FORMATTED_VALUE* properties are not returned unless explicitly requested. (The *CELL_ORDINAL* property is always returned as it is a property of the retrieved data.)

5. Click the OK button in the Cell Properties dialog box to close it.

6. Modify the query to request the *FORMATTED_VALUE* and *FORMAT_STRING* cell properties, purposely omitting the *VALUE* and *CELL_ORDINAL* properties:

```
SELECT
FROM [Chapter 3 Cube]
WHERE (
    [Product].[Subcategory].[Mountain Bikes],
    [Date].[Calendar Year].[All Periods],
    [Date].[Fiscal Year].[All Periods],
    [Product].[Category].[Bikes],
    [Measures].[Measures].[Reseller Sales Amount]
    )
CELL PROPERTIES FORMATTED_VALUE, FORMAT_STRING
```

7. Execute the query.

8. Double-click the returned cell to open the Cell Properties dialog box.

Notice that *VALUE* is omitted from the list of cell properties, but the *CELL_ORDINAL* property is returned with the cell.

9. Review the property values and then click OK to close the dialog box.

The complete list of available cell properties and their descriptions is provided in Table 3-1. Additional information on each property is available through SQL Server Books Online.

TABLE 3-1 Available cell properties

Cell Property	Description
ACTION_TYPE	A bitmask indicating the type of action(s) associated with the cell.
BACK_COLOR	A bitmask indicating the background color to use when displaying the *VALUE* or *FORMATTED_VALUE* property of the cell.
CELL_ORDINAL	The ordinal number of the cell in the cell set.
FONT_FLAGS	A bitmask indicating whether the cell's font should be presented using italic, bold, underline, or strikeout detailing.
FONT_NAME	The name of the font to use when displaying the *VALUE* or *FORMATTED_VALUE* property of the cell.
FONT_SIZE	The font size to use when displaying the *VALUE* or *FORMATTED_VALUE* property of the cell.
FORE_COLOR	A bitmask indicating the foreground color to use when displaying the *VALUE* or *FORMATTED_VALUE* property of the cell.
FORMAT	This is the same as the *FORMAT_STRING* property.
FORMAT_STRING	The format string used to create the value of *FORMATTED_VALUE* property of the cell.
FORMATTED_VALUE	The character string representation of the *VALUE* property formatted per the *FORMAT_STRING* value.
LANGUAGE	The locale against which the *FORMAT_STRING* will be applied.
UPDATEABLE	A value indicating whether the cell can be updated.
VALUE	The unformatted value of the cell.

Working with Partial Tuples

The cube used in this chapter has a very simple structure. With only five attribute-hierarchies (including Measures), points within this cube are identifiable using a five-part tuple. Imagine a more typical cube with tens or even hundreds of attributes. Having to specify a member reference for each attribute-hierarchy within the cube to complete a tuple would simply be overwhelming.

Thankfully, Analysis Services allows you to submit partial tuples. Within a partial tuple one or more member references are omitted. Because a complete tuple is required to locate a point in the cube space, Analysis Services takes responsibility for filling in the missing references. This is done by applying the following rules for each missing attribute-hierarchy member reference:

1. If the member reference is omitted, use the attribute's default member.

2. If the member reference is omitted and no default member is specified, use the attribute's (All) member.

3. If the member reference is omitted, no default member is specified, and the (All) member does not exist, use the attribute's first member.

In the following exercise, you put these rules to work.

Access cells in a cube using partial tuples

1. If you have not already done so, open the MDX Query Editor to the MDX Step-by-Step database.

2. In the code pane, enter the following query specifying a complete tuple:

```
SELECT
FROM [Chapter 3 Cube]
WHERE (
    [Date].[Calendar Year].[All Periods],
    [Date].[Fiscal Year].[All Periods],
    [Product].[Category].[Bikes],
    [Product].[Subcategory].[Mountain Bikes],
    [Measures].[Measures].[Reseller Sales Amount]
    )
```

3. Execute the query and note the result.

Messages	Results
$26,492,684.38	

4. Now, specify a partial tuple by removing the Measures member reference:

```
SELECT
FROM [Chapter 3 Cube]
WHERE (
    [Date].[Calendar Year].[All Periods],
    [Date].[Fiscal Year].[All Periods],
    [Product].[Category].[Bikes],
    [Product].[Subcategory].[Mountain Bikes]
    )
```

> **Note** Be certain to remove the comma following the Mountain Bikes member reference.

5. Execute the query and compare the result to that of the previous query.

Messages	Results
$26,492,684.38	

With the Measures member removed, a partial tuple is submitted to Analysis Services. Analysis Services supplies the missing Measures reference by first checking for a default member. The default member of the Measures attribute-hierarchy is Reseller Sales Amount. That member is applied and the tuple is complete. The process by which the tuple is completed is illustrated in Figure 3-6. Because the completed tuple is the same tuple specified in the first query of this exercise, the same cell is accessed.

Position	Partial Tuple	Rule 1: Default Member	Rule 2: (All) Member	Rule 3: First Member	Completed Tuple
Date. Calendar Year	All Periods	———————————————————————————→			All Periods
Date. Fiscal Year	All Periods	———————————————————————————→			All Periods
Product. Category	Bikes	———————————————————————————→			Bikes
Product. Subcategory	Mountain Bikes	———————————————————————————→			Mountain Bikes
Measures. Measures	(omitted)	Reseller Sales Amount	———————————————→		Reseller Sales Amount

FIGURE 3-6 The process for completing the tuple with a missing Measures member

> **Note** The default member of the Measures attribute-hierarchy is defined at design time when a default measure is assigned to the cube. In this cube, a default measure of Reseller Sales Amount has been assigned. Had this not been explicitly assigned, the third rule would have completed the tuple with Reseller Sales Amount, the first (and only) measure in the cube.

6. Alter the query by removing the two member references associated with the Date dimension:

```
SELECT
FROM [Chapter 3 Cube]
WHERE (
    [Product].[Category].[Bikes],
    [Product].[Subcategory].[Mountain Bikes]
    )
```

7. Execute the query and compare the result to that of the previous query.

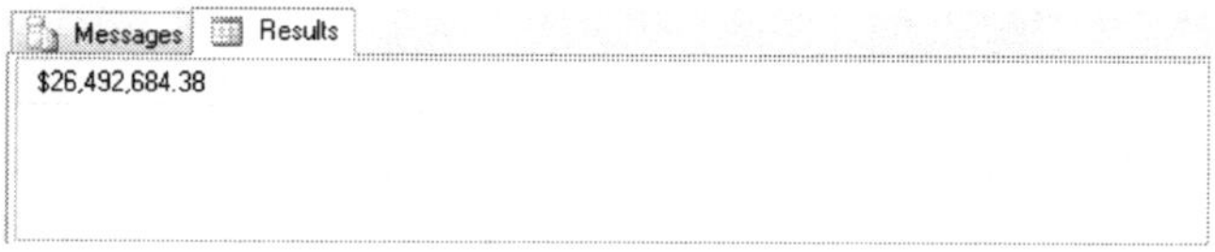

With this query, Analysis Services supplies the Measures member reference by applying the first rule. For the Date dimension's Calendar Year and Fiscal Year attribute-hierarchies, a default member is not defined so the first rule does not address these omitted references. However, an (All) member, All Periods, is defined for these attribute-hierarchies, so the second rule fills in the blanks. The process by which this partial tuple is completed is illustrated in Figure 3-7. As before, the completed tuple is the same as the tuple in the first query of this exercise so that the same cell as before is accessed.

Position	Partial Tuple	Rule 1: Default Member	Rule 2: (All) Member	Rule 3: First Member	Completed Tuple
Date. Calendar Year	(omitted)	(not available)	All Periods ——————————→		All Periods
Date. Fiscal Year	(omitted)	(not available)	All Periods ——————————→		All Periods
Product. Category	Bikes ——————————————————————→				Bikes
Product. Subcategory	Mountain Bikes ——————————————→				Mountain Bikes
Measures. Measures	(omitted)	Reseller Sales Amount ——————→			Reseller Sales Amount

FIGURE 3-7 The process for completing the tuple with missing Measures, Calendar Year, and Fiscal Year members

Now that you understand partial tuples, it should be clear what the basic query introduced in Chapter 2 returns. This query, *SELECT FROM [Step-by-Step]*, returns the cell associated with the partial tuple within which no member references are supplied. Analysis Services completes each member reference using the three preceding rules and accesses the identified cell.

More Member References

Members in user-hierarchies may also be referenced using the form, *[Dimension].[Hierarchy].[Member]*, introduced earlier in this chapter. For example, the calendar year 2003 member of the Calendar-To-Fiscal Year user-hierarchy can be identified as follows:

```
[Date].[Calendar-To-Fiscal Year].[CY 2003]
```

However, because user-hierarchies are assembled from multiple attribute-hierarchies, the member identifier has greater opportunity to be non-unique. This is true not only when member names are employed but also with member keys. To illustrate this, consider the following member reference. Does it reference calendar year 2003 or fiscal year 2003?

```
[Date].[Calendar-To-Fiscal Year].&[2003]
```

This reference is ambiguous. Both the calendar year 2003 and fiscal year 2003 members use the number 2003 as their key. Referencing the member using the form *[Dimension].[Hierarchy].[Level].[Member]* resolves this ambiguity:

```
[Date].[Calendar-To-Fiscal Year].[Calendar Year].&[2003]
```

This new form works with both member keys and member names and is ideal when the member identifier is unique within a specified level but not necessarily unique across the levels of the hierarchy.

Unfortunately, in some situations this new form of member reference is still ambiguous. Consider the Fiscal Year members in Figure 3-8. In particular, pay attention to the two FY 2003 members.

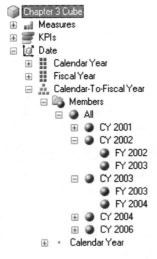

FIGURE 3-8 The relationship between the FY 2003 members and CY 2002 and CY 2003 members

There is one FY 2003 member in the Fiscal Year attribute-hierarchy representing the period July 1, 2002, to June 30, 2003. Since the fiscal year 2003 straddles calendar years 2002 and 2003, two FY 2003 members (one under CY 2002 and the other under CY 2003) are found in the user-hierarchy. Within the user-hierarchy, the FY 2003 member is presented as two distinct members.

In this situation, the only way to differentiate between the two is to identify the Fiscal Year member in relation to its Calendar Year parent. Here are member references identifying these two distinct user-hierarchy members:

```
[Date].[Calendar-To-Fiscal Year].[Calendar Year].[CY 2002].[FY 2003]
[Date].[Calendar-To-Fiscal Year].[Calendar Year].[CY 2003].[FY 2003]
```

Building Tuples with User-Hierarchies

The exercises presented thus far have built tuples exclusively using references to members in attribute-hierarchies. You can also use user-hierarchies to assemble tuples. When a user-hierarchy member reference is employed, Analysis Services translates that reference into one or more attribute-hierarchy member references to assemble a resolvable tuple.

Understanding User-Hierarchy Translation

To translate a user-hierarchy member reference into one or more attribute-hierarchy references, Analysis Services first locates the specified member within the user-hierarchy. With this member located, that member and each member in the levels above it forming the member's lineage in the user-hierarchy is then known. As each level in a user-hierarchy is derived from an attribute-hierarchy, an attribute-hierarchy reference for the specified member and each member in its lineage is then generated. The lone exception to this is the user-hierarchy's (All) member, which does not map to any member in an attribute-hierarchy and is therefore simply ignored in the translation process.

The following exercise demonstrates the process of translating user-hierarchy member references to attribute-hierarchy references.

Access cells with tuples containing user-hierarchies

1. If you have not already done so, open the MDX Query Editor to the MDX Step-by-Step database.

2. In the code pane, enter the following query:

```
SELECT
FROM [Chapter 3 Cube]
WHERE (
    [Date].[Calendar-To-Fiscal Year].[Calendar Year].[CY 2003].[FY 2003]
    )
```

> **Note** When a tuple is specified using a single member reference, the tuple's parentheses can be omitted. Parentheses are applied to the tuple in the preceding query for the purpose of consistency.

3. Execute the query and note the result.

Messages	Results
$12,000,247.33	

To resolve this tuple, Analysis Services first locates the FY 2003 member in the Fiscal Year level associated with the CY 2003 member of the Calendar Year level of the Calendar-To-Fiscal Year user-hierarchy. Analysis Services then determines the lineage of this member, which you already know given the explicit structure of the member reference. Each member in the lineage is then translated into an attribute-hierarchy reference and the tuple is completed as illustrated in Figure 3-9.

Position	User-Hierarchy Translation	Partial Tuple	Rule 1: Default Member	Rule 2: (All) Member	Rule 3: First Member	Completed Tuple
Date. Calendar-To- Fiscal Year	Calendar Year. CY 2003. FY 2003					
Date. Calendar Year	CY 2003					CY 2003
Date. Fiscal Year	FY 2003					FY 2003
Product. Category		*(omitted)*	*(not available)*	All Products		All Products
Product. Subcategory		*(omitted)*	*(not available)*	All Products		All Products
Measures. Measures		*(omitted)*	Reseller Sales Amount			Reseller Sales Amount

FIGURE 3-9 The process for completing the tuple specifying the FY 2003 member associated with CY 2003 in the Calendar-To-Fiscal Year user-hierarchy

To verify this, you can submit the translated (partial) tuple to see that the same cell is returned.

4. Modify the query to reflect the translated (partial) tuple:

```
SELECT
FROM [Chapter 3 Cube]
WHERE (
    [Date].[Calendar Year].[CY 2003],
    [Date].[Fiscal Year].[FY 2003]
    )
```

5. Execute the query and compare the result to that in step 3.

Messages	Results
$12,000,247.33	

When the lineage for FY 2003 is not specified in the user-hierarchy member reference, the reference becomes ambiguous, as described in the previous sidebar "More Member References". Analysis Services retrieves the first FY 2003 member within the Fiscal Year level of the user-hierarchy it encounters. It then proceeds with the translation process, as previously described.

6. Modify the query to use an ambiguous reference to the FY 2003 member of the Calendar-To-Fiscal Year user-hierarchy:

```
SELECT
FROM [Chapter 3 Cube]
WHERE (
    [Date].[Calendar-To-Fiscal Year].[Fiscal Year].[FY 2003]
    )
```

7. Execute the query and note the result.

Messages	Results
$15,921,423.19	

By simply removing the parent member identifier, a different cell is accessed. Analysis Services searches the Fiscal Year level for a member named FY 2003 and the first FY 2003 member encountered just so happens to be the member associated with the CY 2002 member of the Calendar Year level. You can verify this by explicitly requesting this cell and comparing its value to that of the previous query.

8. Modify the query to reflect the translated tuple:

```
SELECT
FROM [Chapter 3 Cube]
WHERE (
    [Date].[Calendar Year].[CY 2002],
    [Date].[Fiscal Year].[FY 2003]
    )
```

9. Execute the query and compare its results to those of the previous query.

Messages	Results
$15,921,423.19	

These steps demonstrate the process by which a reference to a leaf-level member in a user-hierarchy is translated into attribute-hierarchy references. You would expect this process to work the same for references to non-leaf members, and it does. When a reference to a non-leaf member in a user-hierarchy is made, the member is identified along with its ancestors, just as before. Descendant members, those related to the specified member in lower levels of the hierarchy are simply ignored for the purposes of translation.

10. Modify the query, specifying a member from the Calendar Year level of the user-hierarchy:

```
SELECT
FROM [Chapter 3 Cube]
WHERE (
    [Date].[Calendar-To-Fiscal Year].[Calendar Year].[CY 2002]
    )
```

11. Execute the query.

Messages	Results
$24,144,429.65	

The CY 2002 member is located within the Calendar Year level of the Calendar-To-Fiscal Year user-hierarchy. This is a non-leaf level. As before, the specified member, CY 2002, is located. That member and the members in its lineage, of which there are none (of any relevance), are translated into attribute-hierarchy references. No Fiscal Year attribute-hierarchy member reference is created, as illustrated in Figure 3-10.

You can verify this by submitting the translated tuple and comparing its results to that of the prior query.

12. Modify the query to reflect the translated tuple:

```
SELECT
FROM [Chapter 3 Cube]
WHERE (
    [Date].[Calendar Year].[CY 2002]
    )
```

Position	User-Hierarchy Translation	Partial Tuple	Rule 1: Default Member	Rule 2: (All) Member	Rule 3: First Member	Completed Tuple
Date. Calendar-To-Fiscal Year	Calendar Year. CY 2002					
Date. Calendar Year	CY 2002					CY 2002
Date. Fiscal Year		(omitted)	(not available)	All Periods		All Periods
Product. Category		(omitted)	(not available)	All Products		All Products
Product. Subcategory		(omitted)	(not available)	All Products		All Products
Measures. Measures		(omitted)	Reseller Sales Amount			Reseller Sales Amount

FIGURE 3-10 The process for completing the partial tuple specifying the member CY 2002 within the Calendar-To-Fiscal Year user-hierarchy

13. Execute the query and compare the result to those in step 11.

```
Messages  Results
$24,144,429.65
```

Avoiding Reference Conflicts

As has been mentioned, user-hierarchies are assembled from attribute-hierarchies. The translation process described in this chapter deconstructs a user-hierarchy member reference into its associated attribute-hierarchy member references. But, what if a tuple already contains a reference to one of the attribute-hierarchies from which the user-hierarchy is derived? This creates an opportunity for the translation to generate conflicting attribute-hierarchy references.

Access cells with tuples containing overlapping references

1. If you have not already done so, open the MDX Query Editor to the MDX Step-by-Step database.

2. In the code pane, enter the following query to employ references to both the Calendar-To-Fiscal Year user-hierarchy and Fiscal Year attribute-hierarchy:

```
SELECT
FROM [Chapter 3 Cube]
```

```
WHERE (
    [Date].[Calendar-To-Fiscal Year].[Calendar Year].[CY 2002],
    [Date].[Fiscal Year].[FY 2003]
    )
```

3. Execute the query.

Messages	Results
$15,921,423.19	

The process of translation and tuple completion is illustrated in Figure 3-11.

Position	User-Hierarchy Translation	Partial Tuple	Rule 1: Default Member	Rule 2: (All) Member	Rule 3: First Member	Completed Tuple
Date. Calendar-To-Fiscal Year	Calendar Year. CY 2002					
Date. Calendar Year	CY 2002					CY 2002
Date. Fiscal Year		FY 2003				FY 2003
Product. Category		*(omitted)*	*(not available)*	All Products		All Products
Product. Subcategory		*(omitted)*	*(not available)*	All Products		All Products
Measures. Measures		*(omitted)*	Reseller Sales Amount			Reseller Sales Amount

FIGURE 3-11 The process for completing the partial tuple specifying the member CY 2002 within the Calendar-To-Fiscal Year user-hierarchy and FY 2003 within the Fiscal Year attribute-hierarchy

Although the tuple is syntactically valid, the combination of references to an attribute-hierarchy and a user-hierarchy based on that same attribute-hierarchy creates an opportunity for overlapping references following translation. In the previous query, this was avoided. The same is not true in the next query.

4. Modify the query to create an overlapping reference to FY 2003:

```
SELECT
FROM [Chapter 3 Cube]
WHERE (
    [Date].[Calendar-To-Fiscal Year].[Calendar Year].[CY 2002].[FY 2003],
    [Date].[Fiscal Year].[FY 2003]
    )
```

5. Execute the query.

The translation process is illustrated in Figure 3-12.

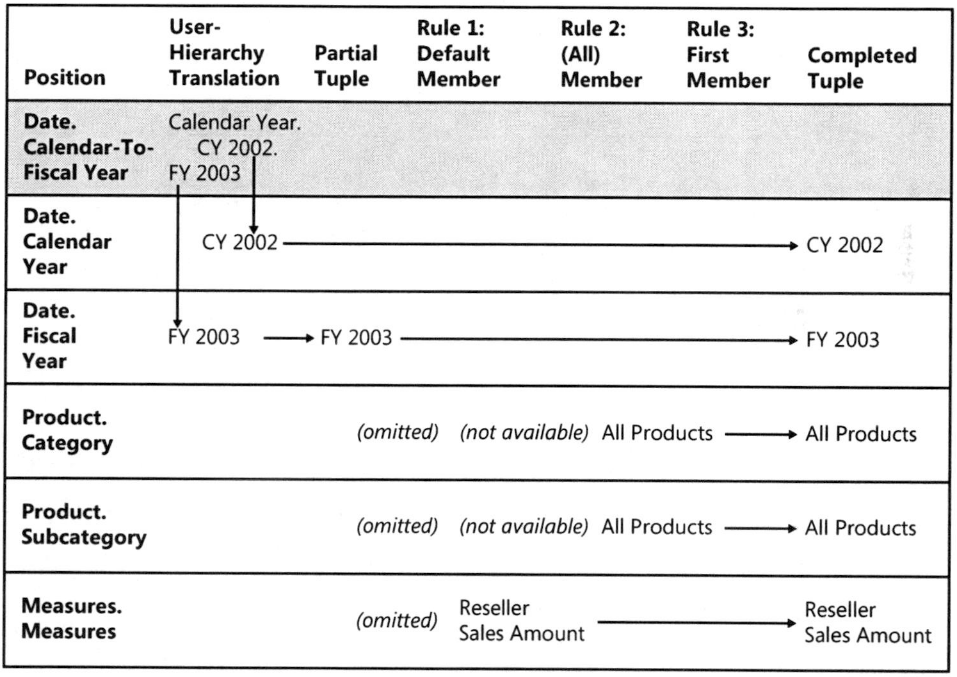

Position	User-Hierarchy Translation	Partial Tuple	Rule 1: Default Member	Rule 2: (All) Member	Rule 3: First Member	Completed Tuple
Date. Calendar-To-Fiscal Year	Calendar Year. CY 2002. FY 2003					
Date. Calendar Year		CY 2002				CY 2002
Date. Fiscal Year	FY 2003	FY 2003				FY 2003
Product. Category		*(omitted)*	*(not available)*	All Products		All Products
Product. Subcategory		*(omitted)*	*(not available)*	All Products		All Products
Measures. Measures		*(omitted)*	Reseller Sales Amount			Reseller Sales Amount

FIGURE 3-12 The process for completing the partial tuple specifying overlapping references to the FY 2003 member

Here, the user-hierarchy member reference is translated to Calendar Year and Fiscal Year attribute-hierarchy references. The tuple already employs a Fiscal Year attribute-hierarchy reference creating overlap. The overlap has a happy ending since the two Fiscal Year attribute-hierarchy member references are identical. Had this not been the case, the overlap would have created a conflict, resulting in an invalid tuple.

6. Modify the query to create an overlapping reference with conflicting Fiscal Year members:

```
SELECT
FROM [Chapter 3 Cube]
WHERE (
    [Date].[Calendar-To-Fiscal Year].[Calendar Year].[CY 2002].[FY 2003],
    [Date].[Fiscal Year].[FY 2002]
    )
```

7. Execute the query.

Messages	Results
(null)

In this query, the user-hierarchy member reference is translated into Calendar Year and Fiscal Year attribute-hierarchy references. As shown in Figure 3-13, the FY 2003 member reference created through this process conflicts with the FY 2002 attribute-hierarchy member reference. The conflict in member references results in an invalid reference to the Fiscal Year attribute-hierarchy, which results in an empty cell being returned.

Position	User-Hierarchy Translation	Partial Tuple	Rule 1: Default Member	Rule 2: (All) Member	Rule 3: First Member	Completed Tuple
Date. Calendar-To-Fiscal Year	Calendar Year. CY 2002. FY 2003					
Date. Calendar Year	CY 2002					CY 2002
Date. Fiscal Year	FY 2003 → FY 2002					*(invalid)*
Product. Category		*(omitted)*	*(not available)*	All Products →		All Products
Product. Subcategory		*(omitted)*	*(not available)*	All Products →		All Products
Measures. Measures		*(omitted)*	Reseller Sales Amount			Reseller Sales Amount

FIGURE 3-13 The process for completing the partial tuple specifying conflicting overlapping members from the Calendar-To-Fiscal Year user-hierarchy and Fiscal Year attribute-hierarchy

For the reason demonstrated here, it is recommended you consider the possibility of overlap when employing references to user-hierarchies in combination with references to the attribute-hierarchies from which they are derived.

> **Note** Analysis Services enforces a rule that a hierarchy can be referenced no more than once in a given tuple. The process of translation as demonstrated in the last two queries can result in redundant (overlapping) member references, which violates this rule without triggering an error. When working with combinations of attribute and user-hierarchies from a given dimension, be certain to understand which attribute-hierarchies are ultimately being referenced, and employ member references in a way that minimizes the potential for overlapping member references.

Member Reference Shortcuts

The last two sidebars introduced you to three forms of member reference. These forms provide greater and greater degrees of precision to address various forms of ambiguity.

However, not all member references are ambiguous. Many members are unique, whether by name or key, across all hierarchies in a dimension. Still others are unique across all hierarchies in all dimensions. In these situations, omitting the dimension or hierarchy identifier in a member reference still allows the specified member to be found without ambiguity.

Although not encouraged, Analysis Services allows you to take these shortcuts in member reference syntax. These shortcuts can include the omission of dimensions and hierarchy identifiers, allowing tuples to be expressed using a more compact format. For example, the first tuple presented in this chapter can be expressed using the shortened form:

```
(
    [Calendar Year].[All Periods],
    [Fiscal Year].[All Periods],
    [Bikes],
    [Subcategory].[Mountain Bikes],
    [Reseller Sales Amount]
)
```

Although this makes the tuple more compact (and therefore reduces the amount of typing you must do), consider some important pitfalls. First, the shortened syntax is less immediately interpretable and may be harder to support in the long run. Second, unless directed to a specific object, Analysis Services searches the various objects within the cube for matches; this results in noticeable performance overhead. Finally, and most important, Analysis Services discontinues its search as soon as a match is found. If you misjudge the ambiguity of the reference, the result of the query may not be what is expected. For this reason, we encourage you to always employ reasonably precise references supplying at a minimum the dimension and hierarchy identifiers along with the member's key or name.

Having said that, there is one shortcut we employ throughout the remainder of this book. Apart from the previous examples in this chapter, you rarely see a measure identified using its fully qualified form. Instead, measures are almost always identified using the simplified form: *[Measures].[Member]*. Although we refer to the Reseller Sales Amount measure as *[Measures].[Measures].[Reseller Sales Amount]* earlier in this chapter to demonstrate a point about measures as members, we now refer to this measure as *[Measures].[Reseller Sales Amount]* (and all other measures with the same form).

Chapter 3 Quick Reference

To	Do this
Reference a member by name	Write the member reference in the form *[Dimension].[Hierarchy].[Member Name]*. For example: `[Product].[Category].[Bikes]`
Reference a member by key	Write the member reference in the form *[Dimension].[Hierarchy].&[Member Key]*. For example: `[Product].[Category].&[1]`

Reference a member by name within a level of a user-hierarchy	Write the member reference in the form *[Dimension].[Hierarchy].[Level].[Member Name]*. For example:
	
	`[Date].[Calendar-To-Fiscal Year].[Calendar Year].[CY 2003]`
	
	In some instances this member reference is ambiguous. To avoid ambiguity, you may use a member reference that includes lineage information, such as this:
	
	`[Date].[Calendar-To-Fiscal Year].[Calendar Year].[CY 2003].[FY 2003]`

Reference a cell using a tuple	Write a parentheses-enclosed, comma-delimited list of member references. For example:
	
	`(`
	`    [Date].[Calendar Year].[All Periods],`
	`    [Product].[Category].[Bikes],`
	`    [Product].[Subcategory].[Mountain Bikes]`
	`)`
	
	Keep in mind user-hierarchy member references will be translated into attribute-hierarchy member references and any missing attribute-hierarchy member references will be supplied by Analysis Services.

Retrieve cell properties as part of the query result set	Include the *CELL PROPERTIES* keyword in the MDX *SELECT* statement, indicating the desired cell properties. For example:
	
	`SELECT`
	`FROM [Chapter 3 Cube]`
	`WHERE (`
	`    [Product].[Subcategory].[Mountain Bikes],`
	`    [Date].[Calendar Year].[All Periods],`
	`    [Date].[Fiscal Year].[All Periods],`
	`    [Product].[Category].[Bikes],`
	`    [Measures].[Measures].[Reseller Sales Amount]`
	`    )`
	`CELL PROPERTIES FORMATTED_VALUE, FORMAT_STRING`
	
	Otherwise, do not specify the *CELL PROPERTIES* keyword to return the default properties *VALUE* and *FORMATTED_VALUE*.

Chapter 4
Working with Sets

After completing this chapter, you will be able to:

- Assemble sets using basic techniques

- Employ sets to retrieve multiple cells through a single query

- Explain the basic components of the *SELECT* statement

In the last chapter, you learned how a tuple is used to locate a cell within a cube. In this chapter, you build upon that concept, using collections of tuples, known as sets, to retrieve multiple cells. Along the way, you expand your understanding of the *SELECT* statement and gain exposure to some basic set-building MDX functions.

Set Basics

In Analysis Services, a *set* is a collection of tuples. Within a set, individual tuples are separated from each other by commas, and the set itself is enclosed in braces ({ }). The following is an example of a basic set:

```
{
    ([Product].[Category].[Accessories]),
    ([Product].[Category].[Bikes]),
    ([Product].[Category].[Clothing]),
    ([Product].[Category].[Components])
}
```

> **Note** The line breaks and indentations are purely for readability.

Notice that each tuple in the preceding set contains a single member reference and each reference is to the same hierarchy, *[Product].[Category]*. These tuples are said to have *shared hierarchality*, which is a requirement for their inclusion within the set.

With multipart tuples, the requirements for set membership become a bit more complex. Not only must the same hierarchies be referenced between tuples, but each tuple must also reference these hierarchies in the same order as the other tuples in the set. This requirement is referred to as *shared dimensionality*. The following is a valid set of multipart tuples exhibiting both shared hierarchality and shared dimensionality:

```
{
    ([Product].[Category].[Accessories], [Date].[Calendar]. [CY 2004]),
    ([Product].[Category].[Bikes], [Date].[Calendar].[CY 2002]),
    ([Product].[Category].[Clothing], [Date].[Calendar].[CY 2003]),
    ([Product].[Category].[Components], [Date].[Calendar].[CY 2001])
}
```

Other than these two constraints, Analysis Services places few limitations on sets. Sets may contain any number of tuples, duplicate tuples are permitted, and tuples may be specified in any order within a set. These concepts are explored in the following exercise.

Assemble a basic set

1. Open the MDX Query Editor to the MDX Step-by-Step database.

2. In the Metadata Browser, select the Step-by-Step cube.

3. Use the Metadata Browser to refresh your understanding of the cube's structure.

   The Step-by-Step cube, first explored in Chapter 2, "Using the MDX Query Editor," is a much more robust cube than Chapter 3 Cube. Within the Step-by-Step cube are multiple measure groups, many with more than one measure, and numerous dimensions containing both user- and attribute-hierarchies. Despite its additional complexity, Analysis Services presents the Step-by-Step cube as a cube space using the same principles described in the last chapter.

4. In the code pane, enter the following query employing two basic sets:

```
SELECT
    {
        ([Date].[Calendar].[CY 2002], [Geography].[Country].[United States]),
        ([Date].[Calendar].[CY 2003], [Geography].[Country].[United States]),
        ([Date].[Calendar].[CY 2004], [Geography].[Country].[United States])
        } ON COLUMNS,
    {
        ([Product].[Category].[Accessories]),
        ([Product].[Category].[Bikes]),
        ([Product].[Category].[Clothing]),
        ([Product].[Category].[Components])
        } ON ROWS
FROM [Step-by-Step]
```

5. Execute the query.

	CY 2002	CY 2003	CY 2004
	United States	United States	United States
Accessories	$61,263.90	$151,136.35	$76,027.18
Bikes	$14,716,804.14	$16,139,984.68	$7,951,335.55
Clothing	$317,939.41	$495,443.62	$197,590.92
Components	$2,526,542.06	$3,284,551.84	$1,137,105.72

Please ignore the details of the *SELECT* statement until the next section of this chapter. Instead, focus your attention on the two sets of tuples defined within the query.
The first set contains three tuples. Each of these three tuples contains two member references, the first associated with the Date dimension's Calendar user-hierarchy and

the second with the Geography dimension's Country attribute-hierarchy. The second set contains four tuples. Each of the four tuples in this second set contains one member reference associated with the Product dimension's Category attribute-hierarchy.

Remember the rule of shared hierarchality requires all tuples within a set to reference members of the same hierarchies. To test this rule, add a fifth tuple to the second set referencing a different hierarchy.

6. Add a tuple referencing the Subcategory attribute-hierarchy's Mountain Bikes member to the second set:

```
SELECT
    {
        ([Date].[Calendar].[CY 2002], [Geography].[Country].[United States]),
        ([Date].[Calendar].[CY 2003], [Geography].[Country].[United States]),
        ([Date].[Calendar].[CY 2004], [Geography].[Country].[United States])
        } ON COLUMNS,
    {
        ([Product].[Category].[Accessories]),
        ([Product].[Category].[Bikes]),
        ([Product].[Category].[Clothing]),
        ([Product].[Category].[Components]),
        ([Product].[Subcategory].[Mountain Bikes])
        } ON ROWS
FROM [Step-by-Step]
```

 Note Be certain to add a comma to separate the newly added tuple from the previous one.

7. Execute the query.

```
Messages
Executing the query ...
Members belong to different hierarchies in the  function.
~
Execution complete
```

As indicated by the message returned, the rule of shared hierarchality is violated and the query fails. All tuples in the second set reference the Category attribute-hierarchy except for the newly added one, which references the Subcategory attribute-hierarchy.

For the second set to be valid, all members must reference the same hierarchy. You may remember from your exploration of the Step-by-Step cube in Chapter 2 that the Product Categories user-hierarchy contains levels derived from the Category and Subcategory (and Product) attribute-hierarchies. Therefore, all the members in the second set—Accessories, Bikes, Clothing, Components, and Mountain Bikes—are found in this one hierarchy. This provides a simple means of addressing this violation while including these members in the set.

8. Alter the hierarchy object identifiers in the second set to point to the Product Categories user-hierarchy:

```
SELECT
    {
        ([Date].[Calendar].[CY 2002], [Geography].[Country].[United States]),
        ([Date].[Calendar].[CY 2003], [Geography].[Country].[United States]),
        ([Date].[Calendar].[CY 2004], [Geography].[Country].[United States])
        } ON COLUMNS,
    {
        ([Product].[Product Categories].[Accessories]),
        ([Product].[Product Categories].[Bikes]),
        ([Product].[Product Categories].[Clothing]),
        ([Product].[Product Categories].[Components]),
        ([Product].[Product Categories].[Mountain Bikes])
        } ON ROWS
FROM [Step-by-Step]
```

9. Execute the query and observe the five members along the *ROWS* axis.

	CY 2002	CY 2003	CY 2004
	United States	United States	United States
Accessories	$61,263.90	$151,136.35	$76,027.18
Bikes	$14,716,804.14	$16,139,984.68	$7,951,335.55
Clothing	$317,939.41	$495,443.62	$197,590.92
Components	$2,526,542.06	$3,284,551.84	$1,137,105.72
Mountain Bikes	$6,970,418.73	$5,832,626.02	$2,539,198.92

Shared dimensionality requires all tuples within a set containing more than one member reference address hierarchies in the same order. The first set in the preceding query contains multipart tuples and provides an opportunity to verify this rule.

10. Alter the first tuple in the first set by transposing the member references:

```
SELECT
    {
        ([Geography].[Country].[United States], [Date].[Calendar].[CY 2002]),
        ([Date].[Calendar].[CY 2003], [Geography].[Country].[United States]),
        ([Date].[Calendar].[CY 2004], [Geography].[Country].[United States])
        } ON COLUMNS,
    {
        ([Product].[Product Categories].[Accessories]),
        ([Product].[Product Categories].[Bikes]),
        ([Product].[Product Categories].[Clothing]),
        ([Product].[Product Categories].[Components]),
        ([Product].[Product Categories].[Mountain Bikes])
        } ON ROWS
FROM [Step-by-Step]
```

11. Execute the query.

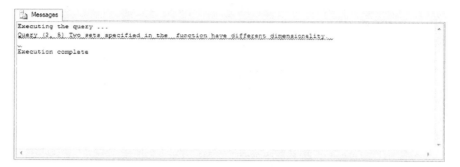

As expected, the query fails complaining of differing dimensionality. The problem is corrected by aligning the sequence in which the hierarchies are referenced within the set's tuples.

12. Align the tuples in the first set by transposing the member references of the second and third tuples:

```
SELECT
    {
        ([Geography].[Country].[United States], [Date].[Calendar].[CY 2002]),
        ([Geography].[Country].[United States], [Date].[Calendar].[CY 2003]),
        ([Geography].[Country].[United States], [Date].[Calendar].[CY 2004])
        } ON COLUMNS,
    {
        ([Product].[Product Categories].[Accessories]),
        ([Product].[Product Categories].[Bikes]),
        ([Product].[Product Categories].[Clothing]),
        ([Product].[Product Categories].[Components]),
        ([Product].[Product Categories].[Mountain Bikes])
        } ON ROWS
FROM [Step-by-Step]
```

13. Execute the query and review the results.

Compare the query results to those depicted in step 9. Notice that the column headers are transposed but, as expected, the cell values are the same.

| | United States | United States | United States |
	CY 2002	CY 2003	CY 2004
Accessories	$61,263.90	$151,136.35	$76,027.18
Bikes	$14,716,804.14	$16,139,984.68	$7,951,335.55
Clothing	$317,939.41	$495,443.62	$197,590.92
Components	$2,526,542.06	$3,284,551.84	$1,137,105.72
Mountain Bikes	$6,970,418.73	$5,832,626.02	$2,539,198.92

Shared hierarchality and shared dimensionality are the two rules you must keep up with when assembling sets. Other than that, Analysis Services is very flexible, allowing tuples to be duplicated and specified in any order.

14. Reverse the order of the tuples in the first set, moving the tuple referencing CY 2002 to the bottom of the set and the tuple referencing CY 2004 to the top:

```
SELECT
    {
        ([Geography].[Country].[United States], [Date].[Calendar].[CY 2004]),
        ([Geography].[Country].[United States], [Date].[Calendar].[CY 2003]),
        ([Geography].[Country].[United States], [Date].[Calendar].[CY 2002])
        } ON COLUMNS,
    {
        ([Product].[Product Categories].[Accessories]),
        ([Product].[Product Categories].[Bikes]),
        ([Product].[Product Categories].[Clothing]),
        ([Product].[Product Categories].[Components]),
        ([Product].[Product Categories].[Mountain Bikes])
        } ON ROWS
FROM [Step-by-Step]
```

15. Add another tuple referencing the Accessories member of the Product Categories user-hierarchy to the top of the second set, creating a duplicate tuple:

```
SELECT
    {
        ([Geography].[Country].[United States], [Date].[Calendar].[CY 2004]),
        ([Geography].[Country].[United States], [Date].[Calendar].[CY 2003]),
        ([Geography].[Country].[United States], [Date].[Calendar].[CY 2002])
        } ON COLUMNS,
    {
        ([Product].[Product Categories].[Accessories]),
        ([Product].[Product Categories].[Accessories]),
        ([Product].[Product Categories].[Bikes]),
        ([Product].[Product Categories].[Clothing]),
        ([Product].[Product Categories].[Components]),
        ([Product].[Product Categories].[Mountain Bikes])
        } ON ROWS
FROM [Step-by-Step]
```

16. Execute the query.

	United States	United States	United States
	CY 2004	CY 2003	CY 2002
Accessories	$76,027.18	$151,136.35	$61,263.90
Accessories	$76,027.18	$151,136.35	$61,263.90
Bikes	$7,951,335.55	$16,139,984.68	$14,716,804.14
Clothing	$197,590.92	$495,443.62	$317,939.41
Components	$1,137,105.72	$3,284,551.84	$2,526,542.06
Mountain Bikes	$2,539,198.92	$5,832,626.02	$6,970,418.73

Notice the order of the calendar years in the column headers of the result set follows the order specified in the set. Notice, too, that the duplicate Accessories member is preserved within the row headers. Analysis Services takes the position that the set you specify is the set you intend and therefore preserves duplicates and ordering as demonstrated in this exercise.

The *Distinct* Function

Duplicate tuples often occur in sets formed through complex logic. You can remove duplicates from sets using the *Distinct* function.

```
Distinct( {Set} )
```

The *Distinct* function takes as its sole argument a set and returns the distinct set of the tuples within it. The following query illustrates its use and impact on sets:

```
SELECT
    {
        ([Geography].[Country].[United States], [Date].[Calendar].[CY 2004]),
        ([Geography].[Country].[United States], [Date].[Calendar].[CY 2003]),
        ([Geography].[Country].[United States], [Date].[Calendar].[CY 2002])
        } ON COLUMNS,
    Distinct(
        {
            ([Product].[Product Categories].[Accessories]),
            ([Product].[Product Categories].[Accessories]),
            ([Product].[Product Categories].[Bikes]),
            ([Product].[Product Categories].[Clothing]),
            ([Product].[Product Categories].[Components]),
            ([Product].[Product Categories].[Mountain Bikes])
            }
        ) ON ROWS
FROM [Step-by-Step]
```

	United States	United States	United States
	CY 2004	CY 2003	CY 2002
Accessories	$76,027.18	$151,136.35	$61,263.90
Bikes	$7,951,335.55	$16,139,984.68	$14,716,804.14
Clothing	$197,590.92	$495,443.62	$317,939.41
Components	$1,137,105.72	$3,284,551.84	$2,526,542.06
Mountain Bikes	$2,539,198.92	$5,832,626.02	$6,970,418.73

Notice that the second set in the MDX query contains two partial tuples with a reference to Accessories, but by employing the *Distinct* function to the set only a single Accessories member is present in the query results.

Understanding the *SELECT* Statement

In the previous exercise, you used the *SELECT* statement to assign sets to two named axes, *ROWS* and *COLUMNS*. The term *axes* (plural of axis) should be very familiar to you from Chapter 3, "Understanding Tuples."

Within that chapter, a cube is described as an n-dimensional space (a cube space), within which the attribute-hierarchies of the cube's dimensions form axes. The members of the attribute-hierarchies reside at positions along their associated axes. The intersection of members of the various axes within the cube form points identifiable through tuples and cells that contain data reside at those points.

The purpose of the *SELECT* statement is to define a new cube space. Within this new cube space are axes, such as *COLUMNS* and *ROWS*, explicitly defined in the *SELECT* statement. Positions along these axes are occupied by the members (or member combinations) of the tuples in the sets assigned to these axes by the statement. This is illustrated in Figure 4-1 for the cube space formed by the first *SELECT* statement in this chapter.

In this figure, three calendar year and country combinations are defined in a set that is assigned to the axis labeled *COLUMNS*. In another set, four categories are defined and assigned to the axis labeled *ROWS*. Together, these two axes form a two-dimensional space with points at the intersection of the positions along these axes.

As before, those intersections are identified by tuples. In Figure 4-1, this is demonstrated for the point at the intersection of the *[CY 2002], [United States]* position along the *COLUMNS* axis and the *[Accessories]* position along the *ROWS* axis. This point has a tuple of *([CY 2002], [United States], [Accessories])*.

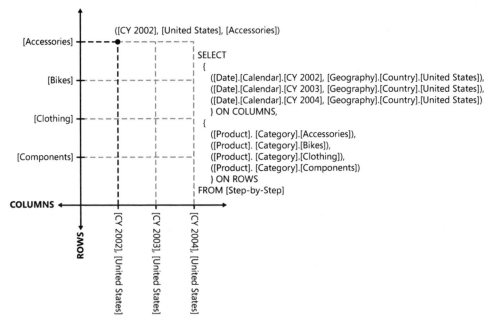

FIGURE 4-1 The first *SELECT* statement in this chapter and the cube space it defines

To resolve the query, each point in the space defined by the *SELECT* statement is resolved against the cube space identified in the statement's *FROM* clause. If the submitted tuple for a given point defined in the query is a partial tuple in the underlying cube space (which is usually the case), Analysis Services fills in the missing references as described in Chapter 3 to access the associated cell. The requested data is then returned as a cell in a cell set, forming the query's result.

The introduction of a *WHERE* clause adds an interesting wrinkle to this logic. You can think of the *WHERE* clause as an additional axis within the query's cube space. This axis, often referred to as the *slicer axis*, has one position occupied by the tuple assigned to the *WHERE* clause. The member or member combinations at this one position influence every tuple in the query's cube space.

This is demonstrated in Figure 4-2, in which the member *[United States]* has been moved from the tuples in the set along the *COLUMNS* axis and into the tuple assigned to the *WHERE* clause. The tuples formed in this new query are the same as those in the last but are formed with the introduction of the third, slicer axis.

> **Note** Though it is referred to as the slicer axis and is presented as a third axis in this model, the *WHERE* clause does not truly form an axis in the same way as *COLUMNS* and *ROWS*. Instead, the *WHERE* clause restricts the cube space defined in the *FROM* clause. The distinction is subtle and, at this point in the learning process, can be largely ignored. Still, the special nature of the *WHERE* clause is the source of some of the behavior described later in this chapter.

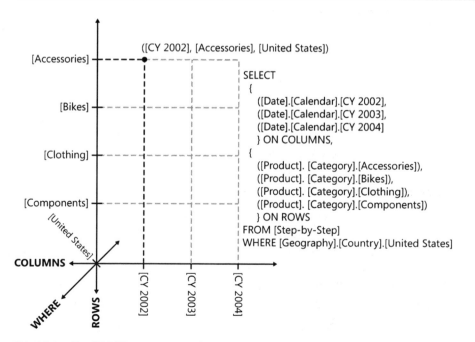

FIGURE 4-2 The *SELECT* statement employing a *WHERE* clause

With this in mind, re-execute the first query from the beginning of this chapter. Follow the preceding logic to understand how each cell in the cell set is resolved.

Explore the *SELECT* statement

1. If you have not already done so, open the MDX Query Editor to the MDX Step-by-Step database.

2. In the code pane, re-enter the following query from the previous exercise:

```
SELECT
    {
        ([Date].[Calendar].[CY 2002], [Geography].[Country].[United States]),
        ([Date].[Calendar].[CY 2003], [Geography].[Country].[United States]),
        ([Date].[Calendar].[CY 2004], [Geography].[Country].[United States])
        } ON COLUMNS,
    {
        ([Product].[Category].[Accessories]),
        ([Product].[Category].[Bikes]),
        ([Product].[Category].[Clothing]),
        ([Product].[Category].[Components])
        } ON ROWS
FROM [Step-by-Step]
```

3. Execute the query and review the results.

	CY 2002	CY 2003	CY 2004
	United States	United States	United States
Accessories	$61,263.90	$151,136.35	$76,027.18
Bikes	$14,716,804.14	$16,139,984.68	$7,951,335.55
Clothing	$317,939.41	$495,443.62	$197,590.92
Components	$2,526,542.06	$3,284,551.84	$1,137,105.72

The *SELECT* statement assembles two axes. The first is named *COLUMNS* and contains the member-combinations CY 2002 and United States, CY 2003 and United States, and CY 2004 and United States. The second axis is named *ROWS* and contains the members Accessories, Bikes, Clothing, and Components.

At the intersection of the three members along the *COLUMNS* axis and the four members along the *ROWS* axis are 12 points, each identified with a tuple formed by the combinations of the tuples along the two axes. For example, the first of these points, the intersection of the CY 2002 and United States members along the *COLUMNS* axis and the Accessories member along the *ROWS* axis, is identified by the tuple *([Date].[Calendar].[CY 2002], [Geography].[Country].[United States], [Product].[Category].[Accessories])*.

This tuple is then applied against the Step-by-Step cube identified in the statement's *FROM* clause. In the context of this cube, the tuple is a partial tuple and is resolved using the logic outlined in Chapter 3. The associated cell in the Step-by-Step cube is returned and serves as the first cell in the query's cell set. Other cells in the cell set are resolved similiarly.

Now consider the *WHERE* clause. The *WHERE* clause affects every tuple in the new cube space by implicitly including each of its member references at the intersection of the members along the *SELECT* statement's axes. The United States member, applied to each tuple in this cell set, is a good candidate to demonstrate the behavior of the *WHERE* clause.

4. Alter the query by removing the references to the United States member from the tuples in the first set:

```
SELECT
    {
        ([Date].[Calendar].[CY 2002]),
        ([Date].[Calendar].[CY 2003]),
        ([Date].[Calendar].[CY 2004])
        } ON COLUMNS,
    {
        ([Product].[Category].[Accessories]),
        ([Product].[Category].[Bikes]),
        ([Product].[Category].[Clothing]),
        ([Product].[Category].[Components])
        } ON ROWS
FROM [Step-by-Step]
```

5. Add a *WHERE* clause with a tuple referencing the United States member:

```
SELECT
    {
        ([Date].[Calendar].[CY 2002]),
        ([Date].[Calendar].[CY 2003]),
        ([Date].[Calendar].[CY 2004])
        } ON COLUMNS,
    {
        ([Product].[Category].[Accessories]),
        ([Product].[Category].[Bikes]),
        ([Product].[Category].[Clothing]),
        ([Product].[Category].[Components])
        } ON ROWS
FROM [Step-by-Step]
WHERE ([Geography].[Country].[United States])
```

6. Execute the query.

	CY 2002	CY 2003	CY 2004
Accessories	$61,263.90	$151,136.35	$76,027.18
Bikes	$14,716,804.14	$16,139,984.68	$7,951,335.55
Clothing	$317,939.41	$495,443.62	$197,590.92
Components	$2,526,542.06	$3,284,551.84	$1,137,105.72

The cell set is the same as before. This is because the tuples formed by the intersection of the tuples along the *COLUMNS* and *ROWS* axes and the slicer axis are identical to those formed by the last query. The difference between the first and the last query is in how the tuples are formed. In the first query, the United States member is part of each member combination along the *COLUMNS* axis. In the last query, the United States member is part of the *WHERE* clause and is appended to the tuples at the intersection of the members along the *COLUMNS* and *ROWS* axes.

SELECT Statement Axes

Within the *SELECT* statement, sets are assigned to axes using the *ON* keyword followed by the name of the axis as illustrated in the preceding exercise. The *SELECT* statement supports up to 128 axes with each axis formally named *Axis(n)* where *n* is the number 0 through 127.

Rarely will you see the formal axis name used. Instead, the axis can be identified just by its number, 0 through 127, or by an alias. The *SELECT* statement supports an alias for each of the first five axes, as identified in Table 4-1.

TABLE 4-1 Formal, short, and alias names for the first five axes of the *SELECT* statement

Formal Name	Short Name	Alias
AXIS(0)	0	COLUMNS
AXIS(1)	1	ROWS
AXIS(2)	2	PAGES
AXIS(3)	3	SECTIONS
AXIS(4)	4	CHAPTERS

Regardless of the naming style you employ, axis assignments within the *SELECT* statement must be consecutive. In other words, if you assign a set to *Axis(1)*, or *ROWS*, you must make an assignment to *Axis(0)*, or *COLUMNS*. That said, you are free to assign sets to any number of consecutive axis or disregard axis assignments altogether, as you did throughout Chapter 3.

Although it has been said you can assign sets to up to 128 axes, you typically make use of no more than the first two axes. Most applications are limited to a two-dimensional display and present data in a tabular format. Individual cells or cell sets employing one or two axis are about all that can be displayed in this manner. Although some tools do support the use of more than two axes, most do so by dividing the data into multiple tabular displays.

Building Sets with Functions

The exercises and examples presented thus far make use of explicit set declarations. In other words, individual sets are assembled from individual tuples using individual member references. Although building sets this way is perfectly valid and at times necessary or even preferable, many other times, especially when set membership is dynamic, sets are best built employing the MDX set-building functions. The most frequently employed of these functions are *Members* and *Crossjoin*.

The *Members* Function

The *Members* function is the most basic and frequently used of the set-building functions. It is a very simple function with no parameters or qualifiers other than the name of the hierarchy or hierarchy level from which a set of members is to be derived.

```
[Dimension].[Hierarchy].Members
[Dimension].[Hierarchy].[Level].Members
```

When employed against a hierarchy with no level specified, the function returns the set of members from all levels of the hierarchy including the (All) member. When a level is specified, only those members from the specified level are returned. This is demonstrated in the following exercise.

> **Note** As mentioned earlier, the *Members* function returns a set of members, but throughout this chapter you have been presented with sets as collections of tuples. Behind the scene, Analysis Services is implicitly converting each individual member returned by the *Members* function into a tuple consisting of a single member reference.
>
> Although not a terrible useful bit of information, this is presented to avoid any confusion in terminology. A set consists of tuples, but collections of members are commonly referred to as sets by many MDX developers (ourselves included). Nothing is wrong with this as long as you keep in mind that an implicit conversion is actually taking place.

Build a set using the *Members* function

1. If you have not already done so, open the MDX Query Editor to the MDX Step-by-Step database.

2. In the code pane, re-enter the following query from the previous exercise:

```
SELECT
    {
        ([Date].[Calendar].[CY 2002]),
        ([Date].[Calendar].[CY 2003]),
        ([Date].[Calendar].[CY 2004])
        } ON COLUMNS,
    {
        ([Product].[Category].[Accessories]),
        ([Product].[Category].[Bikes]),
        ([Product].[Category].[Clothing]),
        ([Product].[Category].[Components])
        } ON ROWS
FROM [Step-by-Step]
WHERE ([Geography].[Country].[United States])
```

3. Execute the query and note the members along the *ROWS* axis.

	CY 2002	CY 2003	CY 2004
Accessories	$61,263.90	$151,136.35	$76,027.18
Bikes	$14,716,804.14	$16,139,984.68	$7,951,335.55
Clothing	$317,939.41	$495,443.62	$197,590.92
Components	$2,526,542.06	$3,284,551.84	$1,137,105.72

In the second set, each member in the leaf level of the Product dimension's Category attribute-hierarchy is explicitly identified. Using the *Members* function, the members of this level (the Category level) can be referenced with much less typing.

> **Note** In an attribute-hierarchy, the leaf level of the hierarchy is named the same as the attribute-hierarchy itself. The topmost level, containing the (All) member, is identified as the (All) level (parentheses included).

4. Alter the second set to extract the members of the Category attribute-hierarchy using the *Members* function:

```
SELECT
    {
        ([Date].[Calendar].[CY 2002]),
        ([Date].[Calendar].[CY 2003]),
        ([Date].[Calendar].[CY 2004])
        } ON COLUMNS,
    {[Product].[Category].[Category].Members} ON ROWS
FROM [Step-by-Step]
WHERE ([Geography].[Country].[United States])
```

5. Execute the query and confirm the results.

	CY 2002	CY 2003	CY 2004
Accessories	$61,263.90	$151,136.35	$76,027.18
Bikes	$14,716,804.14	$16,139,984.68	$7,951,335.55
Clothing	$317,939.41	$495,443.62	$197,590.92
Components	$2,526,542.06	$3,284,551.84	$1,137,105.72

The last two queries produce the same cell set. Thanks to the *Members* function, the second query does it with much less verbiage and in a manner much more flexible should the members of the Category attribute-hierarchy change over time.

> **Note** The order of the members returned by the *Members* function is based on the order assigned to attribute members at design time. When members from multiple levels are extracted, members of higher levels are immediately followed by the members of the lower level to which they are related. This staggered sort is visible in the results of the next two queries.

In the prior query, the set of members returned is limited to those of the leaf level of the attribute-hierarchy. Removing the level identifier causes all members from all levels of the hierarchy to be returned.

6. Alter the previous query to not specify the Category (leaf) level of the Category attribute-hierarchy:

```
SELECT
    {
        ([Date].[Calendar].[CY 2002]),
        ([Date].[Calendar].[CY 2003]),
        ([Date].[Calendar].[CY 2004])
        } ON COLUMNS,
    {[Product].[Category].Members} ON ROWS
FROM [Step-by-Step]
WHERE ([Geography].[Country].[United States])
```

7. Execute the query and review the results.

	CY 2002	CY 2003	CY 2004
All Products	$17,622,549.51	$20,071,116.48	$9,362,059.37
Accessories	$61,263.90	$151,136.35	$76,027.18
Bikes	$14,716,804.14	$16,139,984.68	$7,951,335.55
Clothing	$317,939.41	$495,443.62	$197,590.92
Components	$2,526,542.06	$3,284,551.84	$1,137,105.72

With the level identifier removed, all members from all levels of the hierarchy are returned. With attribute-hierarchies, these include the leaf-level members as well as the (All) member from the level above. With user-hierarchies, the effect of omitting the level identifier is much more dramatic.

8. Alter the query to display the members from all levels of the Product Categories user-hierarchy:

```
SELECT
    {
        ([Date].[Calendar].[CY 2002]),
        ([Date].[Calendar].[CY 2003]),
        ([Date].[Calendar].[CY 2004])
        } ON COLUMNS,
    {[Product].[Product Categories].Members} ON ROWS
FROM [Step-by-Step]
WHERE ([Geography].[Country].[United States])
```

9. Execute the query and evaluate the results. Notice the number of members returned along the *ROWS* axis.

	CY 2002	CY 2003	CY 2004
All Products	$17,622,549.51	$20,071,116.48	$9,362,059.37
Accessories	$61,263.90	$151,136.35	$76,027.18
Bike Racks	(null)	$57,382.62	$36,937.90
Hitch Rack - 4-Bike	(null)	$57,382.62	$36,937.90
Bike Stands	(null)	(null)	(null)
All-Purpose Bike Stand	(null)	(null)	(null)
Bottles and Cages	(null)	$2,186.60	$1,554.90
Mountain Bottle Cage	(null)	(null)	(null)
Road Bottle Cage	(null)	(null)	(null)
Water Bottle - 30 oz.	(null)	$2,186.60	$1,554.90
Cleaners	(null)	$3,379.09	$2,232.34
Bike Wash - Dissolver	(null)	$3,379.09	$2,232.34

By removing the level identifier, each member of each level in the user-hierarchy is returned in the set, regardless of the attribute-hierarchy from which the member is derived.

The *MeasureGroupMeasures* Function

The *Members* function returns all members stored within a hierarchy. When used with the Measures attribute-hierarchy, the *Members* function returns all measures within a cube without regard for the measure groups with which they are associated. To return all measures associated with a specific measure group, use the *MeasureGroupMeasures* function.

```
MeasureGroupMeasures( MeasureGroupName )
```

The *MeasureGroupMeasures* function takes as its lone parameter a string supplying the name of the measure group from which measures should be extracted:

```
SELECT
    {[Product].[Category].Members} ON COLUMNS,
    {MeasureGroupMeasures("Reseller Sales")} ON ROWS
FROM [Step-by-Step]
```

	All Products	Accessories	Bikes	Clothing	Components
Reseller Sales Amount	$80,450,596.98	$571,297.93	$66,302,381.56	$1,777,840.84	$11,799,076.66
Reseller Order Quantity	214,378	25,839	75,015	64,497	49,027
Reseller Extended Amount	$80,978,104.87	$577,985.95	$66,797,022.19	$1,798,805.33	$11,804,291.40
Reseller Tax Amount	$6,436,047.61	$45,703.83	$5,304,190.40	$142,227.25	$943,926.12
Reseller Freight Cost	$2,011,265.92	$14,282.52	$1,657,560.05	$44,446.19	$294,977.15
Discount Amount	$527,507.93	$6,688.03	$494,640.65	$20,964.51	$5,214.74
Reseller Total Product Cost	$79,980,114.38	$375,505.33	$67,293,081.45	$1,545,417.42	$10,766,110.18
Reseller Standard Product Cost	$26,693,830.57	$71,122.89	$22,039,062.39	$294,511.26	$4,289,134.03
Reseller Transaction Count	60,855	5,101	24,800	12,267	18,687
Squared Reseller Sales Amount	380951775420.723	176426996.8961	360359688555.847	495443065.300098	19920216802.6799

The *Crossjoin* Function

Frequently, you will want to combine the tuples of one set with the tuples of another to form more complex, multipart tuples. This is done using the *Crossjoin* function.

```
Crossjoin( {Set1}, {Set2} [, ... {Setn} )
```

The *Crossjoin* function takes as its parameters two or more sets. Each tuple of each set is combined with the tuples of the other sets in a multiplicative operation. Analysis Services supports the use of a cross-join operator (*), employing the same character as is usually reserved for multiplication, as a substitute for the formal use of the *Crossjoin* function.

Build a set using the *Crossjoin* function

1. If you have not already done so, open the MDX Query Editor to the MDX Step-by-Step database.

2. In the code pane, enter the following query:

```
SELECT
    {
        ([Date].[Calendar].[CY 2002]),
        ([Date].[Calendar].[CY 2003]),
        ([Date].[Calendar].[CY 2004])
        } ON COLUMNS,
    {[Product].[Category].[Category].Members} ON ROWS
FROM [Step-by-Step]
WHERE ([Geography].[Country].[United States])
```

3. Execute the query and observe the four members along the *ROWS* axis.

	CY 2002	CY 2003	CY 2004
Accessories	$61,263.90	$151,136.35	$76,027.18
Bikes	$14,716,804.14	$16,139,984.68	$7,951,335.55
Clothing	$317,939.41	$495,443.62	$197,590.92
Components	$2,526,542.06	$3,284,551.84	$1,137,105.72

4. Cross-join the set along the rows with a set containing two measures:

```
SELECT
    {
        ([Date].[Calendar].[CY 2002]),
        ([Date].[Calendar].[CY 2003]),
        ([Date].[Calendar].[CY 2004])
        } ON COLUMNS,
    Crossjoin(
        {[Product].[Category].[Category].Members},
        {
            ([Measures].[Reseller Sales Amount]),
            ([Measures].[Reseller Order Quantity])
            }
        ) ON ROWS
FROM [Step-by-Step]
WHERE ([Geography].[Country].[United States])
```

5. Execute the query.

		CY 2002	CY 2003	CY 2004
Accessories	Reseller Sales Amount	$61,263.90	$151,136.35	$76,027.18
Accessories	Reseller Order Quantity	3,426	6,848	3,125
Bikes	Reseller Sales Amount	$14,716,804.14	$16,139,984.68	$7,951,335.55
Bikes	Reseller Order Quantity	16,079	19,728	9,121
Clothing	Reseller Sales Amount	$317,939.41	$495,443.62	$197,590.92
Clothing	Reseller Order Quantity	11,284	18,028	7,250
Components	Reseller Sales Amount	$2,526,542.06	$3,284,551.84	$1,137,105.72
Components	Reseller Order Quantity	9,602	14,503	5,323

Cross-joining the four (4) product categories by the two (2) measures results in eight (4*2) tuples along the *ROWS* axis. Using the cross-join operator, (*), the query can be rewritten less formally but in a manner reflecting the multiplicative nature of cross-joins.

6. Alter the previous query to make use of the cross-join operator:

```
SELECT
    {
        ([Date].[Calendar].[CY 2002]),
        ([Date].[Calendar].[CY 2003]),
        ([Date].[Calendar].[CY 2004])
        } ON COLUMNS,
    {[Product].[Category].[Category].Members} *
        {
            ([Measures].[Reseller Sales Amount]),
            ([Measures].[Reseller Order Quantity])
            } ON ROWS
FROM [Step-by-Step]
WHERE ([Geography].[Country].[United States])
```

7. Execute the query and verify the same result set as before is returned.

		CY 2002	CY 2003	CY 2004
Accessories	Reseller Sales Amount	$61,263.90	$151,136.35	$76,027.18
Accessories	Reseller Order Quantity	3,426	6,848	3,125
Bikes	Reseller Sales Amount	$14,716,804.14	$16,139,984.68	$7,951,335.55
Bikes	Reseller Order Quantity	16,079	19,728	9,121
Clothing	Reseller Sales Amount	$317,939.41	$495,443.62	$197,590.92
Clothing	Reseller Order Quantity	11,284	18,028	7,250
Components	Reseller Sales Amount	$2,526,542.06	$3,284,551.84	$1,137,105.72
Components	Reseller Order Quantity	9,602	14,503	5,323

Limiting Sets

An important aspect of building a set is limiting its membership. Many techniques exist to assist you with this, but the most basic employ the underlying relationships between data in the cube. These techniques limit members to those which exist in valid combinations with other members in the cube.

Working with Auto-Exists

In the previous exercise, you performed a cross-join operation on two sets and observed a multiplicative effect in the resulting set. This multiplicative effect is characteristic of cross-joins between sets containing members from differing dimensions.

When cross-joins are performed between sets containing members of the same dimension, relationships between the attribute-hierarchies, whether direct or indirect, automatically limit the resulting combinations to those actually observed within the dimension. This is referred to as the auto-exists feature of Analysis Services and its presence is observed in the following exercise.

Limit a set using auto-exists functionality

1. If you have not already done so, open the MDX Query Editor to the MDX Step-by-Step database.

2. In the code pane, enter the following query:

```
SELECT
    {
        ([Date].[Calendar].[CY 2002]),
        ([Date].[Calendar].[CY 2003]),
        ([Date].[Calendar].[CY 2004])
        } *
    {
        ([Measures].[Reseller Sales Amount]),
        ([Measures].[Internet Sales Amount])
        } ON COLUMNS,
    {[Product].[Category].[Category].Members} ON ROWS
FROM [Step-by-Step]
WHERE ([Geography].[Country].[United States])
```

3. Execute the query and observe the multiplicative affect of the cross-join on the *COLUMNS* axis.

	CY 2002	CY 2002	CY 2003	CY 2003	CY 2004	CY 200
	Reseller Sales Amount	Internet Sales Amount	Reseller Sales Amount	Internet Sales Amount	Reseller Sales Amount	Internet Sales
Accessories	$61,263.90	(null)	$151,136.35	$293,709.71	$76,027.18	$407,050
Bikes	$14,716,804.14	$6,530,343.53	$16,139,984.68	$9,359,102.62	$7,951,335.55	$9,162.32
Clothing	$317,939.41	(null)	$495,443.62	$138,247.97	$197,590.92	$201,524
Components	$2,526,542.06	(null)	$3,284,551.84	(null)	$1,137,105.72	(null)

As before, the cross-join of two sets of tuples containing members of differing dimensions results in a perfect cross-product. The three tuples in the first set are multiplied by the two tuples of the second set to produce six tuples along the *COLUMNS* axis. The same effect is not observed between tuples with members of the same dimension.

4. Cross-join the set along the *ROWS* axis with the set of leaf-level members from the Product dimension's Subcategory attribute-hierarchy:

```
SELECT
    {
        ([Date].[Calendar].[CY 2002]),
        ([Date].[Calendar].[CY 2003]),
        ([Date].[Calendar].[CY 2004])
        } *
```

```
        {
            ([Measures].[Reseller Sales Amount]),
            ([Measures].[Internet Sales Amount])
        } ON COLUMNS,
    {[Product].[Category].[Category].Members} *
        {[Product].[Subcategory].[Subcategory].Members} ON ROWS
FROM [Step-by-Step]
WHERE ([Geography].[Country].[United States])
```

5. Execute the query.

		CY 2002	CY 2002	CY 2003	CY 2003	CY 200
		Reseller Sales Amount	Internet Sales Amount	Reseller Sales Amount	Internet Sales Amount	Reseller Sales
Accessories	Bike Racks	(null)	(null)	$57,382.62	$16,440.00	$36,937.
Accessories	Bike Stands	(null)	(null)	(null)	$18,921.00	(null)
Accessories	Bottles and Cages	(null)	(null)	$2,186.60	$23,280.27	$1,554.5
Accessories	Cleaners	(null)	(null)	$3,379.09	$3,044.85	$2,232.3
Accessories	Fenders	(null)	(null)	(null)	$19,408.34	(null)
Accessories	Helmets	$49,586.49	(null)	$61,131.18	$92,583.54	$24,542.
Accessories	Hydration Packs	(null)	(null)	$19,561.85	$16,771.95	$10,639.
Accessories	Lights	(null)	(null)	(null)	(null)	(null)
Accessories	Locks	$6,339.46	(null)	$3,890.52	(null)	(null)
Accessories	Panniers	(null)	(null)	(null)	(null)	(null)

6. Review the messages pane and note the number of rows returned.

```
Executing the query ...
Obtained object of type: Microsoft.AnalysisServices.AdomdClient.CellSet
Formatting.
Cell set consists of 39 rows and 8 columns.
Done formatting.
Execution complete
```

The leaf level of the Category attribute-hierarchy contains 4 members. The leaf level of the Subcategory attribute-hierarchy contains 37 members. In a perfect cross-join, a set of 4 x 37, or 148, member combinations would be produced. However, the messages pane indicates only 39 rows are returned. Two of these rows are for the column headers occupied by the Calendar Year and Measures members. This leaves 37 member combinations along the *ROWS* axis.

The direct relationship between Subcategory and Category dictates that each Subcategory member is related to one and only one Category member. In other words, with 37 subcategories and one category per subcategory, no more than 37 subcategory-category combinations are possible. These 37 combinations are exactly what are returned.

When members are associated through indirect relationships between attribute-hierarchies in a given dimension, predicting the number of combinations returned can be harder. Still, auto-exists is employed, limiting the set to those combinations actually observed in the dimension.

7. Alter the set along the *ROWS* axis to cross-join the Category leaf-level members with the leaf-level members of the indirectly related Color attribute-hierarchy:

```
SELECT
    {
        ([Date].[Calendar].[CY 2002]),
        ([Date].[Calendar].[CY 2003]),
        ([Date].[Calendar].[CY 2004])
        } *
    {
        ([Measures].[Reseller Sales Amount]),
        ([Measures].[Internet Sales Amount])
        } ON COLUMNS,
    {[Product].[Category].[Category].Members} *
        {[Product].[Color].[Color].Members} ON ROWS
FROM [Step-by-Step]
WHERE ([Geography].[Country].[United States])
```

8. Execute the query.

		CY 2002	CY 2002	CY 2003	CY 2003	CY 2004
		Reseller Sales Amount	Internet Sales Amount	Reseller Sales Amount	Internet Sales Amount	Reseller Sales Amou
Accessories	Black	$16,302.48	(null)	$20,293.73	$31,176.09	$8,314.99
Accessories	Blue	$17,569.55	(null)	$21,556.86	$29,986.43	$9,198.05
Accessories	Grey	(null)	(null)	(null)	(null)	(null)
Accessories	NA	$11,677.41	(null)	$70,443.32	$184,354.22	$40,844.67
Accessories	Red	$15,714.46	(null)	$19,280.58	$31,421.02	$7,029.84
Accessories	Silver	(null)	(null)	$19,561.85	$16,771.95	$10,639.64
Bikes	Black	$6,314,977.53	$1,728,251.55	$6,358,849.63	$3,775,240.23	$2,446,852.45
Bikes	Blue	(null)	(null)	$1,578,302.59	$817,376.85	$1,366,761.47
Bikes	Red	$4,665,086.86	$3,935,630.74	$2,189,360.17	$921,782.03	$159,795.09
Bikes	Silver	$3,043,003.18	$720,397.36	$2,567,325.63	$2,027,634.94	$1,274,149.65

The leaf level of the Category attribute-hierarchy contains 4 members; Color contains 10. A perfect cross-product produces 4 x 10, or 40, potential member combinations, although only 23 are actually observed. Auto-exists exploits the indirect relationships between the attribute-hierarchy members defined within the Product dimension to determine the set of valid combinations.

The effect of auto-exists is not only observed in cross-joins. Sets along axes are also limited by related members in the *WHERE* clause.

9. Alter the query to limit the set of Category and Color members along the *ROWS* axis to those associated with the Mountain Bikes subcategory:

```
SELECT
    {
        ([Date].[Calendar].[CY 2002]),
        ([Date].[Calendar].[CY 2003]),
        ([Date].[Calendar].[CY 2004])
        } *
```

```
    {
        ([Measures].[Reseller Sales Amount]),
        ([Measures].[Internet Sales Amount])
    } ON COLUMNS,
    {[Product].[Category].[Category].Members} *
        {[Product].[Color].[Color].Members} ON ROWS
FROM [Step-by-Step]
WHERE ([Geography].[Country].[United States],
        [Product].[Subcategory].[Mountain Bikes])
```

10. Execute the query.

		CY 2002	CY 2002	CY 2003	CY 2003	CY 2004	CY 2
		Reseller Sales Amount	Internet Sales Amount	Reseller Sales Amount	Internet Sales Amount	Reseller Sales Amount	Internet Sal
Bikes	Black	$3,927,415.56	$842,059.40	$3,265,300.39	$1,962,003.53	$1,265,049.27	$1,775.:
Bikes	Silver	$3,043,003.18	$720,397.36	$2,567,325.63	$2,027,634.94	$1,274,149.65	$2,039.4

In the prior query, a cross-join between the leaf-level members of the Category and Color attribute-hierarchies is performed to define a set along the *ROWS* axis. Auto-exists limits the resulting set to the 23 valid combinations observed within the Product dimension.

But in this latest query, only two combinations are observed. With the Mountain Bikes member of the Product dimension's Subcategory hierarchy introduced in the *WHERE* clause, the set along the *ROWS* axis is restricted to those color and category combinations found in association with this particular member in their shared dimension.

This demonstrates a special feature of the *WHERE* clause. Through auto-exists functionality, members in the tuple of the *WHERE* clause influence membership in sets along the axes. This same influence is not observed between the sets along the traditional query axes.

The *Exists* Function

The previous exercise demonstrates the limiting effect of auto-exists. When two sets containing members of the same dimension are cross-joined, the resulting set is limited to those combinations of members actually observed in that dimension. When the *WHERE* clause contains a member of a dimension, sets along the axes containing members from that same dimension are limited as well.

A common thread in these two examples is that the members on both sides of the limiting effect are present in the tuples generated by the query. Frequently, you may wish to limit one set by another using auto-exists functionality but without the members of the second set present in the results. In these situations, the *Exists* function can be employed.

```
Exists( {Set1}, {Set2} )
```

The *Exists* function employs auto-exists to limit the members of the first set to those observed in combination with the members of the second based on relationships in their common dimension. Though the second set exerts influence over set membership, the returned set only contains members from the first set.

Limit a set using the *Exists* function

1. If you have not already done so, open the MDX Query Editor to the MDX Step-by-Step database.

2. If required, enter the following query from the previous exercise:

```
SELECT
    {
        ([Date].[Calendar].[CY 2002]),
        ([Date].[Calendar].[CY 2003]),
        ([Date].[Calendar].[CY 2004])
        } *
        {
            ([Measures].[Reseller Sales Amount]),
            ([Measures].[Internet Sales Amount])
            } ON COLUMNS,
    {[Product].[Category].[Category].Members} *
        {[Product].[Color].[Color].Members} ON ROWS
FROM [Step-by-Step]
WHERE ([Geography].[Country].[United States],
        [Product].[Subcategory].[Mountain Bikes])
```

3. Execute the query and review the results:

		CY 2002	CY 2002	CY 2003	CY 2003	CY 2004	CY 2
		Reseller Sales Amount	Internet Sales Amount	Reseller Sales Amount	Internet Sales Amount	Reseller Sales Amount	Internet Sale
Bikes	Black	$3,927,415.56	$842,059.40	$3,265,300.39	$1,962,003.53	$1,265,049.27	$1,775,
Bikes	Silver	$3,043,003.18	$720,397.36	$2,567,325.63	$2,027,634.94	$1,274,149.65	$2,039,

When the Mountain Bikes Subcategory member is assigned to the *WHERE* clause, it limits the set along the *ROWS* axis to those combinations of Category and Color members associated with the Mountain Bikes member (and each other). It also influences the tuples produced so that each cell returned is associated with the Mountain Bikes Subcategory member.

To illustrate this, consider the first cell in the cell set, which has the value $3,927,415.56. The query produces the following tuple to access this cell:

```
(
    [Date].[Calendar].[CY 2002],
    [Measures].[Reseller Sales Amount],
    [Product].[Category].[Bikes],
    [Product].[Color].[Black],
    [Geography].[Country].[United States],
    [Product].[Subcategory].[Mountain Bikes]
)
```

Using the *Exists* function, you can use the Mountain Bikes Subcategory member to limit the set of Category and Color members along the *ROWS* axis to those associated with the Mountain Bikes member but without the presence of the Mountain Bikes member in the tuples formed by the query.

4. Alter the query to limit the set along the *ROWS* axis to those member combinations associated with the Mountain Bikes Subcategory member but without limiting the values returned to Mountain Bikes:

```
SELECT
    {
        ([Date].[Calendar].[CY 2002]),
        ([Date].[Calendar].[CY 2003]),
        ([Date].[Calendar].[CY 2004])
        } *
    {
        ([Measures].[Reseller Sales Amount]),
        ([Measures].[Internet Sales Amount])
        } ON COLUMNS,
    Exists(
        {[Product].[Category].[Category].Members} *
            {[Product].[Color].[Color].Members},
        {([Product].[Subcategory].[Mountain Bikes])}
        ) ON ROWS
FROM [Step-by-Step]
WHERE ([Geography].[Country].[United States])
```

5. Execute the query.

		CY 2002	CY 2002	CY 2003	CY 2003	CY 2004	CY 2
		Reseller Sales Amount	Internet Sales Amount	Reseller Sales Amount	Internet Sales Amount	Reseller Sales Amount	Internet Sale
Bikes	Black	$6,314,977.53	$1,728,251.55	$6,358,849.63	$3,775,240.23	$2,446,852.45	$2,809,1
Bikes	Silver	$3,043,003.18	$720,397.36	$2,567,325.63	$2,027,634.94	$1,274,149.65	$2,039,1

The cell set has the same structure as before, but notice that the values have changed. The first cell of the cell set now has a value of $6,314,977.53 whereas it had a value of

$3,927,415.56 in the previous query. This is because the tuple associated with the cell no longer contains the Mountain Bikes Subcategory member:

```
(
    [Date].[Calendar].[CY 2002],
    [Measures].[Reseller Sales Amount],
    [Product].[Category].[Bikes],
    [Product].[Color].[Black],
    [Geography].[Country].[United States]
)
```

You can verify this by using the previous tuple to retrieve this cell from the cube.

6. Enter the following query to retrieve the cell using the tuple identified in the previous step:

```
SELECT
FROM [Step-by-Step]
WHERE (
    [Date].[Calendar].[CY 2002],
    [Measures].[Reseller Sales Amount],
    [Product].[Category].[Bikes],
    [Product].[Color].[Black],
    [Geography].[Country].[United States]
    )
```

7. Execute the query and verify the value matches that of the first cell in the cell set of the previous query.

The *NON EMPTY* Keyword and the Other-Form of the *Exists* Function

Cross-joins between members of hierarchies from differing dimensions can result in many, many member combinations not likely to be found in the data warehouse. Take for example, the following query, within which reseller sales for employees in the month of May 2002 is retrieved:

```
SELECT
    {[Measures].[Reseller Sales Amount]} ON COLUMNS,
    {[Date].[Month].[May 2002]} *
        {[Employee].[Employee].Members} ON ROWS
FROM [Step-by-Step]
```

		Reseller Sales Amount
May 2002	All Employees	$2,269,116.71
May 2002	A. Scott Wright	(null)
May 2002	Alan J. Brewer	(null)
May 2002	Alejandro E. McGuel	(null)
May 2002	Alex M. Nayberg	(null)
May 2002	Alice O. Ciccu	(null)
May 2002	Amy E. Alberts	(null)
May 2002	Andreas T. Berglund	(null)
May 2002	Andrew M. Cencini	(null)
May 2002	Andrew R. Hill	(null)
May 2002	Andy M. Ruth	(null)
May 2002	Angela W. Barbariol	(null)

The Employee and Month attribute-hierarchies are from differing dimensions, so that a perfect cross-join is performed. However, not every employee has sales for this month, as evidenced by the large number of empty (null) cells returned. This makes the query appear to contain a lot of junk combinations along the rows. One way to eliminate these empty cells is to employ the *NON EMPTY* keyword along the *ROWS* axis:

```
SELECT
    {[Measures].[Reseller Sales Amount]} ON COLUMNS,
    NON EMPTY {[Date].[Month].[May 2002]} *
        {[Employee].[Employee].Members} ON ROWS
FROM [Step-by-Step]
```

		Reseller Sales Amount
May 2002	All Employees	$2,269,116.71
May 2002	David R. Campbell	$115,901.80
May 2002	Garrett R. Vargas	$172,622.35
May 2002	Jillian Carson	$464,167.31
May 2002	José Edvaldo Saraiva	$212,020.26
May 2002	Linda C. Mitchell	$401,687.56
May 2002	Michael G. Blythe	$172,429.58
May 2002	Pamela O. Ansman-Wolfe	$252,116.05
May 2002	Shu K. Ito	$103,508.43
May 2002	Tsvi Michael Reiter	$374,663.36

Very frequently, you see the *NON EMPTY* keyword employed in queries generated by tools such as the Microsoft SQL Server Reporting Services Report Designer and Microsoft Office Excel. The *NON EMPTY* keyword forces Analysis Services to remove member combinations along the specified axis with which nothing but empty cells are associated.

The assumption behind the use of the *NON EMPTY* keyword is that an entry along an axis with which nothing but empty cells is associated is a junk entry or otherwise of no value in the query result. This can be an invalid assumption.

To illustrate this, reconsider the preceding query. Not every employee has sales for the month of May 2002, but this might be for a number of reasons. One employee may have no sales responsibilities, so you would not expect sales associated with him or her. Another employee may have sales responsibility and is not fulfilling those obligations. Eliminating employees of the first group (those without sales responsibility) from the set of employees on the *ROWS* axis adds value to the query. Eliminating employees of the second group (those with sales responsibility) from the set detracts value. A variant of the *Exists* function can help you limit the set of employees appropriately.

This variant of the *Exists* function allows you to compare two sets derived from differing dimensions. The relationship between these sets is derived from their association in the facts recorded in a specified measure group. Those members in the first set related to members in the second set as recorded in the identified measure group are returned by the function.

The Step-by-Step database contains a measure group called Sales Targets within which quarterly sales targets for employees are recorded. With May 2002 belonging to the second quarter of calendar year 2002, you can use the *Exists* function to limit the set of Employees along the *ROWS* axis to those for whom a Q2 target has been specified. Notice that in the result set, Stephen Y. Jiang is now present but with no sales in this month.

```
SELECT
    {[Measures].[Reseller Sales Amount]} ON COLUMNS,
    {[Date].[Month].[May 2002]} *
        Exists(
            {[Employee].[Employee].Members},
            {[Date].[Calendar].[Q2 CY 2002]},
            "Sales Targets"
            ) ON ROWS
FROM [Step-by-Step]
```

		Reseller Sales Amount
May 2002	All Employees	$2,269,116.71
May 2002	David R. Campbell	$115,901.80
May 2002	Garrett R. Vargas	$172,622.35
May 2002	Jillian Carson	$464,167.31
May 2002	José Edvaldo. Saraiva	$212,020.26
May 2002	Linda C. Mitchell	$401,687.56
May 2002	Michael G. Blythe	$172,429.58
May 2002	Pamela O. Ansman-Wolfe	$252,116.05
May 2002	Shu K. Ito	$103,508.43
May 2002	Stephen Y. Jiang	(null)
May 2002	Tsvi Michael. Reiter	$374,663.36

Chapter 4 Quick Reference

To	Do this

Assemble a fixed set of tuples	Assemble the tuples in a comma-delimited list of tuples and enclose the list in braces ({ }). For example:
	
	`{`
	    `([Product].[Category].[Accessories]),`
	    `([Product].[Category].[Bikes])`
	`}`
	
	Each tuple in the set must contain the same number of member references from the same hierarchies, and those hierarchies must be referenced in the same order.

To	Do this
Assemble the set of all members from a hierarchy or hierarchy level	Append the *Members* function to the name of the hierarchy or hierarchy level, as demonstrated here: ``` [Product].[Category].Members [Product].[Category].[Category].Members ```

Remove duplicate tuples from a set	Use the *Distinct* function with a set. For example:
	
	``
	SELECT
	    Distinct(
	        {
	            ([Product].[Category].[Bikes]),
	            ([Product].[Category].[Bikes])
	        }
	    ) ON COLUMNS
	FROM [Step-by-Step]
	``

To assemble the cross-product of one or more sets	Use the *Crossjoin* function. The following query assembles the combination of May 2002 and all employees:
	
	``
	SELECT
	    Crossjoin(
	        {[Date].[Month].[May 2002]},
	        {[Employee].[Employee].Members}
	        ) ON COLUMNS
	FROM [Step-by-Step]
	``
	
	Alternatively, you can employ the cross-join operator to perform the same operation:
	
	``
	SELECT
	    {[Date].[Month].[May 2002]} *
	        {[Employee].[Employee].Members} ON COLUMNS
	FROM [Step-by-Step]
	``

Return the members of a set related to the members of another	Use the *Exists* function. The following query limits the set of colors to those found in association with the Mountain Bikes Subcategory:
	
	``
	SELECT
	    Exists(
	        {[Product].[Color].[Color].Members},
	        {([Product].[Subcategory].[Mountain Bikes])}
	        ) ON COLUMNS
	FROM [Step-by-Step]
	``

Eliminate empty cells from an axis of a *SELECT* statement	Use the *NON EMPTY* keyword along the appropriate axis. In the following query, the *NON EMPTY* keyword is used to eliminate combinations of May 2002 and Employees with which no reseller sales are associated:
	
	``
	SELECT
	    {([Measures].[Reseller Sales Amount])} ON COLUMNS,
	    NON EMPTY {[Date].[Month].[May 2002]}
	        * {[Employee].[Employee].Members} ON ROWS
	FROM [Step-by-Step]
	``

Chapter 5
Working with Expressions

After completing this chapter, you will be able to:

- Assemble expressions employing constants, tuples, members, and sets

- Explain the concept of expression context

- Successfully employ context to build dynamic expressions

Although Analysis Services is highly efficient at storing and retrieving values, the ability to calculate new values—values difficult to derive from the relational data warehouse—is where Analysis Services really shines. Expressions provide this capability.

The subject of expressions is very broad in nature. In this chapter, you focus on a particular type of expression known as a calculated member. Calculated members are frequently employed for calculating new values in Analysis Services cubes and provide an accessible starting point for exploring expression concepts.

Expression Basics

You can think of an expression as a formula. Within this formula, one or more values are combined to produce a result. The following example is a simple but valid expression within which two constant values are combined to form a resulting value of 2:

`1 + 1`

Most expressions return numeric values, but results are not limited to this. Expressions may return numeric, string, date, Boolean, and other types of values.

Expression results are formed by combining values using operators. Table 5-1 presents the comparison, logical, numeric, string, and set operators supported by MDX.

TABLE 5-1 Operators Supported by Analysis Services

Symbol	Operator	Returns	Description
IS	Object Comparison	Boolean	Performs an equivalency comparison between two objects
-	Except	Set	Returns the difference between two sets, removing duplicates
-	Negative	Number	Returns the negative value of a numeric expression
-	Subtract	Number	Subtracts one number from another number

TABLE 5-1 Operators Supported by Analysis Services

Symbol	Operator	Returns	Description
*	Cross-Join	Set	Returns the cross product of two sets
*	Multiply	Number	Multiplies two numbers
/	Divide	Number	Divides one number by another number
^	Power	Number	Raises one number by another number
:	Range	Set	Returns a naturally ordered set of all members between inclusive of the specified members
+	Add	Number	Adds two numbers
+	Positive	Number	Returns the positive value of a numeric expression
+	String Concatenation	String	Concatenates two character strings or tuples
+	Union	Set	Returns a union of two sets, removing duplicates
<	Less Than	Boolean	Performs a less than comparison between two values
<=	Less Than or Equal To	Boolean	Performs a less than or equal to comparison between two values
<>	Not Equal To	Boolean	Performs a not equal to comparison between two values
=	Equal To	Boolean	Performs an equal to comparison between two values
>	Greater Than	Boolean	Performs a greater than comparison between two values
>=	Greater Than or Equal To	Boolean	Performs a greater than or equal to comparison between two values
AND	Logical Conjunction	Boolean	Performs a logical conjunction on two values
IS	Logical Comparison	Boolean	Performs a logical comparison on two values
NOT	Logical Inverse	Boolean	Performs a logical negation on a Boolean value
OR	Logical Disjunction	Boolean	Performs a logical disjunction on two values
XOR	Logical Exclusion	Boolean	Performs a logical exclusion on two values

When multiple operators are in use, Analysis Services evaluates an expression using a standard order of operations, as documented in SQL Server Books Online. Though precise and clearly defined, relying on the order of operations in your expressions can make them challenging to interpret. Instead of relying on this feature, it is strongly recommended that you make use of parentheses to determine the order within which parts of an expression are evaluated.

Functions provide another means by which values are combined within an expression. Analysis Services supports a wide range of native MDX functions, many of which are presented in this book. This set of functions can be extended through assemblies, four of which come pre-installed with Analysis Services. Some of the more useful non-native functions made available through these assemblies are the VBA functions listed in Table 5-2.

TABLE 5-2 VBA Functions Available Through Built-in Assemblies

Abs	CSng	DateDiff	IPmt	LTrim	Oct	Round	Time
Array	CStr	DatePart	InStr	Left	PPmt	SLN	TimeSerial
Asc	CVDate	DateSerial	InStrB	LeftB	PV	SYD	TimeValue
AscB	Ccur	DateValue	Int	Len	Partition	Second	Timer
AscW	Choose	Day	IsDate	LenB	Pmt	Sgn	Trim
Atn	Chr	Exp	IsEmpty	Log	QBColor	Sin	TypeName
CBool	ChrW	FileLen	IsError	Mid	RGB	Sqr	UCase
CByte	Cos	Fix	IsNull	MidB	RTrim	Str	Val
CDate	Cvar	Format	IsNumeric	Minute	Rate	StrComp	Weekday
CDbl	DDB	Hex	IsObject	Month	Right	String	Year
CInt	Date	Hour	Item	NPer	RightB	Switch	
CLng	DateAdd	IIf	LCase	Now	Rnd	Tan	

When calling a non-native function, you may need to identify the assembly through which the function is provided. You do this by preceding the function with the assembly's registered name and an exclamation point (!). This is demonstrated in the following expression, which returns the first character on the left of the string ABC:

```
VBAMDX!Left( "ABC", 1)
```

Finally, expressions can be quite long and complex. It is recommended that you make use of comments within expressions to improve interpretability. Inline comments are supported through double dashes (--) and double forward slashes (//). Multiline comments are supported through blocks of paired forward slashes and asterisks (/* ... */), as demonstrated here:

```
/* This expression adds one
and one to produce a result
of 2. */
1 + 1
```

Working with *Null* in Expressions

A cell to which no value has been assigned is referred to as an empty cell. The value associated with such a cell is the *Null* value.

The *Null* value is special within databases in that it represents an absence of data. A *Null* value can be interpreted in a number of ways, but in general the value is said to be unknown. This often causes problems with the evaluation of the *Null* value.

Analysis Services handles this by converting the *Null* value to a default value depending on the operation being performed against it. When involved in an addition, subtraction or power operation, Analysis Services treats the *Null* value as a 0 numeric value. In a string concatenation operation, the *Null* value is treated as an empty string, and in a Boolean operation, the *Null* value is treated as a *False* value. (Surprisingly, in a multiplication operation and when employed as the divisor in a division operation, the *Null* value is preserved so that the result of the operation is *Null*.)

If you need to determine whether a value is equivalent to *Null*, you may use the *IsEmpty* function. This function evaluates a value and returns *True* if the value is *Null* and *False* if it is not. Alternatively, you may use the *IS* operator to compare a value to the keyword *Null*. This expression returns *True* if the two are equivalent; otherwise it returns *False*.

Calculated Members

You can think of a calculated member as just another member of an existing attribute or user-hierarchy. However, unlike traditional members, calculated members have no data actually stored at the points in the cube space associated with them. Instead, calculated members are assigned an MDX expression. That expression is evaluated as a cell associated with the calculated member is accessed to determine the cell's value. The following exercise provides a simple demonstration of a calculated member.

Construct a Simple Calculated Member

1. Open the MDX Query Editor to the MDX Step-by-Step database.

2. In the code pane, enter the following query:

```
SELECT
    {
        ([Date].[Calendar Year].[CY 2003]),
        ([Date].[Calendar Year].[CY 2004])
        } ON COLUMNS,
    {
        ([Product].[Category].[Accessories]),
        ([Product].[Category].[Bikes]),
        ([Product].[Category].[Clothing]),
        ([Product].[Category].[Components])
        } ON ROWS
FROM [Step-by-Step]
```

3. Execute the query and review the results.

    This is a simple query, much like the ones you explored in the last chapter. The *COLUMNS* axis is assigned two members of the Calendar Year attribute-hierarchy, and the *ROWS* axis is assigned four members of the Category attribute-hierarchy. Each of these six members—the

	CY 2003	CY 2004
Accessories	$296,532.88	$161,794.33
Bikes	$25,551,775.07	$13,399,243.18
Clothing	$371,864.19	$386,013.16
Components	$5,482,497.29	$2,091,011.92

two calendar years and the four categories—along with the values of the cells at their intersections are directly derived from the cube's data source, the relational data warehouse.

A calculated member differs from these members in that the calculated member does not originate from the data source. In addition, the cells with which it is associated do not contain stored data. Instead, the values of these cells are defined through an expression.

4. Alter the query to define a calculated member of the Category attribute-hierarchy named X employing a simple expression:

```
WITH
MEMBER [Product].[Category].[All Products].[X] AS
    1+1
SELECT
    {
        ([Date].[Calendar Year].[CY 2003]),
        ([Date].[Calendar Year].[CY 2004])
        } ON COLUMNS,
    {
        ([Product].[Category].[Accessories]) ,
        ([Product].[Category].[Bikes]),
        ([Product].[Category].[Clothing]),
        ([Product].[Category].[Components])
        } ON ROWS
FROM [Step-by-Step]
```

5. Add the calculated member X to the *ROWS* axis:

```
WITH
MEMBER [Product].[Category].[All Products].[X] AS
    1+1
SELECT
    {
       ([Date].[Calendar Year].[CY 2003]),
       ([Date].[Calendar Year].[CY 2004])
    } ON COLUMNS,
    {
       ([Product].[Category].[Accessories]) ,
       ([Product].[Category].[Bikes]),
       ([Product].[Category].[Clothing]),
       ([Product].[Category].[Components]),
       ([Product].[Category].[X])
       } ON ROWS
FROM [Step-by-Step]
```

6. Execute the query and observe the newly defined calculated member X.

	CY 2003	CY 2004
Accessories	$296,532.88	$161,794.33
Bikes	$25,551,775.07	$13,399,243.18
Clothing	$871,864.19	$386,013.16
Components	$5,482,497.29	$2,091,011.92
X	2	2

Calculated members, like any member in a cube, must be associated with a hierarchy. In the previous query, the calculated member X is assigned to the Product dimension's Category attribute-hierarchy. This member is assigned an expression of 1+1 that evaluates to a value of 2. This expression is highly simplistic but it affords you an opportunity to explore how cells associated with the calculated member are resolved.

To refresh your memory of how cells in a query are resolved, start with the first cell, the one at the intersection of CY 2003 and Accessories. With no *WHERE* clause, the tuple for this cell is *([Date].[Calendar Year].[CY 2003], [Product].[Category].[Accessories])*. This tuple is handed over to Analysis Services as a partial tuple, which it completes through the application of its three rules. The completed tuple is then used to locate a point within the cube space formed by the Step-by-Step cube and access the associated cell. The value of that cell is then returned.

Now, apply that logic to the cell at the intersection of CY 2003 and the calculated member X. With no *WHERE* clause, the partial tuple for that cell is *([Date].[Calendar Year].[CY 2003], [Product].[Category].[X])*. Analysis Services applies its rules to complete the tuple and then uses this tuple to locate a point within the cube space.

At this point, we have no stored cell—only an instruction for how to determine the value of the cell being accessed. This instruction, the calculated member's expression, states that the value of this cell should be 1+1, which evaluates to a value of 2. This is the value returned with the query.

The *AllMembers* Function

In the last chapter, you were presented with the *Members* function. The *Members* function returns the members stored within an attribute or user-hierarchy. This does not include calculated members, as demonstrated in the following query:

```
WITH
MEMBER [Product].[Category].[All Products].[X] AS
    1+1
```

```
SELECT
    {
        ([Date].[Calendar Year].[CY 2003]),
        ([Date].[Calendar Year].[CY 2004])
        } ON COLUMNS,
    {[Product].[Category].[Category].Members} ON ROWS
FROM [Step-by-Step]
```

	CY 2003	CY 2004
Accessories	$296,532.88	$161,794.33
Bikes	$25,551,775.07	$13,399,243.18
Clothing	$871,864.19	$386,013.16
Components	$5,482,497.29	$2,091,011.92

To retrieve all members associated with a hierarchy, regardless of whether they are stored or calculated, use the *AllMembers* function.

```
[Dimension].[Hierarchy].AllMembers
[Dimension].[Hierarchy].[Level].AllMembers
```

The syntax of the *AllMembers* function is the same as that of the *Members* function. Use the *AllMembers* function when you wish to retrieve both the stored and calculated members associated with a hierarchy, as demonstrated in the following example:

```
WITH
MEMBER [Product].[Category].[All Products].[X] AS
    1+1
SELECT
    {
        ([Date].[Calendar Year].[CY 2003]),
        ([Date].[Calendar Year].[CY 2004])
        } ON COLUMNS,
    {[Product].[Category].[Category].AllMembers} ON ROWS
FROM [Step-by-Step]
```

	CY 2003	CY 2004
Accessories	$296,532.88	$161,794.33
Bikes	$25,551,775.07	$13,399,243.18
Clothing	$871,864.19	$386,013.16
Components	$5,482,497.29	$2,091,011.92
X	2	2

Declaring Calculated Members

Calculated members are declared as members of a hierarchy using a member reference format. In the form employed in the previous exercise, the calculated member is declared in relation to a parent member within a hierarchy. This format defines the calculated member as a child of the identified parent. For example, the calculated member X is defined as a child of the (All) member of the Product dimension's Category attribute-hierarchy.

Alternatively, a calculated member can simply be assigned to a hierarchy without an identified parent member. When this form is used, the calculated member is assigned to the topmost level of the hierarchy as a sibling of any other member(s) in this level. This is the form typically employed when assigning a calculated member to the Measures attribute-hierarchy.

Calculated members may be defined within the *WITH* clause of a *SELECT* statement, as demonstrated by the previous exercise. This creates a calculated member that is said to be *query-scoped*. In other words, the calculated member is only available in the query within which it is declared. Other statements defining session-scoped and cube-scoped calculated members are supported in the MDX language. Cube-scoped calculated members are addressed in Chapter 10, "Enhancing the Cube."

Building Dynamic Expressions

In Analysis Services, a tuple identifies a cell and that cell provides access to a value. It's a small logical leap, but you could say that a tuple simply represents a value. Doing so allows you to incorporate tuples into expressions as placeholders for values. These tuple placeholders differ from the constant values you employed in the last exercise in that their value is variable, depending on the context within which the expression is being resolved. In this way, incorporating tuples allows you to build dynamic expressions. The following exercise demonstrates these concepts.

Construct a dynamic calculated member

1. If you have not already done so, open the MDX Query Editor to the MDX Step-by-Step database.

2. If required, enter the following query from the previous exercise:

```
WITH
MEMBER [Product].[Category].[All Products].[X] AS
    1+1
```

```
SELECT
    {
        ([Date].[Calendar Year].[CY 2003]),
        ([Date].[Calendar Year].[CY 2004])
        } ON COLUMNS,
    {[Product].[Category].AllMembers} ON ROWS
FROM [Step-by-Step]
```

3. Replace the first constant in the expression with a tuple containing nothing more than a member reference to the Bikes member of the Category attribute-hierarchy:

```
WITH
MEMBER [Product].[Category].[All Products].[X] AS
    ([Product].[Category].[Bikes])+1
SELECT
    {
        ([Date].[Calendar Year].[CY 2003]),
        ([Date].[Calendar Year].[CY 2004])
        } ON COLUMNS,
    {[Product].[Category].AllMembers} ON ROWS
FROM [Step-by-Step]
```

4. Execute the query and compare the values associated with X to those associated with Bikes.

	CY 2003	CY 2004
All Products	$32,202,669.43	$16,038,062.60
Accessories	$296,532.88	$161,794.33
Bikes	$25,551,775.07	$13,399,243.18
Clothing	$871,864.19	$386,013.16
Components	$5,482,497.29	$2,091,011.92
X	$25,551,776.07	$13,399,244.18

The values associated with the calculated member X are evaluated using a tuple with a member reference to the Bikes Category member. If you look closely at the values associated with X, you see they are the same as the values associated with Bikes plus the constant value 1. And just like the values associated with Bikes, the values associated with X vary between calendar years.

Before explaining how this works, complete the expression by replacing the second constant with another tuple.

5. Replace the remaining constant in the expression with a tuple containing nothing more than a member reference for the Accessories member of the Category attribute-hierarchy:

```
WITH
MEMBER [Product].[Category].[All Products].[X] AS
    ([Product].[Category].[Bikes]) + ([Product].[Category].[Accessories])
```

```
SELECT
    {
        ([Date].[Calendar Year].[CY 2003]),
        ([Date].[Calendar Year].[CY 2004])
        } ON COLUMNS,
    {[Product].[Category].AllMembers} ON ROWS
FROM [Step-by-Step]
```

6. Rename the calculated member Bikes & Accessories:

```
WITH
MEMBER [Product].[Category].[All Products].[Bikes & Accessories] AS
    ([Product].[Category].[Bikes]) + ([Product].[Category].[Accessories])
SELECT
    {
        ([Date].[Calendar Year].[CY 2003]),
        ([Date].[Calendar Year].[CY 2004])
        } ON COLUMNS,
    {[Product].[Category].AllMembers} ON ROWS
FROM [Step-by-Step]
```

7. Execute the query and compare the values associated with Bikes & Accessories with those associated with the individual Bikes and Accessories members.

	CY 2003	CY 2004
All Products	$32,202,669.43	$16,038,062.60
Accessories	$296,532.88	$161,794.33
Bikes	$25,551,775.07	$13,399,243.18
Clothing	$871,864.19	$386,013.16
Components	$5,482,497.29	$2,091,011.92
Bikes & Accessori...	$25,848,307.95	$13,561,037.52

The calculated member, now named Bikes & Accessories, employs an expression containing two tuples: One references the Category attribute-hierarchy member Bikes, and the other references Accessories from the same hierarchy. The calculated member adds these values together to serve as its return value.

> **Note** You may notice a slight difference in the last decimal place between the Bikes & Accessories value and the value you would expect by manually adding the Bikes and Accessories values as displayed on screen. Keep in mind that what is displayed through the results pane is a formatted value. Applying formatting to numeric values introduces rounding, which can lead to these slight variations. You may notice similar rounding issues in queries throughout this book.

Notice that the values associated with the calculated member vary between calendar years just as the values associated with the Bikes and Accessories members do. Applying the logic introduced in the preceding section of this chapter, you can see why this is the case.

Consider the cell at the intersection of the CY 2003 and Bikes & Accessories. This cell has a partial tuple of *([Date].[Calendar Year].[CY 2003], [Product].[Category].[Bikes & Accessories])*. Analysis Services completes this tuple by applying its three rules, as described in Chapter 3, "Understanding Tuples." The partial tuple for this cell and the process by which it is completed are illustrated in Figure 5-1.

> **Note** Figure 5-1 does not present all attribute-hierarchies within the Step-by-Step cube. The attribute-hierarchies displayed are those displayed in Chapter 3 for the purpose of presenting this information in a familiar form.

Position	Partial Tuple	Three Rules	Completed Tuple
Date. Calendar Year	CY 2003 ———————————————→		CY 2003
Date. Fiscal Year	*(omitted)*	All Periods	All Periods
Product. Category	Bikes & Accessories ———————→		Bikes & Accessories
Product. Subcategory	*(omitted)*	All Products	All Products
Measures. Measures	*(omitted)*	Reseller Sales Amount	Reseller Sales Amount

FIGURE 5-1 The process by which the partial tuple *([Date].[Calendar Year].[CY 2003], [Product].[Category].[Bikes & Accessories])* is completed

After applying its three rules, Analysis Services now has a completed tuple it can use to access a cell in the cube space. However, the completed tuple contains a calculated member and therefore does not point to a location at which a cell has been actually recorded. Instead, Analysis Services must apply the expression for the calculated member to derive the cell at this location.

The expression for the calculated member Bikes & Accessories combines the values associated with two partial tuples: *([Product].[Category].[Bikes])* and *([Product].[Category] .[Accessories])*. To determine the values associated with these partial tuples, Analysis Services must now complete them. Instead of applying the three rules to fill in the missing member references, Analysis Services completes the partial tuples by taking any missing member references from the completed tuple associated with the current cell. To say this another way, the completed tuple containing the calculated member provides the *context* within which the expression's partial tuples are resolved.

To illustrate this process, consider the first partial tuple in the expression, *([Product].[Category].[Bikes])*, as presented in Figure 5-2. In this partial tuple, a member reference to the Category attribute-hierarchy is provided. All other member references are omitted. These omitted references are completed using the member references supplied by the expression's context. This same logic applies to the other partial tuple in the expression.

Position	Context	Partial Tuple	Completed Tuple
Date. Calendar Year	CY 2003 ——— (omitted) ——→		CY 2003
Date. Fiscal Year	All Periods ——— (omitted) ——→		All Periods
Product. Category	Bikes & Accessories	Bikes	Bikes
Product. Subcategory	All Products ——— (omitted) ——→		All Products
Measures. Measures	Reseller Sales Amount — (omitted) ——→		Reseller Sales Amount

FIGURE 5-2 The process by which the partial tuple *([Product].[Category].[Bikes])* in the expression for the calculated member Bikes & Accessories is resolved

The purpose of this example is to illustrate why the value associated with Bikes & Accessories varies by calendar year. You can now see by relying on the context for missing references, such as Calendar Year, the partial tuples in the expression support this variability. When the context points to calendar year 2003 and a reference to Calendar Year is omitted in the expression's partial tuples, the partial tuple uses CY 2003 for this member reference. When the context points to calendar year 2004, the partial tuple uses CY 2004. In this way, you can think of partial tuples in expressions as variables in a formula.

Resolving Contextual Conflicts

The process of resolving cells associated with calculated members as described in the last exercise creates two critical opportunities for problems. These are problems with infinite recursion and solve order.

Avoiding Infinite Recursion

In the previous exercise, you created a calculated member Bikes & Accessories, which was assigned to the Product dimension's Category attribute-hierarchy. Partial tuples in this calculated member's expression contain references to the Category attribute-hierarchy so that when these partial tuples are completed using context, the calculated member in the context is displaced.

Had the calculated member not been displaced, the partial tuples would have been completed and these completed tuples would have retained the calculated member Bikes & Accessories. Analysis Services could attempt to resolve this calculated member, but in doing so it would only end up with tuples still containing a reference to this calculated member. This un-resolvable, circular process is referred to as *infinite recursion*. Analysis Services detects this problem and throws an *infinite recursion error*.

To avoid infinite recursion, it is important you give careful consideration to which hierarchy you assign your calculated members. Make sure each tuple in the calculated member's expression contains an explicit reference to a member of the hierarchy to which the calculated member is assigned. If one (or more) of these references is to another calculated member, make sure that calculated member does not point back, directly or indirectly, to your calculated member.

Generate an infinite recursion error

1. If you have not already done so, open the MDX Query Editor to the MDX Step-by-Step database.

2. In the code pane, re-enter the following query from the previous exercise:

```
WITH
MEMBER [Product].[Category].[All Products].[Bikes & Accessories] AS
    ([Product].[Category].[Bikes]) + ([Product].[Category].[Accessories])
SELECT
    {
        ([Date].[Calendar Year].[CY 2003]),
        ([Date].[Calendar Year].[CY 2004])
        } ON COLUMNS,
    {[Product].[Category].AllMembers} ON ROWS
FROM [Step-by-Step]
```

3. Replace the tuples in the calculated member's expression with tuples containing member references to the United States and Canada members of the Geography dimension's Country attribute-hierarchy:

```
WITH
MEMBER [Product].[Category].[All Products].[Bikes & Accessories] AS
    ([Geography].[Country].[United States]) + ([Geography].[Country].[Canada])
SELECT
    {
        ([Date].[Calendar Year].[CY 2003]),
        ([Date].[Calendar Year].[CY 2004])
    } ON COLUMNS,
    {[Product].[Category].AllMembers} ON ROWS
FROM [Step-by-Step]
```

4. Execute the query and note the resulting error associated with the calculated member.

	CY 2003	CY 2004
Accessories	$296,532.88	$161,794.33
Bikes	$25,551,775.07	$13,399,243.18
Clothing	$871,864.19	$386,013.16
Components	$5,482,497.29	$2,091,011.92
Bikes & Accessori...	#Error	#Error

Notice that the cells associated with the calculated member Bikes & Accessories each contain an error message.

5. Double-click the first cell of the last row to open the Cell Properties dialog box. Review the error message displayed in the dialog box. You may find it helpful to expand the dialog box.

Property	Value
CellOrdinal	8
VALUE	#Error Infinite recursion detected. The loop of dependencies is: Bikes & Accessories -> Bikes & Accessories.
FORMATTED_VALUE	#Error Infinite recursion detected. The loop of dependencies is: Bikes & Accessories -> Bikes & Accessories.

6. Click OK to close the dialog box.

The calculated member Bikes & Accessories is associated with the Product dimension's Category attribute-hierarchy. The tuples in the expression associated with this calculated member contain no reference to this attribute-hierarchy.

When context is applied to complete the tuples in the calculated member's expression, the calculated member is not displaced. As a result, the calculated member is referenced within the tuples in its own expression. Analysis Services detects this and throws an error for these cells.

Controlling Solve Order

Consider the following formula:

```
1 + 1 * 2
```

If the standard order of operations is followed, the multiplication operation is performed first, followed by the addition operation, resulting in a value of 3. If the standard order of operations is ignored and the expression is calculated from left to right, a value of 4 is produced. When multiple operations are performed within a formula to produce a value, the order in which those operations are performed affects the outcome.

The same is true in MDX expressions. When a tuple contains more than one calculated member and those calculated members employ operations with differing precedence in the standard order of operations, the value returned is said to be dependent upon *solve order*. Just as you use parentheses in formulas to explicitly control the order in which parts of a formula are executed, you use the *SOLVE_ORDER* property of calculated members to affect the order in which calculated members within a tuple are resolved.

The value associated with a tuple can also be dependent on solve order when multiple calculated members are referenced and the expressions associated with these employ conflicting references to the same hierarchies. This occurs less frequently than the scenario described earlier and is demonstrated in the following exercise.

Use solve order to control the precedence of calculated members

1. If you have not already done so, open the MDX Query Editor to the MDX Step-by-Step database.

2. In the code pane, enter the following query to calculate the percentage of bikes relative to all categories for the current measure:

```
WITH
MEMBER [Product].[Category].[All Products].[Percent Bikes] AS
    ([Product].[Category].[Bikes])/([Product].[Category].[All Products])
    ,FORMAT_STRING="Percent"
```

```
SELECT
    {
        ([Measures].[Reseller Sales Amount]),
        ([Measures].[Internet Sales Amount])
        } ON COLUMNS,
    {[Product].[Category].AllMembers} ON ROWS
FROM [Step-by-Step]
```

3. Execute the query and review the calculated member Percent Bikes.

	Reseller Sales Amount	Internet Sales Amount
All Products	$80,450,596.98	$29,358,677.22
Accessories	$571,297.93	$700,759.96
Bikes	$66,302,381.56	$28,318,144.65
Clothing	$1,777,840.84	$339,772.61
Components	$11,799,076.66	(null)
Percent Bikes	82.41%	96.46%

In the previous exercise, you noticed that sales amounts of products in the Bikes far exceed the sales amounts of other categories. In this query, a calculated member determining the percentage contribution of Bikes is defined.

 Note The calculated member introduces the *FORMAT_STRING* property, which is explained in the sidebar "Formatting Calculated Members."

The results of the query show that the Bikes category accounts for 82.41% of the Reseller Sales Amount measure. For Internet Sales Amount, the percentage is even higher, 96.46%. What about across combined reseller and Internet sales?

4. Add a calculated member associated with the Measures attribute-hierarchy that calculates combined reseller and Internet sales amounts:

```
WITH
MEMBER [Measures].[Combined Sales Amount] AS
    ([Measures].[Reseller Sales Amount])+([Measures].[Internet Sales Amount])
MEMBER [Product].[Category].[All Products].[Percent Bikes] AS
    ([Product].[Category].[Bikes])/([Product].[Category].[All Products])
    ,FORMAT_STRING="Percent"
SELECT
    {
        ([Measures].[Reseller Sales Amount]),
        ([Measures].[Internet Sales Amount])
        } ON COLUMNS,
    {[Product].[Category].AllMembers} ON ROWS
FROM [Step-by-Step]
```

5. Add the new calculated member to the *COLUMNS* axis:

```
WITH
MEMBER [Measures].[Combined Sales Amount] AS
    ([Measures].[Reseller Sales Amount])+([Measures].[Internet Sales Amount])
MEMBER [Product].[Category].[All Products].[Percent Bikes] AS
    ([Product].[Category].[Bikes])/([Product].[Category].[All Products])
    ,FORMAT_STRING="Percent"
SELECT
    {
        ([Measures].[Reseller Sales Amount]),
        ([Measures].[Internet Sales Amount]),
        ([Measures].[Combined Sales Amount])
        } ON COLUMNS,
    {[Product].[Category].AllMembers} ON ROWS
FROM [Step-by-Step]
```

6. Execute the query and observe the values associated with the Combined Sales Amount calculated member, especially the value for Percent Bikes.

	Reseller Sales Amount	Internet Sales Amount	Combined Sales Amount
All Products	$80,450,596.98	$29,358,677.22	$109,809,274.20
Accessories	$571,297.93	$700,759.96	$1,272,057.89
Bikes	$66,302,381.56	$28,318,144.65	$94,620,526.21
Clothing	$1,777,840.84	$339,772.61	$2,117,613.45
Components	$11,799,076.66	(null)	$11,799,076.66
Percent Bikes	82.41%	96.46%	178.87%

As before, Bikes account for 82.41% and 96.46% of reseller sales and Internet sales amounts, respectively. Combined, Bikes account for 178.87%. Wait a minute. That's not right, is it?

Of course it isn't. Analysis Services, when presented with a tuple containing both the Percent Bikes and Combined Sales Amount calculated members, elected to resolve the Percent Bikes calculated member first, causing the percentage associated with Reseller Sales Amount and the other percentage associated with Internet Sales Amount to be added together.

What should have happened is that the Combined Sales Amount should have been calculated first followed by Percent Bikes. To enforce this order of operations, the *SOLVE_ORDER* property is applied to the two expressions.

7. Assign solve order instructions to the two expressions, requiring Analysis Services to resolve Combined Sales Amount first followed by Percent Bikes:

```
WITH
MEMBER [Measures].[Combined Sales Amount] AS
    ([Measures].[Reseller Sales Amount])+([Measures].[Internet Sales Amount])
    ,SOLVE_ORDER=1
```

```
MEMBER [Product].[Category].[All Products].[Percent Bikes] AS
    ([Product].[Category].[Bikes])/([Product].[Category].[All Products])
    ,FORMAT_STRING="Percent"
    ,SOLVE_ORDER=2
SELECT
    {
        ([Measures].[Reseller Sales Amount]),
        ([Measures].[Internet Sales Amount]),
        ([Measures].[Combined Sales Amount])
    } ON COLUMNS,
    {[Product].[Category].AllMembers} ON ROWS
FROM [Step-by-Step]
```

8. Execute the query and note the new value associated with Combined Sales Amount and Percent Bikes.

	Reseller Sales Amount	Internet Sales Amount	Combined Sales Amount
All Products	$80,450,596.98	$29,358,677.22	$109,809,274.20
Accessories	$571,297.93	$700,759.96	$1,272,057.89
Bikes	$66,302,381.56	$28,318,144.65	$94,620,526.21
Clothing	$1,777,840.84	$339,772.61	$2,117,613.45
Components	$11,799,076.66	(null)	$11,799,076.66
Percent Bikes	82.41%	96.46%	86.17%

The *SOLVE_ORDER* property defines the order in which calculated members are resolved when a tuple contains two or more calculated members. The calculated member with the lowest *SOLVE_ORDER* property value is resolved first.

The *SOLVE_ORDER* property takes a wide range of values; you aren't required to assign sequential values such as those used in the preceding exercise. Generally speaking, you should not assign a *SOLVE_ORDER* value of less than 1 and cannot assign a value of greater than 65,535.

Formatting Calculated Members

The last exercise introduced the *FORMAT_STRING* property for calculated member expressions. This property provides Analysis Services instruction on how to translate a cell's value to the value presented as the cell's *FORMATTED_VALUE* property. (Remember that the MDX Query Editor is displaying the value of the *FORMATTED_VALUE* property.)

The *FORMAT_STRING* property accepts a number of standard formats as identified in Tables 5-3 and 5-4. The precise definition of each of these formats, along with instructions on the assembly of custom formats, is available through SQL Server Books Online.

TABLE 5-3 Standard Numeric Formats

General Number	Standard	Yes/No
Currency	Scientific	True/False
Fixed	Percent	On/Off

TABLE 5-4 Standard Date Formats

General Date	Medium Date	Long Time	Short Time
Long Date	Short Date	Medium Time	

Building Complex Expressions

The expressions you've worked with in this chapter have been relatively simple, employing nothing more than constants and tuples. Many business problems can be solved with just these basic elements. Still, you will frequently need to implement more complex expressions.

Two frequently employed elements of complex expressions are the current member and sets. In the sections that follow, you learn some of the basics of employing these in your expressions. This provides you with the foundation you need to explore even more complex expressions in the following chapters of this book.

Working with the Current Member

Quite frequently, you will need to obtain a reference to the member identified for a particular hierarchy in the current context. This is referred to as that hierarchy's *current member* and is accessed using the *CurrentMember* function:

```
[Dimension].[Hierarchy].CurrentMember
```

The *CurrentMember* function returns a member reference. This reference can be used to assemble a tuple, pass the member to a function, or investigate properties of the member.

Member properties are quite useful in expressions. Not only can member properties be returned as part of the expression's value, but properties can also be used to conditionally evaluate an expression. This is facilitated by the *IIF* function:

```
IIF( Logical Expression, Expression1, Expression2)
```

The *inline-IF* function, *IIF,* is used to evaluate a logical expression. If this expression returns *True*, the first of two expressions is evaluated. If this expression returns *False*, the second of two expressions is evaluated. The MDX *IIF* function is very similar to inline-*IF* functions found in many other languages.

MDX makes accessible a number of member properties through specialized functions. These include *Name, UniqueName, MemberValue,* and *Member_Caption.* Each of these functions is explained in Table 5-5.

TABLE 5-5 Member Property Functions

Function	Syntax	Description
Name	*member.Name*	Returns the member's name.
UniqueName	*member.UniqueName*	Returns the member's key-based member reference.
MemberValue	*member.MemberValue*	Returns the member's value. If a value has not been explicitly defined, this is the member's name.
Member_Caption	*member.Member_Caption*	Returns the member's caption. If a caption has not been explicitly defined, this is the member's name.

In addition to these specialized functions, MDX supports the more generic *Properties* function:

```
member.Properties( Name [, TYPED] )
```

Through the *Properties* function, a number of intrinsic and user-defined member properties can be retrieved by name. A list of intrinsic member properties supported by Analysis Services is provided in Table 5-6. Each of these properties is returned as a string unless the *Properties* function's optional *TYPED* flag is employed, forcing the property to be returned in its underlying data type.

TABLE 5-6 Intrinsic Member Properties Frequently Accessed Through the *Properties* Function

Name	Description
CAPTION	The caption associated with the member. If a caption is not explicitly defined, the *MEMBER_NAME* property is returned. This property is equivalent to *MEMBER_CAPTION*.
CHILDREN_CARDINALITY	The number of children associated with the member. This number may not be exact.
CUBE_NAME	The name of the cube with which this member is associated.

TABLE 5-6 **Intrinsic Member Properties Frequently Accessed Through the *Properties* Function**

Name	Description
DIMENSION_UNIQUE_NAME	The unique name of the dimension with which this member is associated.
HIERARCHY_UNIQUE_NAME	The unique name of the hierarchy with which this member is associated.
IS_DATAMEMBER	A True/False value indicating whether the member has measure group data directly attributed to it.
KEY	The member's key value. If a member has a composite key, you should use the *KEYx* property.
KEYx	The member's key value. The *x* is a number starting with 0 identifying which part of a composite key to return. If *KEY0* is used with a non-composite key, the value returned is equivalent to the value associated with the *KEY* property.
LEVEL_NUMBER	The ordinal value of the level with which the member is associated. The root level has a value of 0.
LEVEL_UNIQUE_NAME	The unique name of the level with which the member is associated.
MEMBER_CAPTION	The caption associated with the member. If a caption is not explicitly defined, the *MEMBER_NAME* property is returned. This property is equivalent to *CAPTION*.
MEMBER_NAME	The name of the member. This property is equivalent to *NAME*.
MEMBER_UNIQUE_NAME	The name uniquely identifying the member.
MEMBER_VALUE	The value of a member. If a member value has not been explicitly defined, this is the member's name.
NAME	The name of the member. This property is equivalent to *MEMBER_NAME*.
PARENT_COUNT	The number of parent members associated with this member.
PARENT_LEVEL	The ordinal value of the level with which the member's parent is associated.
PARENT_UNIQUE_NAME	The name uniquely identifying the member's parent.

Use the current member and member properties in an expression

1. If you have not already done so, open the MDX Query Editor to the MDX Step-by-Step database.

2. In the code pane, enter the following query to return the Product Categories current member's parent members name:

```
WITH
MEMBER [Measures].[Parent Member Name] AS
```

```
        [Product].[Product Categories].CurrentMember.Parent.Name
SELECT
    {([Measures].[Parent Member Name])} ON COLUMNS,
    {[Product].[Product Categories].AllMembers} ON ROWS
FROM [Step-by-Step]
```

3. Execute the query and note the values associated with the Parent Member Name calculated member, especially the value for All Products.

	Parent Member Name
All Products	(null)
Accessories	All Products
Bike Racks	Accessories
Hitch Rack - 4-Bike	Bike Racks
Bike Stands	Accessories
All-Purpose Bike Stand	Bike Stands
Bottles and Cages	Accessories
Mountain Bottle Cage	Bottles and Cages
Road Bottle Cage	Bottles and Cages
Water Bottle - 30 oz	Bottles and Cages
Cleaners	Accessories
Bike Wash - Dissolver	Cleaners

In the expression for the calculated member Parent Member Name, the *CurrentMember* function is used to access the current member of the Product Categories hierarchy. The *Parent* function, which is discussed further in Chapter 8, "Navigating Hierarchies," is used to access the current member's parent member in the Product Categories hierarchy. The *Name* function is then used to return the parent member's *Name* property.

The All Products member is the topmost member of this user-hierarchy. As such it has no parent member. Instead of returning a *Null* value for its parent member's name, it might be more appropriate to indicate the concept of a parent member is not appropriate for it.

4. Alter the query to determine whether a member is the topmost member of the hierarchy. If it is, return the string *Not Applicable* for the Parent Member Name calculated member:

```
WITH
MEMBER [Measures].[Parent Member Name] AS
    IIF(
        [Product].[Product Categories].CurrentMember.Properties
                ("Level_Number",TYPED)=0,
        "Not Applicable",
        [Product].[Product Categories].CurrentMember.Parent.Name
        )
SELECT
    {([Measures].[Parent Member Name])} ON COLUMNS,
    {[Product].[Product Categories].AllMembers} ON ROWS
FROM [Step-by-Step]
```

5. Execute the query and note the new value for the value associated with Parent Member Name for the All Products member.

Parent Member Name	
All Products	Not Applicable
Accessories	All Products
Bike Racks	Accessories
Hitch Rack - 4-Bike	Bike Racks
Bike Stands	Accessories
All-Purpose Bike Stand	Bike Stands
Bottles and Cages	Accessories
Mountain Bottle Cage	Bottles and Cages
Road Bottle Cage	Bottles and Cages
Water Bottle - 30 oz.	Bottles and Cages
Cleaners	Accessories
Bike Wash - Dissolver	Cleaners

The *IIF* function allows you to apply conditional logic in the expression. Using the current member's level number property, you evaluate whether the current member represents the topmost level of the hierarchy. If it does, the string *Not Applicable* is returned as the value of the expression. Otherwise, the parent name is accessed as before. Although interesting from a cosmetic perspective, the real power of combining properties with conditional evaluation is that certain errors can be avoided.

6. Alter the query to include a new calculated member Percent of Parent based on Reseller Sales Amount:

```
WITH
MEMBER [Measures].[Parent Member Name] AS
    IIF(
        [Product].[Product Categories].CurrentMember.Properties
                ("Level_Number",TYPED)=0,
        "Not Applicable",
        [Product].[Product Categories].CurrentMember.Parent.Name
        )
MEMBER [Measures].[Percent of Parent] AS
    ([Measures].[Reseller Sales Amount])/
        ([Product].[Product Categories].CurrentMember.Parent,
                [Measures].[Reseller Sales Amount])
    ,FORMAT_STRING="Percent"
SELECT
    {
        ([Measures].[Parent Member Name]),
        ([Measures].[Reseller Sales Amount]),
        ([Measures].[Percent of Parent])
        } ON COLUMNS,
    {[Product].[Product Categories].AllMembers} ON ROWS
FROM [Step-by-Step]
```

7. Execute the query and note the values associated with Percent of Parent, especially the value for All Products.

	Parent Member Name	Reseller Sales Amount	Percent of Parent
All Products	Not Applicable	$80,450,596.98	1.#INF
Accessories	All Products	$571,297.93	0.71%
Bike Racks	Accessories	$197,736.16	34.61%
Hitch Rack - 4-Bike	Bike Racks	$197,736.16	100.00%
Bike Stands	Accessories	(null)	(null)
All-Purpose Bike Stand	Bike Stands	(null)	(null)
Bottles and Cages	Accessories	$7,476.60	1.31%
Mountain Bottle Cage	Bottles and Cages	(null)	(null)
Road Bottle Cage	Bottles and Cages	(null)	(null)
Water Bottle - 30 oz.	Bottles and Cages	$7,476.60	100.00%
Cleaners	Accessories	$11,188.37	1.96%
Bike Wash - Dissolver	Cleaners	$11,188.37	100.00%

The Percent of Parent member divides the Reseller Sales Amount value associated with the current cell by the same amount associated with the parent of the Product Categories member in that cell. This works fine for most members except the All Products member, which does not have a parent. In this instance, the parent value of (null) is replace with 0 (ZERO), resulting in a division by ZERO. Just as before, you need to provide conditional logic to control how the calculated member's value is derived.

8. Alter the Percent of Parent expression to more elegantly address those members without parents:

```
WITH
MEMBER [Measures].[Parent Member Name] AS
    IIF(
        [Product].[Product Categories].CurrentMember.Properties
                ("Level_Number",TYPED)=0,
        "Not Applicable",
        [Product].[Product Categories].CurrentMember.Parent.Name
        )
MEMBER [Measures].[Percent of Parent] AS
    IIF(
        [Product].[Product Categories].CurrentMember.Properties
                ("Level_Number",TYPED)=0,
        "Not Applicable",
        ([Measures].[Reseller Sales Amount])/
            ([Product].[Product Categories].CurrentMember.Parent,
                    [Measures].[Reseller Sales Amount])
        )
    ,FORMAT_STRING="Percent"
SELECT
    {
        ([Measures].[Parent Member Name]),
        ([Measures].[Reseller Sales Amount]),
        ([Measures].[Percent of Parent])
        } ON COLUMNS,
    {[Product].[Product Categories].AllMembers} ON ROWS
FROM [Step-by-Step]
```

9. Execute the query and note the new value associated with All Products and Percent of Parent.

	Parent Member Name	Reseller Sales Amount	Percent of Parent
All Products	Not Applicable	$80,450,596.98	Not Applicable
Accessories	All Products	$571,297.93	0.71%
Bike Racks	Accessories	$197,736.16	34.61%
Hitch Rack - 4-Bike	Bike Racks	$197,736.16	100.00%
Bike Stands	Accessories	(null)	(null)
All-Purpose Bike Stand	Bike Stands	(null)	(null)
Bottles and Cages	Accessories	$7,476.60	1.31%
Mountain Bottle Cage	Bottles and Cages	(null)	(null)
Road Bottle Cage	Bottles and Cages	(null)	(null)
Water Bottle - 30 oz	Bottles and Cages	$7,476.60	100.00%
Cleaners	Accessories	$11,188.37	1.96%
Bike Wash - Dissolver	Cleaners	$11,188.37	100.00%

Special Member Functions

In addition to *CurrentMember*, Analysis Services supports several functions to provide access to special members: *DefaultMember*, *UnknownMember*, and *DataMember*:

```
[Dimension].[Hierarchy].DefaultMember
[Dimension].[Hierarchy].UnknownMember
[Dimension].[Hierarchy].DataMember
```

The *DefaultMember* function returns the default member of a given hierarchy. If no default member is defined, the function returns the (All) member, and if no (All) member is defined, the function returns the first member of the hierarchy. In other words, the *DefaultMember* function provides access to the member of a hierarchy Analysis Services selects when no member for that hierarchy is specified within a tuple.

The *UnknownMember* function returns the unknown member associated with a given hierarchy. If an unknown member does not exist, the function typically returns *Null*. In the case of the Measures attribute-hierarchy with which the concept of an unknown member is inappropriate, the *UnknownMember* function returns an error.

Finally, the *DataMember* function returns the member with which fact data is directly attributed. This typically only makes sense in the context of a parent-child hierarchy within which a non-leaf member of the hierarchy may have data directly attributed to both it and its children.

Working with Sets in Expressions

When employed in an expression, sets are not affected by the current cell's context. As a result, the auto-exists functionality limiting sets demonstrated in Chapter 4, "Working with Sets," does not come into play.

Quite frequently, you will need a set to be constrained by the expression's context. This is done through the use of the *EXISTING* keyword, as demonstrated in the following exercise.

Force a set to be evaluated within an expression's context

1. If you have not already done so, open the MDX Query Editor to the MDX Step-by-Step database.

2. In the code pane, enter the following query to count the number of products:

```
WITH
MEMBER [Measures].[Number of Products] AS
    Count(
        [Product].[Product].[Product].Members
        )
SELECT
    {
        ([Measures].[Reseller Sales Amount]),
        ([Measures].[Number of Products])
        } ON COLUMNS,
    {[Product].[Category].Members} ON ROWS
FROM [Step-by-Step]
```

3. Execute the query and note the value for Number of Products associated with each Category member.

	Reseller Sales Amount	Number of Products
All Products	$80,450,596.98	397
Accessories	$571,297.93	397
Bikes	$66,302,381.56	397
Clothing	$1,777,840.84	397
Components	$11,799,076.66	397

The calculated member generates a set of products. The *Count* function, explored in Chapter 7, "Performing Aggregation," counts the members in this set.

There are 397 products within the cube, but as you evaluate the calculated member in the context of varying product categories you would expect the number of related products to vary. However, the same number of products, 397, is repeated for each.

This is because the set of products is not evaluated within the calculated member's context. As a result, the auto-exists functionality that would limit this set to just those products associated with a given product category is not employed. Using the *EXISTING* keyword, you can force the current context to be taken into consideration.

4. Alter the query to force the set of products to be restricted per the current context:

```
WITH
MEMBER [Measures].[Number of Products] AS
    Count(
        EXISTING [Product].[Product].[Product].Members
        )
SELECT
    {
        ([Measures].[Reseller Sales Amount]),
        ([Measures].[Number of Products])
        } ON COLUMNS,
    {[Product].[Category].Members} ON ROWS
FROM [Step-by-Step]
```

5. Execute the query and note the change in the values associated with Number of Products and the various Category members.

The Number of Products now produces the correct count in accordance with the context in which it is being presented.

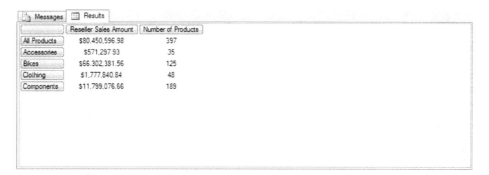

It is critical when employing sets within expressions that you carefully consider context. This is a topic you revisit as you work with more set functions in the subsequent chapters of this book.

Chapter 5 Quick Reference

To	Do this

Construct a calculated member within a query	Add a *MEMBER* sub-statement to the *SELECT* statement's *WITH* clause. Employ constants, tuples, operators, and functions in an expression to determine the calculated member's value. For example, the following statement assembles a calculated member named Bikes & Accessories:
	
	`WITH`
	`MEMBER [Product].[Category].[All Products].[Bikes & Accessories] AS`
	`    ([Product].[Category].[Bikes]) +`
	`        ([Product].[Category].[Accessories])`

To	Do this
| | ```
SELECT
    {
        ([Date].[Calendar Year].[CY 2003]),
        ([Date].[Calendar Year].[CY 2004])
        } ON COLUMNS,
    {
        ([Product].[Category].[Accessories]) ,
        ([Product].[Category].[Bikes]),
        ([Product].[Category].[Bikes & Accessories])
        } ON ROWS
FROM [Step-by-Step]
``` |
| Return all members of a hierarchy or hierarchy level including calculated members | Use the *AllMembers* function. For example, the following assembles a set of all Category attribute-hierarchy members including the calculated member Bikes & Accessories along the *ROWS* axis:<br><br>```
WITH
MEMBER [Product].[Category].[All Products].[Bikes & Accessories] AS
    ([Product].[Category].[Bikes]) +
        ([Product].[Category].[Accessories])
SELECT
    {
        ([Date].[Calendar Year].[CY 2003]),
        ([Date].[Calendar Year].[CY 2004])
        } ON COLUMNS,
    {[Product].[Category].AllMembers} ON ROWS
FROM [Step-by-Step]
``` |
| Avoid infinite recursion errors | Be certain to assign the calculated member to a hierarchy referenced by each tuple within the calculated member's expression. |
| Resolve solve order issues | Assign a value to the relevant calculated members' *SOLVE_ORDER* property to explicitly define the order in which they are resolved. For example, the use of the *SOLVE_ORDER* property in the following two calculated members ensures the Percent Bikes calculated member is calculated correctly for combined sales:<br><br>```
WITH
MEMBER [Measures].[Combined Sales Amount] AS
    ([Measures].[Reseller Sales Amount])+
        ([Measures].[Internet Sales Amount])
    ,SOLVE_ORDER=1
MEMBER [Product].[Category].[All Products].[Percent Bikes] AS
    ([Product].[Category].[Bikes])/
        ([Product].[Category].[All Products])
    ,FORMAT_STRING="Percent"
    ,SOLVE_ORDER=2
SELECT
    {
        ([Measures].[Reseller Sales Amount]),
        ([Measures].[Internet Sales Amount]),
        ([Measures].[Combined Sales Amount])
        } ON COLUMNS,
    {[Product].[Category].AllMembers} ON ROWS
FROM [Step-by-Step]
``` |
```

To	Do this
Reference the current member in the expression context	Use the *CurrentMember* function to obtain the member reference associated with a particular hierarchy. This member reference can then be employed like any other member reference within the expression. For example, the following query demonstrates the evaluation of the Product Categories user-hierarchy's current member to determine whether the current member has a parent member and performs expression evaluation appropriately:

```
WITH
MEMBER [Measures].[Parent Member Name] AS
    IIF(
        [Product].[Product Categories].CurrentMember
            .Properties("Level_Number",TYPED)=0,
        "Not Applicable",
        [Product].[Product Categories].CurrentMember
            .Parent.Name
        )
MEMBER [Measures].[Percent of Parent] AS
    IIF(
        [Product].[Product Categories].CurrentMember
            .Properties("Level_Number",TYPED)=0,
        "Not Applicable",
        ([Measures].[Reseller Sales Amount])/
            ([Product].[Product Categories].CurrentMember
                .Parent, [Measures].[Reseller Sales Amount])
        )
    ,FORMAT_STRING="Percent"
SELECT
    {
        ([Measures].[Parent Member Name]),
        ([Measures].[Reseller Sales Amount]),
        ([Measures].[Percent of Parent])
        } ON COLUMNS,
    {[Product].[Product Categories].AllMembers} ON ROWS
FROM [Step-by-Step]
```

To	Do this
Evaluate a set within the current context	Use the *EXISTING* keyword. For example, the following forces the set of products to be evaluated within the current context to appropriately determine the number of products in each product category.

```
WITH
MEMBER [Measures].[Number of Products] AS
    Count(
        EXISTING [Product].[Product].[Product].Members
        )
SELECT
    {
        ([Measures].[Reseller Sales Amount]),
        ([Measures].[Number of Products])
        } ON COLUMNS,
    {[Product].[Category].Members} ON ROWS
FROM [Step-by-Step]
```

Part II
MDX Functions

Chapter 6
Building Complex Sets

After completing this chapter, you will be able to:

- Assemble an ordered set

- Apply criteria to control set membership

- Apply set logic and advanced set building techniques

Part I introduced you to the fundamental concepts of tuples, sets, and expressions. In Part II, you build upon this foundation as you explore some of the more frequently used MDX functions.

Part II marks the book's transition from theory to application. Although the theoretical concepts explored in Part I are now largely relegated to the background, you are strongly encouraged to continually apply those concepts to the examples presented in these chapters to deepen your understanding of the MDX language.

In this chapter, you explore the assembly of complex sets using a variety of MDX functions. Building just the right set is critical to retrieving the data you need from your cubes, and having a repertoire of functions at your disposal makes this possible.

Assembling Ordered Sets

In Chapter 4, "Working with Sets," you explored the basics of set order. With explicitly defined sets, tuples are returned in the order specified in the set definition. With the *Members* function, the order of the tuples in the returned set mirrors the order of the members in the hierarchy from which they are derived.

Quite frequently, you will need to provide an alternative sort order for the tuples of a set. In reports, this is done to make data easier to locate, often with the most critical data presented at the top of the set. In MDX, the reordering of tuples in a set is performed using the *Order* function:

```
Order( {Set}, Expression [, Flag])
```

The *Order* function sorts the tuples of a set based on the value returned by an expression. In the function's first argument, the set to be sorted is identified. Each tuple in that set is then applied to the expression serving as the function's second argument. The numeric or string value returned by the expression is then used as the basis for sorting the tuples in the set.

Unless one of four flags is provided as the function's third argument, the set is sorted in ascending order. With the *ASC* flag specified, Analysis Services is instructed to sort the set in that same default ascending order. The *DESC* flag triggers a descending sort.

The ascending and descending sort orders specified with these flags are hierarchical sorts and work a little differently than you might first expect. With a hierarchical sort, each member reference is first sorted according to its order within the hierarchy with which it is associated. The last member reference in the tuple is then sorted in ascending or descending order based on the value of the expression specified for the second argument of the *Order* function and the provided flag.

The hierarchical sort can be very useful in some situations, but more often than not you will want to break the hierarchical constraints to sort the set in ascending or descending order across all members in the tuples. This is achieved using the break-hierarchy flags, *BASC* and *BDESC*.

Use the *Order* function to sort a set by an expression

1. Open the MDX Query Editor to the MDX Step-by-Step database.

2. In the code pane, enter the following query to return reseller sales by product:

```
SELECT
    {([Measures].[Reseller Sales Amount])} ON COLUMNS,
    {[Product].[Product].[Product].Members} ON ROWS
FROM [Step-by-Step]
```

3. Execute the query and note the sort order of the products along the rows.

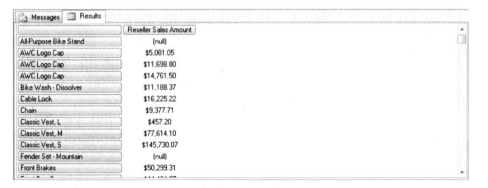

The query returns products along the *ROWS* axis sorted by name, the product's default sort order which is determined by properties set during the design of the dimension. This sort order is useful if you need to locate products by name, but what if you want to identify which products performed better than others? In this situation, sorting by sales might make more sense.

4. Alter the query to sort the set of products by reseller sales in descending order:

```
SELECT
    {([Measures].[Reseller Sales Amount])} ON COLUMNS,
    Order(
        {[Product].[Product].[Product].Members},
        ([Measures].[Reseller Sales Amount]),
        DESC
        ) ON ROWS
FROM [Step-by-Step]
```

5. Execute the query and note the new sort order for the products along the rows.

	Reseller Sales Amount
Mountain-200 Black, 38	$1,634,647.94
Mountain-200 Black, 38	$1,471,078.72
Road-350-W Yellow, 48	$1,380,253.88
Touring-1000 Blue, 60	$1,370,784.22
Mountain-200 Black, 42	$1,360,828.02
Mountain-200 Black, 42	$1,285,524.65
Road-350-W Yellow, 40	$1,238,754.64
Touring-1000 Yellow, 60	$1,184,363.30
Mountain-200 Silver, 38	$1,181,945.82
Mountain-200 Silver, 42	$1,175,932.52
Mountain-100 Black, 38	$1,174,622.74
Mountain-200 Silver, 38	$1,172,269.42

Using the *Order* function, each tuple in the set of products is evaluated using the expression *([Measures].[Reseller Sales Amount])*. The value returned for each tuple is then used to sort the set in descending order as indicated by the *DESC* flag.

The reseller sales value used to sort the set of products is reflected in the query's cell set. However, the values on which the sort is based are not required to be present in the query's results.

6. Alter the query to sort the products by the absolute difference between Internet and reseller sales amounts. Include the Internet sales amount in the cell set returned by the query, but not the difference in sales on which the sort is based:

```
SELECT
    {
        ([Measures].[Reseller Sales Amount]),
        ([Measures].[Internet Sales Amount])
        } ON COLUMNS,
    Order(
        {[Product].[Product].[Product].Members},
        VBAMDX!ABS(
            ([Measures].[Reseller Sales Amount]) -
            ([Measures].[Internet Sales Amount])
            ),
        DESC
        ) ON ROWS
FROM [Step-by-Step]
```

Note This example uses the VBA function *ABS* to calculate the absolute value between the Reseller Sales Amount and the Internet Sales Amount measures. The VBA functions were briefly introduced in Chapter 5, "Working with Expressions."

7. Execute the query and review the sort order.

	Reseller Sales Amount	Internet Sales Amount
Mountain-200 Black, 38	$1,471,078.72	$340,150.30
Touring-1000 Blue, 60	$1,370,784.22	$350,458.29
Mountain-100 Black, 38	$1,174,622.74	$165,374.51
Road-350-W Yellow, 48	$1,380,253.88	$394,629.68
Mountain-200 Black, 42	$1,360,828.02	$383,181.36
Mountain-100 Black, 44	$1,163,352.98	$202,499.40
Mountain-100 Black, 42	$1,102,848.18	$151,874.55
Mountain-100 Silver, 42	$1,043,695.27	$142,799.58
Mountain-100 Silver, 38	$1,094,669.28	$197,199.42
Mountain-100 Silver, 44	$1,050,610.85	$166,599.51
Road-150 Red, 48	$334,926.07	$1,205,876.99
Touring-1000 Yellow, 60	$1,184,363.30	$333,769.80

The products are clearly not sorted by either Internet or reseller sales. A quick (manual) inspection of the absolute difference between these two values reveals that the products are in fact sorted per the expression in the *Order* function, even though that value is not present in the cell set.

Use the *Order* function to sort a set while breaking hierarchical constraints

1. If you have not already done so, open the MDX Query Editor to the MDX Step-by-Step database.

2. In the code pane, enter the following query to return the set of product subcategories against reseller sales:

```
SELECT
    {([Measures].[Reseller Sales Amount])} ON COLUMNS,
    {[Product].[Subcategory].[Subcategory].Members} ON ROWS
FROM [Step-by-Step]
```

3. Execute the query and note the sort order of subcategory members.

	Reseller Sales Amount
Bib-Shorts	$166,739.71
Bike Racks	$197,736.16
Bike Stands	(null)
Bottles and Cages	$7,476.60
Bottom Brackets	$51,826.37
Brakes	$66,018.71
Caps	$31,541.35
Chains	$9,377.71
Cleaners	$11,188.37
Cranksets	$203,942.62
Derailleurs	$70,209.50
Fenders	(null)

The subcategories are presented in their default sort order. This is an alphabetical order by subcategory name. Although this alphabetical listing could be useful in some situations, subcategories might be easier for you to understand in the context of their parent categories.

4. Alter the set along the *ROWS* axis to include members of the Categories attribute-hierarchy:

```
SELECT
    {([Measures].[Reseller Sales Amount])} ON COLUMNS,
    {[Product].[Category].[Category].Members} *
        {[Product].[Subcategory].[Subcategory].Members} ON ROWS
FROM [Step-by-Step]
```

5. Execute the query and note the new sort order of the members along the *ROWS* axis.

		Reseller Sales Amount
Accessories	Bike Racks	$197,736.16
Accessories	Bike Stands	(null)
Accessories	Bottles and Cages	$7,476.60
Accessories	Cleaners	$11,188.37
Accessories	Fenders	(null)
Accessories	Helmets	$258,712.93
Accessories	Hydration Packs	$65,518.75
Accessories	Lights	(null)
Accessories	Locks	$16,225.22
Accessories	Panniers	(null)
Accessories	Pumps	$13,514.69
Accessories	Tires and Tubes	$925.21
Bikes	Mountain Bikes	$26,492,684.38
Bikes	Road Bikes	$29,358,206.96
Bikes	Touring Bikes	$10,451,490.22
Clothing	Bib-Shorts	$166,739.71
Clothing	Caps	$31,541.35

The set of cross-joined Category and Subcategory members preserves the default sort order of the Category members. Under each category, the Subcategory members are then sorted in their default alphabetical order, but because of the influence of the Category member's sort, the order of the Subcategory members is different from what was seen earlier.

> **Note** The sorting of Subcategory members within Category members is a residual of how Analysis Services performs the cross-join operation and not the relationship between these two attribute-hierarchies. Their relationship only serves to limit the number of tuples produced by the cross-join operation. You will get the same sorting behavior described here if two unrelated attributes are cross-joined.

As before, the order of these members is driven by their default sort order, which may not be the most useful for analysis. The *Order* function can be applied to re-sort these members by an expression.

6. Alter the query to sort the set along the *ROWS* axis in descending order by reseller sales:

```
SELECT
    {([Measures].[Reseller Sales Amount])} ON COLUMNS,
    Order(
        {[Product].[Category].[Category].Members} *
            {[Product].[Subcategory].[Subcategory].Members},
        ([Measures].[Reseller Sales Amount]),
        DESC
        ) ON ROWS
FROM [Step-by-Step]
```

7. Execute the query and note the sort order of the members along the *ROWS* axis.

		Reseller Sales Amount
Accessories	Helmets	$258,712.93
Accessories	Bike Racks	$197,736.16
Accessories	Hydration Packs	$65,518.75
Accessories	Locks	$16,225.22
Accessories	Pumps	$13,514.69
Accessories	Cleaners	$11,188.37
Accessories	Bottles and Cages	$7,476.60
Accessories	Tires and Tubes	$925.21
Accessories	Bike Stands	(null)
Accessories	Fenders	(null)
Accessories	Lights	(null)
Accessories	Panniers	(null)
Bikes	Road Bikes	$29,358,206.96
Bikes	Mountain Bikes	$26,492,684.38
Bikes	Touring Bikes	$10,451,490.22
Clothing	Jerseys	$579,308.71
Clothing	Shorts	$342,202.72

Notice subcategories are now sorted in descending order. However, as you make your way down the rows, notice this sort is only being applied within the context of the Category members that themselves are sorted in their default order. This is because the *ASC* and *DESC* sorts are hierarchical. In other words, these sorts operate against the last member of the tuples in a set. The order of the preceding members in those tuples is preserved. To break this hierarchical constraint, employ the break-hierarchy flags, *BASC* and *BDESC*.

8. Alter the query to perform a break-hierarchy sort in descending order:

```
SELECT
    {([Measures].[Reseller Sales Amount])} ON COLUMNS,
    Order(
        {[Product].[Category].[Category].Members} *
            {[Product].[Subcategory].[Subcategory].Members},
        ([Measures].[Reseller Sales Amount]),
        BDESC
        ) ON ROWS
FROM [Step-by-Step]
```

9. Execute the query and note the new sort order of the members along the *ROWS* axis.

		Reseller Sales Amount
Bikes	Road Bikes	$29,358,206.96
Bikes	Mountain Bikes	$26,492,684.38
Bikes	Touring Bikes	$10,451,490.22
Components	Mountain Frames	$4,713,672.15
Components	Road Frames	$3,849,853.34
Components	Touring Frames	$1,642,327.69
Components	Wheels	$679,070.07
Clothing	Jerseys	$579,308.71
Clothing	Shorts	$342,202.72
Accessories	Helmets	$258,712.93
Clothing	Vests	$223,801.37
Clothing	Gloves	$207,775.17
Components	Cranksets	$203,942.62
Clothing	Tights	$201,833.01
Accessories	Bike Racks	$197,736.16
Components	Handlebars	$170,591.32
Clothing	Bib-Shorts	$166,739.71

The break-hierarchy sort now forces the tuples to be sorted purely by the value associated with them, without regard for the internal ordering of member references within the tuples. When you deal with multi-part tuples, you frequently employ the break-hierarchy sort flags to produce sort orders like the one demonstrated here.

The *Hierarchize* Function

The assembly of complex sets can often result in sets with non-meaningful orders. Although you can use the *Order* function to sort a set by a value, you may simply wish to return a set with the default order of the members in its tuples. The *Hierarchize* function performs this operation:

```
Hierarchize( {Set} [, POST])
```

The *Hierarchize* function sorts all members of the tuples in the set specified in its first argument by their default order. When members of different levels of a hierarchy are encountered, higher-level members are sorted ahead of their children, as demonstrated in the following sample:

```
SELECT
    {([Measures].[Reseller Sales Amount])} ON COLUMNS,
    Hierarchize(
        {
            ([Product].[Product Categories].[Subcategory].[Road Bikes]),
            ([Product].[Product Categories].[All Products]),
            ([Product].[Product Categories].[Subcategory].[Mountain Bikes]),
            ([Product].[Product Categories].[Category].[Bikes]),
            ([Product].[Product Categories].[Subcategory].[Touring Bikes])
        }
    ) ON ROWS
FROM [Step-by-Step]
```

	Reseller Sales Amount
All Products	$80,450,596.98
Bikes	$66,302,381.56
Mountain Bikes	$26,492,684.38
Road Bikes	$29,358,206.96
Touring Bikes	$10,451,490.22

Specifying the optional *POST* flag instructs Analysis Services to sort higher-level members after their children, as demonstrated in the following example. Sorting in this manner is often done in reports to represent subtotals.

```
SELECT
    {([Measures].[Reseller Sales Amount])} ON COLUMNS,
    Hierarchize(
        {
            ([Product].[Product Categories].[Subcategory].[Road Bikes]),
            ([Product].[Product Categories].[All Products]),
            ([Product].[Product Categories].[Subcategory].[Mountain Bikes]),
            ([Product].[Product Categories].[Category].[Bikes]),
            ([Product].[Product Categories].[Subcategory].[Touring Bikes])
        },
        POST
    ) ON ROWS
FROM [Step-by-Step]
```

	Reseller Sales Amount
Mountain Bikes	$26,492,684.38
Road Bikes	$29,358,206.96
Touring Bikes	$10,451,490.22
Bikes	$66,302,381.56
All Products	$80,450,596.98

The Range Operator

The range operator (:) provides another means of assembling an ordered set. Using this operator, two members from the same level of a hierarchy are specified as the starting and ending members of a range. Employing the default ordering of the members in the level, Analysis Services returns these two members along with each member located between them as a set. The members in this set retain the default ordering of the attribute. As demonstrated in the following example, the range operator makes short work of assembling an ordered set:

```
SELECT
     {([Measures].[Reseller Sales Amount])} ON COLUMNS,
     {[Date].[Calendar].[CY 2001]:[Date].[Calendar].[CY 2004]} ON ROWS
FROM [Step-by-Step]
```

	Reseller Sales Amount
CY 2001	$8,065,435.31
CY 2002	$24,144,429.65
CY 2003	$32,202,669.43
CY 2004	$16,038,062.60

Retrieving the First or Last Tuples of a Set

As mentioned in the previous section, ordering sets by a value is often used to help focus attention on the most critical data. Quite frequently, this "most critical" data is the only data of interest. Business intelligence reports and dashboards are often littered with information on top or bottom performers. In the MDX language, the limiting of sets in this manner is performed through the *TopCount* and *BottomCount* functions:

```
TopCount( {Set}, n [, Expression])
BottomCount( {Set}, n [, Expression])
```

With the *TopCount* function, the first of a specified number of tuples is returned from a set. If an expression is provided, the set is sorted in break-hierarchy descending order. If no expression is provided, the set retains its default order. The specified number of tuples is then retrieved.

The *BottomCount* function works in a very similar way, with a specified number of tuples being returned from a given set. If no expression is provided, the last of a specified number of tuples are taken from the set, sorted in its default order. However, if an expression is provided, the set is sorted in break-hierarchy ascending order before the specified number of tuples is retrieved from the set's top. The fact that *BottomCount* employs an ascending sort and takes from the top of the ordered set when an expression is provided can cause some confusion when you first start using the function.

Use the *TopCount* and *BottomCount* functions to extract best and worst performers

1. If you have not already done so, open the MDX Query Editor to the MDX Step-by-Step database.

2. In the code pane, enter the following query to retrieve product subcategories sorted by reseller sales:

```
SELECT
    {([Measures].[Reseller Sales Amount])} ON COLUMNS,
    Order(
        {[Product].[Subcategory].[Subcategory].Members},
        ([Measures].[Reseller Sales Amount]),
        BDESC
        ) ON ROWS
FROM [Step-by-Step]
```

3. Execute the query.

	Reseller Sales Amount
Road Bikes	$29,358,206.96
Mountain Bikes	$26,492,684.38
Touring Bikes	$10,451,490.22
Mountain Frames	$4,713,672.15
Road Frames	$3,849,853.34
Touring Frames	$1,642,327.69
Wheels	$679,070.07
Jerseys	$579,308.71
Shorts	$342,202.72
Helmets	$258,712.93
Vests	$223,801.37
Gloves	$207,775.17

The set returned on the *ROWS* axis contains subcategories sorted in descending order based on reseller sales. From the set, you can quickly locate the best and worst performers by looking at the top and the bottom of the cell set. Although this is useful for validating the results of your queries, you may be interested in focusing your attention on only the top or bottom five subcategories of this set.

4. Alter the query to limit the set of subcategories to the top five performers based on reseller sales:

```
SELECT
    {([Measures].[Reseller Sales Amount])} ON COLUMNS,
    TopCount(
        {[Product].[Subcategory].[Subcategory].Members},
        5,
        ([Measures].[Reseller Sales Amount])
        ) ON ROWS
FROM [Step-by-Step]
```

5. Execute the query and review the results.

6. Alter the query again to limit the set of subcategories to the bottom five performers based on reseller sales:

```
SELECT
    {([Measures].[Reseller Sales Amount])} ON COLUMNS,
    BottomCount(
        {[Product].[Subcategory].[Subcategory].Members},
        5,
        ([Measures].[Reseller Sales Amount])
        ) ON ROWS
FROM [Step-by-Step]
```

7. Execute the query and review the results.

A number of interesting things are going on here. Notice the result set of the preceding query includes four members with a null value. If you consider the business problem solved by this MDX query, this is a logical result. In essence, the results indicate that four subcategories have no reseller sales. If you happen to be interested in the bottom five product subcategories that do have reseller sales, you need to use additional logic to exclude all members with no values from the set against which you will determine the bottom five. You can limit the set in this manner by using the *Filter* or *NonEmpty* functions explored later in this chapter.

Notice, too, the returned set contains a number of tuples with matching values: In other words, the first four entries all have no sales. These represent "ties," but the *BottomCount* function (like the *TopCount* function) has no concept of tied values. Instead, it only knows to order the set and then take some number of tuples from it. If you had specified a bottom count of 3, you would have returned Panniers, Lights, and Fenders, whereas Bike Stands would be excluded for arbitrary reasons. It's important when looking at top and bottom counts to be aware of this behavior.

Finally, notice the returned set is in ascending order, as mentioned earlier. These are the bottom five performers, but because of how the *BottomCount* function works internally, they are returned in ascending order. This is easily addressed by applying the *Order* function to the set returned by the *BottomCount* function or by using *Tail* with an ordered set, as described in the next sidebar, "The *Head* and *Tail* Functions."

The *Head* and *Tail* Functions

The *TopCount* and *BottomCount* functions are closely related to the *Head* and *Tail* functions. The *Head* and *Tail* functions return a specified number of tuples from the top and bottom of a set, respectively:

```
Head( {Set} [, n])
Tail( {Set} [, n])
```

The chief difference between *Head* and *Tail* and the *TopCount* and *BottomCount* functions is the former do not sort the tuples in their sets. In addition, the *Head* and *Tail* functions do not require you to specify a number of tuples. If the number of tuples to return is not specified with the *Head* and *Tail* functions, a set containing the topmost or bottommost tuple is returned, respectively.

The *Head* and *Tail* functions are useful for constraining the size of the result set when developing long-running queries returning a large number of cells. More frequently, the *Head* and *Tail* functions are used to retrieve tuples from a set with a meaningful default order, such as a set of dates. Alternatively, you can combine the *Head* and *Tail* functions with the *Order* function to assemble your own top and bottom counts. This is useful for addressing the sorting issue with the *BottomCount* function described in the preceding exercise.

The following query demonstrates the use of the *Tail* function combined with the *Order* function to perform a bottom count operation that leaves the set in a descending sort order:

```
SELECT
    {([Measures].[Reseller Sales Amount])} ON COLUMNS,
    Tail(
        Order(
            {[Product].[Subcategory].[Subcategory].Members},
            ([Measures].[Reseller Sales Amount]),
            BDESC
            ),
        5
        ) ON ROWS
FROM [Step-by-Step]
```

Messages	Results	
	Reseller Sales Amount	
Tires and Tubes	$925.21	
Bike Stands	(null)	
Fenders	(null)	
Lights	(null)	
Panniers	(null)	

The *Item* Function

The *TopCount, BottomCount, Head,* and *Tail* functions all return sets. Occasionally, you will need to extract a single tuple from a set. For example, in ordered sets, the tuple to be extracted is often the first tuple in the ordered set. To retrieve a tuple from a set, ordered or otherwise, MDX provides the *Item* function:

```
{Set} | (Tuple).Item( i )
{Set}.Item( String1 [, String2, ..., Stringn] )
```

To retrieve a tuple by position within a set, use the first form of the function. In this form, each tuple in a set is identified using an ordinal value with the first tuple in the set identified by the value 0.

In its alternate form, a tuple in a set can be retrieved using a string-based representation of the tuple of interest. This second form is a bit complex and seldom used. If you need this form of the *Item* function, we recommend that you get more information on it from SQL Server Books Online.

The *Item* function is not limited to use against a set. When applied to a tuple, the *Item* function can be used to retrieve a specific member. When you use the *Item* function against a tuple, members in the tuple can only be identified using the zero-based ordinal position of the member in the tuple. The following example illustrates the use of the *Item* function to retrieve the top product by Internet sales for each of the four years:

```
WITH
MEMBER [Measures].[Top Product Sales] AS
    {
        EXISTING
        TopCount(
            [Product].[Product].[Product].Members,
            1,
            ([Measures].[Internet Sales Amount])
            ) *
            {[Measures].[Internet Sales Amount]}
        }.Item(0)
    ,FORMAT_STRING="Currency"
MEMBER [Measures].[Top Product Name] AS
    {
        EXISTING
        TopCount(
            [Product].[Product].[Product].Members,
            1,
            ([Measures].[Internet Sales Amount])
            )
        }.Item(0).Item(0).Name
SELECT
    {
        ([Measures].[Internet Sales Amount]),
        ([Measures].[Top Product Sales]),
        ([Measures].[Top Product Name])
        } ON COLUMNS,
    {
        ([Date].[Calendar Year].[CY 2001]),
        ([Date].[Calendar Year].[CY 2002]),
        ([Date].[Calendar Year].[CY 2003]),
        ([Date].[Calendar Year].[CY 2004])
        } ON ROWS
FROM [Step-by-Step]
```

	Internet Sales Amount	Top Product Sales	Top Product Name
CY 2001	$3,266,373.66	$593,992.82	Road-150 Red, 62
CY 2002	$6,530,343.53	$658,401.68	Road-150 Red, 48
CY 2003	$9,791,060.30	$431,458.12	Mountain-200 Black, 46
CY 2004	$9,770,899.74	$589,277.46	Mountain-200 Silver, 38

A lot is going on in this query that deserves explanation. First, a set of calendar years is placed along the *ROWS* axis. Internet sales for each year are returned, as are the sales of the top-selling product in that year. Finally, the name of that product is returned.

To retrieve the sales and name of the top-selling product in a given year, you use the *TopCount* function to produce a set containing a single tuple. (That tuple contains a single member reference to the Product attribute-hierarchy.) The *EXISTING* keyword forces this set to be evaluated in the context of the given year.

To obtain the name of the product, you use the *Item* function to extract the tuple from the set produced by *TopCount*. You then use the *Item* function against that tuple to extract the first and only member reference it contains, the reference to the Product attribute-hierarchy. Then you apply the *Name* function to retrieve the product's name.

To obtain sales, the goal is to produce a tuple containing the top-selling product and the Internet Sales Amount measure. As a kind of shortcut, the set produced by *TopCount* is cross-joined against a set containing this lone measure. This generates a set with a single tuple but two member references, one to Product and the other to Measures. The *Item* function is then used to obtain that tuple, which is then evaluated to return the Internet sales for that product.

> **Note** This is a lot to absorb. The *Item* function is often employed in very tricky situations.

Filtering Sets

Effective data analysis requires you to narrow your focus to the most critical and revealing data. This data is often identified through complex criteria that go beyond positioning at the top or bottom of a set or the exploitation of relationships as explored in Chapter 4. To support the evaluation of complex criteria for set membership, MDX provides the *Filter* function:

```
Filter( {Set}, Expression)
```

The *Filter* function works by evaluating each tuple in the set provided in the function's first argument by a logical expression provided in the function's second argument. Those tuples for which the expression evaluates to True are included in the set returned by the function.

The logical expression consists of one or more logical comparisons. If more than one logical comparison is employed, the truth value of these individual statements is consolidated using the logical operators *AND, OR,* and *XOR*. As with other expressions, parentheses control the order of evaluation.

Limit set membership using the *Filter* function

1. If you have not already done so, open the MDX Query Editor to the MDX Step-by-Step database.

2. In the code pane, enter the following query to view reseller and Internet sales across products:

```
SELECT
    {
        ([Measures].[Reseller Sales Amount]),
        ([Measures].[Internet Sales Amount])
        } ON COLUMNS,
    {[Product].[Product].[Product].Members} ON ROWS
FROM [Step-by-Step]
```

3. Execute the query and review the results. Be sure to review the number of rows returned in the messages pane.

	Reseller Sales Amount	Internet Sales Amount
All-Purpose Bike Stand	(null)	$39,591.00
AWC Logo Cap	$5,081.05	(null)
AWC Logo Cap	$11,698.80	(null)
AWC Logo Cap	$14,761.50	$19,688.10
Bike Wash - Dissolver	$11,188.37	$7,218.60
Cable Lock	$16,225.22	(null)
Chain	$9,377.71	(null)
Classic Vest, L	$457.20	$12,382.50
Classic Vest, M	$77,614.10	$12,636.50
Classic Vest, S	$145,730.07	$10,668.00
Fender Set - Mountain	(null)	$46,619.58
Front Brakes	$50,299.31	(null)

```
Messages   Results
Executing the query ...
Obtained object of type: Microsoft.AnalysisServices.AdomdClient.CellSet
Formatting.
Cell set consists of 398 rows and 3 columns.
Done formatting.
Execution complete
```

The query returns quite a few products to consider. Use the *Filter* function to limit these to only those with Internet-based sales in excess of reseller-based sales.

4. Alter the query to focus on those products with Internet sales greater than reseller sales:

```
SELECT
    {
        ([Measures].[Reseller Sales Amount]),
        ([Measures].[Internet Sales Amount])
        } ON COLUMNS,
```

```
Filter(
    {[Product].[Product].[Product].Members},
    ([Measures].[Internet Sales Amount]) > ([Measures].[Reseller Sales Amount])
    ) ON ROWS
FROM [Step-by-Step]
```

5. Execute the query and review the results.

A quick glance at the data reveals a mixture of accessories, clothing, and components. Let's assume component sales are not of interest at this time. Narrowing the criteria a bit more, you can focus your attention on clothing and accessories only.

6. Alter the query to restrict the products to those in the accessory and clothing categories:

```
SELECT
    {
        ([Measures].[Reseller Sales Amount]),
        ([Measures].[Internet Sales Amount])
        } ON COLUMNS,
    Filter(
        {[Product].[Product].[Product].Members},
        ([Measures].[Internet Sales Amount]) > ([Measures].[Reseller Sales Amount])
        AND
        (
            [Product].[Category].CurrentMember Is [Product].[Category].[Clothing] OR
            [Product].[Category].CurrentMember Is [Product].[Category].[Accessories]
            )
        ) ON ROWS
FROM [Step-by-Step]
```

7. Execute the query.

The results are now limited to products in the clothing and accessories categories. Just out of curiosity, what products are you not looking at by limiting products to just these categories?

8. Alter the query to look at products that are not in the clothing and accessories categories but meet the other criteria:

```
SELECT
    {
        ([Measures].[Reseller Sales Amount]),
        ([Measures].[Internet Sales Amount])
        } ON COLUMNS,
    Filter(
        {[Product].[Product].[Product].Members},
        ([Measures].[Internet Sales Amount]) >
            ([Measures].[Reseller Sales Amount]) AND
        NOT (
            [Product].[Category].CurrentMember Is [Product].[Category].[Clothing] OR
            [Product].[Category].CurrentMember Is [Product].[Category].[Accessories]
            )
        ) ON ROWS
FROM [Step-by-Step]
```

9. Execute the query and review the results. Notice the products presented along the *ROWS* axis are not included in the previous query result.

The *NonEmpty* Function

In Chapter 4, you were introduced to the *NON EMPTY* keyword as a way to remove members from an axis for which all associated cells are empty. The *NON EMPTY* keyword is a powerful and frequently used (and abused) feature of the MDX *SELECT* statement for cleaning up query results. Occasionally, you may wish to employ this same behavior to filter a set, but without performing the non-empty evaluation across the final cell set. The *NonEmpty* function facilitates this:

```
NonEmpty( {Set1} [,{Set2}])
```

To understand the *NonEmpty* function, consider the following query:

```
SELECT
    {([Measures].[Reseller Sales Amount])} ON COLUMNS,
    NON EMPTY {[Product].[Product].[Product].Members} ON ROWS
FROM [Step-by-Step]
```

	Reseller Sales Amount
AWC Logo Cap	$5,081.05
AWC Logo Cap	$11,698.80
AWC Logo Cap	$14,761.50
Bike Wash - Dissolver	$11,188.37
Cable Lock	$16,225.22
Chain	$9,377.71
Classic Vest, L	$457.20
Classic Vest, M	$77,614.10
Classic Vest, S	$145,730.07
Front Brakes	$50,299.31
Front Derailleur	$44,484.27
Full-Finger Gloves, L	$69,622.20

The *NON EMPTY* keyword limits the products to those with non-empty reseller sales amounts. This same set of products can be returned using the *NonEmpty* function:

```
SELECT
    {([Measures].[Reseller Sales Amount])} ON COLUMNS,
    NonEmpty(
        {[Product].[Product].[Product].Members},
        {([Measures].[Reseller Sales Amount])}
        ) ON ROWS
FROM [Step-by-Step]
```

	Reseller Sales Amount
AWC Logo Cap	$5,081.05
AWC Logo Cap	$11,698.80
AWC Logo Cap	$14,761.50
Bike Wash - Dissolver	$11,188.37
Cable Lock	$16,225.22
Chain	$9,377.71
Classic Vest, L	$457.20
Classic Vest, M	$77,614.10
Classic Vest, S	$145,730.07
Front Brakes	$50,299.31
Front Derailleur	$44,484.27
Full-Finger Gloves, L	$69,622.20

Though the set of products returned is the same, how that set is determined is very different. The elimination of members in the set of products is driven by their evaluation against the measures along the second set of the function, not the other axes of the query. By handling empty member exclusion this way, you can build more complex queries, such as a query showing Internet sales amounts for products known to have reseller sales amounts:

```
SELECT
    {([Measures].[Internet Sales Amount])} ON COLUMNS,
    NonEmpty(
        {[Product].[Product].[Product].Members},
        {([Measures].[Reseller Sales Amount])}
        ) ON ROWS
FROM [Step-by-Step]
```

	Internet Sales Amount
AWC Logo Cap	(null)
AWC Logo Cap	(null)
AWC Logo Cap	$19,688.10
Bike Wash - Dissolver	$7,218.60
Cable Lock	(null)
Chain	(null)
Classic Vest, L	$12,382.50
Classic Vest, M	$12,636.50
Classic Vest, S	$10,668.00
Front Brakes	(null)
Front Derailleur	(null)
Full-Finger Gloves, L	(null)

It's important to understand one critical aspect of the *NonEmpty* function that sets it apart from many other set functions in the MDX language. When the tuples of the first set are evaluated against the tuples of the second set, the evaluation is done in the query's context. In other words, the *WHERE* clause of your query is considered in determining whether a tuple in the first set is empty.

Note Limitations imposed by nested queries and subcube statements, neither of which have yet been discussed, also impact this evaluation. These are considered fairly advanced topics. We touch on nested queries in Chapter 12, "Building Reports," but we refer you to SQL Server Books Online for more information on these topics.

Combining Sets

You can accomplish quite a bit with the set-building functions previously described. That said, some logic is much more easily employed through the use of basic set operations.

If you are like us, you were probably first introduced to set operations as a series of overlapping circles referred to as Venn diagrams. These diagrams, presented in Figure 6-1, represent various ways that two sets—visualized as circles in the diagrams—can be combined to form a new set.

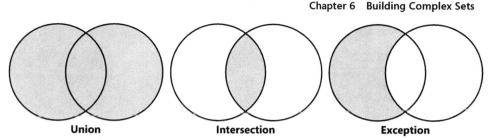

FIGURE 6-1 Venn diagram representations of the union, intersection, and exception operations

Through the union operation, membership in either the first or the second set confers membership in the resulting set. With the intersection operation, membership in the first and second set is required for membership in the resulting set. And through the exception operation, membership in the resulting set is granted with membership in the first set and not in the second set.

In MDX, the union, intersection, and exception operations are supported through the *Union, Intersect,* and *Except* functions:

```
Union( {Set1}, {Set2} [, ALL])
Intersect( {Set1}, {Set2} [, ALL])
Except( {Set1}, {Set2} [, ALL])
```

Each of these functions requires the two sets on which the operation is being performed be of the same dimensionality. The set returned by each function is a distinct set of tuples from the combined sets, unless the *ALL* flag is provided.

Of the three set operations, union and exception are the most frequently employed. For this reason, the MDX language provides the union and exception operators (+ and –) for use in place of the *Union* and *Except* functions. These operators behave just like their associated functions without the *ALL* flag.

Use the *Union, Intersect,* and *Except* functions to construct sets

1. If you have not already done so, open the MDX Query Editor to the MDX Step-by-Step database.

2. In the code pane, enter the following query to identify the top 10 performing products by reseller sales in calendar year 2004:

```
SELECT
    {([Measures].[Reseller Sales Amount])} ON COLUMNS,
    TopCount(
        {[Product].[Product].[Product].Members},
        10,
        ([Measures].[Reseller Sales Amount], [Date].[Calendar Year].[CY 2004])
        ) ON ROWS
FROM [Step-by-Step]
```

3. Execute the query and review the results.

	Reseller Sales Amount
Mountain-200 Black, 38	$1,634,647.94
Road-350-W Yellow, 48	$1,380,253.88
Touring-1000 Yellow, 60	$1,184,363.30
Touring-1000 Blue, 60	$1,370,784.22
Road-350-W Yellow, 40	$1,238,754.64
Mountain-200 Black, 42	$1,285,524.65
Mountain-200 Silver, 38	$1,181,945.82
Touring-1000 Yellow, 46	$1,016,312.83
Touring-1000 Blue, 46	$1,164,973.18
Mountain-200 Black, 46	$995,927.43

4. Alter the query to combine the top 10 performers of 2004 with the top 10 performers of 2003:

```
SELECT
    {([Measures].[Reseller Sales Amount])} ON COLUMNS,
    Union(
        TopCount(
            {[Product].[Product].[Product].Members},
            10,
            ([Measures].[Reseller Sales Amount], [Date].[Calendar Year].[CY 2003])
            ),
        TopCount(
            {[Product].[Product].[Product].Members},
            10,
            ([Measures].[Reseller Sales Amount], [Date].[Calendar Year].[CY 2004])
            )
        ) ON ROWS
FROM [Step-by-Step]
```

5. Execute the query and review the results.

	Reseller Sales Amount
Mountain-200 Black, 38	$1,634,647.94
Touring-1000 Blue, 60	$1,370,784.22
Road-350-W Yellow, 48	$1,380,253.88
Mountain-200 Black, 42	$1,285,524.65
Mountain-200 Black, 38	$1,471,078.72
Road-350-W Yellow, 40	$1,238,754.64
Touring-1000 Blue, 46	$1,164,973.18
Mountain-200 Silver, 38	$1,181,945.82
Mountain-200 Black, 42	$1,360,828.02
Touring-1000 Yellow, 60	$1,184,363.30
Touring-1000 Yellow, 46	$1,016,312.83
Mountain-200 Black, 46	$995,927.43

The preceding query combines the top 10 performers of 2004 with the top 10 of 2003. A quick review of the members along the rows identifies 12 products. Obviously, some products exist in one set and not the other. Those that fell from the top between 2003 and 2004 would be interesting to identify for further analysis.

6. Alter the query to identify those products in the top 10 for 2003 but not for 2004:

```
SELECT
    {([Measures].[Reseller Sales Amount])} ON COLUMNS,
    Except(
        TopCount(
            {[Product].[Product].[Product].Members},
            10,
            ([Measures].[Reseller Sales Amount], [Date].[Calendar Year].[CY 2003])
            ),
        TopCount(
            {[Product].[Product].[Product].Members},
            10,
            ([Measures].[Reseller Sales Amount], [Date].[Calendar Year].[CY 2004])
            )
        ) ON ROWS
FROM [Step-by-Step]
```

7. Execute the query and review the results.

The results indicate that two products fell out of the top 10 between 2003 and 2004. Reversing the order of the sets in the *Except* function allows you to more easily identify those products in the top 10 in 2004 but not 2003.

8. Alter the order of the exception to identify products in the top 10 of 2004 that were not there in 2003:

```
SELECT
    {([Measures].[Reseller Sales Amount])} ON COLUMNS,
    Except(
        TopCount(
            {[Product].[Product].[Product].Members},
            10,
            ([Measures].[Reseller Sales Amount], [Date].[Calendar Year].[CY 2004])
            ),
        TopCount(
            {[Product].[Product].[Product].Members},
            10,
            ([Measures].[Reseller Sales Amount], [Date].[Calendar Year].[CY 2003])
            )
        ) ON ROWS
FROM [Step-by-Step]
```

9. Execute the query.

	Reseller Sales Amount
Touring-1000 Yellow, 46	$1,016,312.83
Mountain-200 Black, 46	$995,927.43

Although the last two queries focused on those products that fell and rose from the top 10 between the years 2003 and 2004, a number of products were consistently in the top 10 between these two years. The following query identifies these products.

10. Use the *Intersect* function to identify those products in the top 10 for both 2003 and 2004:

```
SELECT
    {([Measures].[Reseller Sales Amount])} ON COLUMNS,
    Intersect(
        TopCount(
            {[Product].[Product].[Product].Members},
            10,
            ([Measures].[Reseller Sales Amount], [Date].[Calendar Year].[CY 2004])
            ),
        TopCount(
            {[Product].[Product].[Product].Members},
            10,
            ([Measures].[Reseller Sales Amount], [Date].[Calendar Year].[CY 2003])
            )
        ) ON ROWS
FROM [Step-by-Step]
```

11. Execute the query and review the results.

	Reseller Sales Amount
Mountain-200 Black, 38	$1,634,647.94
Road-350-W Yellow, 48	$1,380,253.88
Touring-1000 Yellow, 60	$1,184,363.30
Touring-1000 Blue, 60	$1,370,784.22
Road-350-W Yellow, 40	$1,238,754.64
Mountain-200 Black, 42	$1,285,524.65
Mountain-200 Silver, 38	$1,181,945.82
Touring-1000 Blue, 46	$1,164,973.18

Performing Advanced Set Construction

The MDX language provides access to some powerful if somewhat esoteric functions for building complex sets. In this final section of the chapter, you take a look at how two of these functions, *Generate* and *Extract*, can help you address common challenges.

Assembling Sets with the Generate Function

If you've worked with a procedural language such as C# or Visual Basic, you are familiar with the concept of a For Each loop. With a For Each loop, you iterate over the objects in a collection. For each of these objects, some operation is performed. Substitute a set of tuples for the collection of objects, use a set-building expression for the operations, and you've got the basic idea behind the *Generate* function:

```
Generate( {Set}, {Set Expression} [, ALL])
```

With each tuple in the set over which the *Generate* function iterates, a set-building expression is evaluated. The set returned with each iteration is combined with the sets produced by the other iteration to produce a unioned result set. The optional *ALL* flag instructs the union operation to retain duplicates.

The applications of the *Generate* function are not always immediately apparent, but should you find yourself encountering the need to assemble a set with For Each–type logic, the *Generate* function may be able to assist you.

Build a complex set using the *Generate* function

1. If you have not already done so, open the MDX Query Editor to the MDX Step-by-Step database.

2. In the code pane, enter the following query identifying the top five products based on reseller sales:

```
SELECT
    {([Measures].[Reseller Sales Amount])} ON COLUMNS,
    TopCount(
        {[Product].[Product].[Product].Members},
        5,
        ([Measures].[Reseller Sales Amount])
        ) ON ROWS
FROM [Step-by-Step]
```

3. Execute the query.

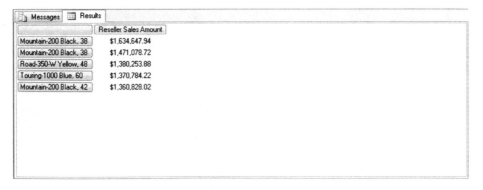

The preceding query is very similar to a query you built earlier in this chapter. It identifies the top five products by reseller sales. A quick review of these reveals all of the top five products are bicycles. With AdventureWorks Cycles, we expect the five top-selling products to be bicycles. To gain some insight into the top five products for each of the various categories of products sold by this company, use the *Generate* function.

4. Alter the query to identify the top five for each of the product categories:

```
SELECT
    {([Measures].[Reseller Sales Amount])} ON COLUMNS,
    Generate(
        {[Product].[Category].[Category].Members},
        TopCount(
            {[Product].[Product].[Product].Members},
            5,
            ([Measures].[Reseller Sales Amount])
        )
    ) ON ROWS
FROM [Step-by-Step]
```

5. Execute the query and review the results.

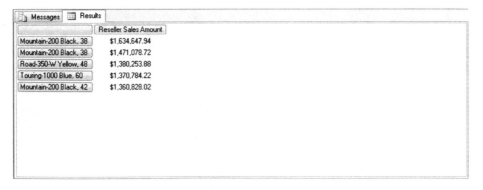

The query returns the exact same result. If you add the *ALL* flag, you can more clearly see why.

6. Alter the query to use the *ALL* flag with the *Generate* function:

```
SELECT
    {([Measures].[Reseller Sales Amount])} ON COLUMNS,
    Generate(
        {[Product].[Category].[Category].Members},
        TopCount(
            {[Product].[Product].[Product].Members},
            5,
            ([Measures].[Reseller Sales Amount])
            ),
        ALL
        ) ON ROWS
FROM [Step-by-Step]
```

7. Execute the query and review the results.

	Reseller Sales Amount
Mountain-200 Black, 38	$1,634,647.94
Mountain-200 Black, 38	$1,471,078.72
Road-350-W Yellow, 48	$1,380,253.88
Touring-1000 Blue, 60	$1,370,784.22
Mountain-200 Black, 42	$1,360,828.02
Mountain-200 Black, 38	$1,634,647.94
Mountain-200 Black, 38	$1,471,078.72
Road-350-W Yellow, 48	$1,380,253.88
Touring-1000 Blue, 60	$1,370,784.22
Mountain-200 Black, 42	$1,360,828.02
Mountain-200 Black, 38	$1,634,647.94
Mountain-200 Black, 38	$1,471,078.72

The results of this last query show that the *Generate* function is assembling a set of 20 products. By now, you are very familiar with the fact that there are four product categories. Four categories means four iterations of the loop. Each iteration returns 5 products, resulting in a 20-tuple returned set. The problem here is that the set of top five is being assembled outside the current context. You must force the top five products to be evaluated within the current context—the product category associated with the iteration. Using the *EXISTING* keyword forces the set to be assembled in this manner.

8. Use the *EXISTING* keyword to force the set expression to employ the current context:

```
SELECT
    {([Measures].[Reseller Sales Amount])} ON COLUMNS,
    Generate(
        {[Product].[Category].[Category].Members},
        TopCount(
            EXISTING {[Product].[Product].[Product].Members},
            5,
            ([Measures].[Reseller Sales Amount])
            ),
        ALL
        ) ON ROWS
FROM [Step-by-Step]
```

9. Execute the query and review the results.

	Reseller Sales Amount
Hitch Rack - 4-Bike	$197,736.16
Hydration Pack - 70 oz.	$65,518.75
Sport-100 Helmet, Black	$43,950.46
Sport-100 Helmet, Blue	$43,926.02
Sport-100 Helmet, Red	$39,328.16
Mountain-200 Black, 38	$1,634,647.94
Mountain-200 Black, 38	$1,471,078.72
Road-350-W Yellow, 48	$1,380,253.88
Touring-1000 Blue, 60	$1,370,784.22
Mountain-200 Black, 42	$1,360,828.02
Classic Vest, S	$145,730.07
Women's Mountain Shorts, S	$115,887.17

The query returns the top five products by category. However, if you aren't familiar with each of these products, it's a bit difficult to see exactly which category each product is associated with. A cross-join can assist with this.

> **Note** This business problem has a number of possible solutions. We selected the option employed here to keep the focus on the *Generate* function.

10. Apply the current member of the Category attribute-hierarchy to the set of products to produce the desired set:

```
SELECT
    {([Measures].[Reseller Sales Amount])} ON COLUMNS,
    Generate(
        {[Product].[Category].[Category].Members},
        {([Product].[Category].CurrentMember)} *
            TopCount(
                EXISTING {[Product].[Product].[Product].Members},
                5,
                ([Measures].[Reseller Sales Amount])
                ),
        ALL
        ) ON ROWS
FROM [Step-by-Step]
```

11. Execute the query and review the results.

		Reseller Sales Amount
Accessories	Hitch Rack - 4-Bike	$197,736.16
Accessories	Hydration Pack - 70 oz.	$65,518.75
Accessories	Sport-100 Helmet, Black	$43,950.46
Accessories	Sport-100 Helmet, Blue	$43,926.02
Accessories	Sport-100 Helmet, Red	$39,328.16
Bikes	Mountain-200 Black, 38	$1,634,647.94
Bikes	Mountain-200 Black, 38	$1,471,078.72
Bikes	Road-350-W Yellow, 48	$1,380,253.88
Bikes	Touring-1000 Blue, 60	$1,370,784.22
Bikes	Mountain-200 Black, 42	$1,360,828.02
Clothing	Classic Vest, S	$145,730.07
Clothing	Women's Mountain Shorts, S	$115,887.17

Assembling Sets with the *Extract* Function

Think of the *Extract* function as a way to assemble a set of tuples by reducing the dimensionality of another set of tuples. This allows you to define a base set based on complex evaluation and then identify those members or member combinations represented across that set:

```
Extract( {Set}, Hierarchy1 [, Hierarchy2, … HierarchyN])
```

The first argument of the *Extract* function is a set. This set is often assembled using the set-building functions defined in this and other chapters. In the second and subsequent arguments, the hierarchies to be represented in the extracted tuples are identified. Analysis Services then extracts the combinations of members associated with these hierarchies found in the provided set and returns a new distinct set of those combinations.

Assemble a set using the *Extract* function

1. If you have not already done so, open the MDX Query Editor to the MDX Step-by-Step database.

2. In the code pane, enter the following query to identify products and month combinations:

```
SELECT
    {([Measures].[Reseller Sales Amount])} ON COLUMNS,
    {[Product].[Product].[Product].Members} *
        {[Date].[Calendar].[Month].Members} ON ROWS
FROM [Step-by-Step]
```

3. Execute the query and review the results.

		Reseller Sales Amount
All-Purpose Bike Stand	July 2001	(null)
All-Purpose Bike Stand	August 2001	(null)
All-Purpose Bike Stand	September 2001	(null)
All-Purpose Bike Stand	October 2001	(null)
All-Purpose Bike Stand	November 2001	(null)
All-Purpose Bike Stand	December 2001	(null)
All-Purpose Bike Stand	January 2002	(null)
All-Purpose Bike Stand	February 2002	(null)
All-Purpose Bike Stand	March 2002	(null)
All-Purpose Bike Stand	April 2002	(null)
All-Purpose Bike Stand	May 2002	(null)
All-Purpose Bike Stand	June 2002	(null)

In this query, you can see reseller sales for the combination of each month and product in the cube. This is quite a bit of data to review. You might wish to focus your attention on those products that sold significantly more than others in one or more months. In the next step, you use the sales value of $160,000 to define a (relatively arbitrary) cutoff for evaluation.

4. Use the *Filter* function to restrict this set to those product and month combinations having reseller sales greater than $160,000:

```
SELECT
    {([Measures].[Reseller Sales Amount])} ON COLUMNS,
    Filter(
        {[Product].[Product].[Product].Members} *
            {[Date].[Calendar].[Month].Members},
        ([Measures].[Reseller Sales Amount])>160000
        ) ON ROWS
FROM [Step-by-Step]
```

5. Execute the query and verify the returned set.

		Reseller Sales Amount
Mountain-100 Black, 44	November 2001	$185,019.65
Mountain-100 Silver, 38	November 2001	$175,439.48
Mountain-100 Silver, 42	November 2001	$187,679.45
Mountain-100 Silver, 44	May 2002	$169,319.50
Mountain-200 Black, 38	August 2002	$162,288.57
Mountain-200 Black, 38	November 2002	$168,435.87
Mountain-200 Black, 38	August 2003	$206,764.83
Mountain-200 Black, 38	September 2003	$191,639.24
Mountain-200 Black, 38	November 2003	$180,472.28
Mountain-200 Black, 38	June 2004	$166,616.27
Mountain-200 Black, 42	September 2002	$162,365.42
Mountain-200 Black, 42	November 2002	$178,271.54

The results show a number of month and product combinations with more than $160,000 in sales. However, only a few distinct products pop up across these combinations. The *Extract* function can help you focus your attention on the products in this set.

6. Use the *Extract* function to isolate those products for which reseller sales in any given month were greater than $160,000:

```
SELECT
    {([Measures].[Reseller Sales Amount])} ON COLUMNS,
    Extract(
        Filter(
            {[Product].[Product].[Product].Members} *
                {[Date].[Calendar].[Month].Members},
            ([Measures].[Reseller Sales Amount])>160000
            ),
        [Product].[Product]
        ) ON ROWS
FROM [Step-by-Step]
```

7. Execute the query and review the results.

The *Extract* function extracts the set of products from the combined set of products and months for which reseller sales exceeded $160,000. A distinct listing of these products is now found along the *ROWS* axis. Although duplicate products seem to appear within this set, they are in fact unique based on their member key values.

Messages	Results	
	Reseller Sales Amount	
Mountain-100 Black, 44	$1,163,352.98	
Mountain-100 Silver, 38	$1,094,669.28	
Mountain-100 Silver, 42	$1,043,695.27	
Mountain-100 Silver, 44	$1,050,610.85	
Mountain-200 Black, 38	$1,471,078.72	
Mountain-200 Black, 38	$1,634,647.94	
Mountain-200 Black, 42	$1,360,828.02	
Mountain-200 Silver, 42	$1,175,932.52	
Mountain-200 Silver, 46	$1,157,224.28	
Touring-1000 Blue, 60	$1,370,784.22	

Note The Reseller Sales Amount value in the preceding cell set reflects sales for each product across all time. This is because once the set of products is assembled, it is a set just like any other. The details of how that set was assembled is no longer relevant to resolving the tuples of the final cell set.

Chapter 6 Quick Reference

To	Do this
Order a set by an expression	Use the *Order* function to sort the set. For example, the following query orders all products by reseller sales in descending order:

```
SELECT
  {([Measures].[Reseller Sales Amount])} ON COLUMNS,
  Order(
    {[Product].[Product].[Product].Members},
    ([Measures].[Reseller Sales Amount]),
    DESC
    ) ON ROWS
FROM [Step-by-Step]
```

Use the *ASC* or *DESC* flag to perform a hierarchal sort in ascending or descending order, and use the *BASC* or *BDESC* flag to sort across hierarchies in ascending or descending order, respectively.

To	Do this
Restore the order of a set to its natural order	Use the *Hierarchize* function to sort a set by its natural order. For example:

```
SELECT
  {([Measures].[Reseller Sales Amount])} ON COLUMNS,
  Hierarchize(
    {
      ([Product].[Product Categories].[Road Bikes]),
      ([Product].[Product Categories].[All Products]),
      ([Product].[Product Categories].[Mountain Bikes]),
```

To	Do this
	``
    ([Product].[Product Categories].[Bikes]),
    ([Product].[Product Categories].[Touring Bikes])
  },
  POST
) ON ROWS
FROM [Step-by-Step]
```
The optional *POST* flag instructs Analysis Services to sort child members in front of their parent members. |
| Retrieve the first or last tuples of a set | Use the *TopCount* or *BottomCount* functions to retrieve the first or last number of tuples from a set, respectively. Both functions allow you to sort the set by an expression prior to retrieving the specified number of tuples. The following example retrieves the top five product subcategories by reseller sales:
```
SELECT
  {([Measures].[Reseller Sales Amount])} ON COLUMNS,
  TopCount(
    {[Product].[Subcategory].[Subcategory].Members},
    5,
    ([Measures].[Reseller Sales Amount])
) ON ROWS
FROM [Step-by-Step]
```
Alternatively, you can use the *Head* and *Tail* functions to retrieve the first or last number of tuples from a set, as demonstrated here:
```
SELECT
  {([Measures].[Reseller Sales Amount])} ON COLUMNS,
  Tail(
    Order(
      {[Product].[Subcategory].[Subcategory].Members},
      ([Measures].[Reseller Sales Amount]),
      BDESC
    ),
    5
) ON ROWS
FROM [Step-by-Step]
``` |
| Filter a set by an expression | Use the *Filter* function to constrain a set. In the following example, the *Filter* function is used to assemble a set that contains all products with Internet sales in excess of $25,000.00:
```
SELECT
  {
    ([Measures].[Reseller Sales Amount]),
    ([Measures].[Internet Sales Amount])
  } ON COLUMNS,
  Filter(
    {[Product].[Product].[Product].Members},
    ([Measures].[Internet Sales Amount]) > 25000
  ) ON ROWS
FROM [Step-by-Step]
``` |
```

To	Do this
Exclude empty tuples from a set	Use the *NonEmpty* function. This is demonstrated in the following example, which presents Internet sales for those products having reseller sales:

```
SELECT
  {([Measures].[Internet Sales Amount])} ON COLUMNS,
  NonEmpty(
    {[Product].[Product].[Product].Members},
    {([Measures].[Reseller Sales Amount])}
    ) ON ROWS
FROM [Step-by-Step]
```

To	Do this
Merge two sets	Use the *Union* function. This is demonstrated in the following example, in which a set of the top 10 products for 2003 is combined with the set of top 10 products for 2004:

```
SELECT
  {([Measures].[Reseller Sales Amount])} ON COLUMNS,
  Union(
    TopCount(
      {[Product].[Product].[Product].Members},
      10,
      ([Measures].[Reseller Sales Amount],
       [Date].[Calendar Year].[CY 2003])
      ),
    TopCount(
      {[Product].[Product].[Product].Members},
      10,
      ([Measures].[Reseller Sales Amount],
       [Date].[Calendar Year].[CY 2004])
      )
    ) ON ROWS
FROM [Step-by-Step]
```

Use the optional *ALL* flag to preserve duplicate tuples between the sets.

To	Do this
Identify the tuples in one set but not another	Use the *Except* function. In the following example, the products in the top 10 for 2003 but not for 2004 are identified:

```
SELECT
  {([Measures].[Reseller Sales Amount])} ON COLUMNS,
  Except(
    TopCount(
      {[Product].[Product].[Product].Members},
      10,
      ([Measures].[Reseller Sales Amount],
        [Date].[Calendar Year].[CY 2003])
      ),
    TopCount(
      {[Product].[Product].[Product].Members},
      10,
      ([Measures].[Reseller Sales Amount],
        [Date].[Calendar Year].[CY 2004])
      )
    ) ON ROWS
FROM [Step-by-Step]
```

The optional *ALL* flag preserves duplicates in the resulting set.

To	Do this
Identify the tuples common between two sets	Use the *Intersect* function. In the following example, the products in the top 10 for both 2003 and 2004 are identified:

```
SELECT
  {([Measures].[Reseller Sales Amount])} ON COLUMNS,
  Intersect(
    TopCount(
      {[Product].[Product].[Product].Members},
      10,
      ([Measures].[Reseller Sales Amount],
        [Date].[Calendar Year].[CY 2004])
      ),
    TopCount(
      {[Product].[Product].[Product].Members},
      10,
      ([Measures].[Reseller Sales Amount],
        [Date].[Calendar Year].[CY 2003])
      )
    ) ON ROWS
FROM [Step-by-Step]
```

Use the optional *ALL* flag to preserve duplicates in the resulting set.

To	Do this
Assemble a merged set through iteration over another set	Use the *Generate* function. In the following example, the *Generate* function is used to produce the set of top five products for each product category:

```
SELECT
  {([Measures].[Reseller Sales Amount])} ON COLUMNS,
  Generate(
    {[Product].[Category].[Category].Members},
    {([Product].[Category].CurrentMember)} *
      TopCount(
        EXISTING
          {[Product].[Product].[Product].Members},
        5,
        ([Measures].[Reseller Sales Amount])
        ),
    ALL
    ) ON ROWS
FROM [Step-by-Step]
```

To	Do this
Extract member references from a set to form a new set of distinct combinations	Use the *Extract* function. This is demonstrated in the following example, which returns the set of products having greater than $160,000 in sales for any given month:

```
SELECT
  {([Measures].[Reseller Sales Amount])} ON COLUMNS,
  Extract(
    Filter(
      {[Product].[Product].[Product].Members} *
        {[Date].[Calendar].[Month].Members},
      ([Measures].[Reseller Sales Amount])>160000
      ),
    [Product].[Product]
    ) ON ROWS
FROM [Step-by-Step]
```

Chapter 7
Performing Aggregation

After completing this chapter, you will be able to:

- Perform basic aggregations using MDX functions
- Employ appropriate strategies for calculating aggregate values

Analysis Services records and returns measures as aggregate values. The singular aggregate value returned for a given measure may represent hundreds, thousands, or even millions of individually recorded fact table entries. An aggregation function assigned to the measure at design time determines how these many fact table values are combined to form the singular value returned.

You can perform additional aggregation on top of these aggregate values through the use of the MDX aggregation functions. These functions provide insight into the magnitude and distribution of values across a given set.

Important Throughout this chapter, we discuss the MDX aggregation functions in relationship to the aggregate functions assigned to measures during the cube's design. The terminology used overlaps considerably and can be a bit confusing. For this reason, we will refer to the functions assigned to measures within the cube as the aggregate functions and identify these in all lowercase characters. We'll identify the MDX aggregation functions using standard capitalization.

Performing Summation

When the subject of aggregation is introduced, many folks initially think of summation. Summation involves the simple addition of values and provides insight into the overall magnitude of a given measure. Within the cube, summation is supported through the assignment of the sum aggregate function to a measure. Within a query, summation is supported through the MDX *Sum* function:

```
Sum( {Set} [, Expression])
```

The first argument of the MDX *Sum* function is a set of tuples. The function works by resolving each tuple to a value using the supplied expression or the current measure and then adding these values.

The MDX *Sum* function is highly simplistic in that measure values are added together without regard for how those values are derived. For measure values based on the sum or count aggregate functions, this is no big deal. For other measure values, such as those employing distinct count, max, or min aggregate functions, summing the values across a set frequently produces inappropriate results. In these situations, what is typically required is for measures to be aggregated based on whichever aggregate function is assigned to them within the cube. This is handled by the MDX *Aggregate* function:

```
Aggregate( {Set} [, Expression])
```

Just like the MDX *Sum* function, the MDX *Aggregate* function aggregates values across a specified set. Instead of employing simple summation, the MDX *Aggregate* function works to evaluate measures in a manner consistent with their assigned aggregate functions. In this way the aggregation of a set of values based on the sum or count aggregate function returns a sum, a set of values based on the max aggregate function returns a max, a set of values based on a distinct count aggregate function returns a distinct count, and so on and so on. The actual mechanics of how Analysis Services pulls this off can be quite complex, so when using the MDX *Aggregate* function it is always recommended you double-check the calculated value.

Define a calculated member summarizing the values of the top five subcategories

1. Open the MDX Query Editor to the MDX Step-by-Step database.

2. In the code pane, enter the following query to review the top five product subcategories based on reseller sales as well as the total across all subcategories:

```
SELECT
    {
        ([Measures].[Reseller Sales Amount]),
        ([Measures].[Reseller Transaction Count]),
        ([Measures].[Reseller Order Count])
        } ON COLUMNS,
    TopCount(
        {[Product].[Subcategory].[Subcategory].Members},
        5,
        ([Measures].[Reseller Sales Amount])
        ) +
        {([Product].[Subcategory].[All Products])} ON ROWS
FROM [Step-by-Step]
```

3. Execute the query and review the results.

	Reseller Sales Amount	Reseller Transaction Count	Reseller Order Count
Road Bikes	$29,358,206.96	12,850	1,460
Mountain Bikes	$26,492,684.38	7,487	1,215
Touring Bikes	$10,451,490.22	4,463	478
Mountain Frames	$4,713,672.15	4,476	860
Road Frames	$3,849,853.34	4,708	1,013
All Products	$80,450,596.98	60,855	3,796

This query presents the Reseller Sales Amount, Reseller Transaction Count, and Reseller Order count measures for each of the top five product subcategories as well as the subcategory (All) member. Each of these three measures derives from a single fact table in the underlying relational data warehouse but is calculated in different ways:

❑ **Reseller Sales Amount** The Reseller Sales Amount measure represents a sum of the Sales Amount field in this table. In the cube, it employs the sum aggregate function to aggregate the values from this field.

❑ **Reseller Transaction Count** The Reseller Transaction Count measure represents a count of the records in the underlying fact table and therefore employs the count aggregate function. In the AdventureWorks model, this measure provides a count of the line items in an order.

❑ **Reseller Order Count** The Reseller Order Count performs a count of the order numbers in the underlying fact table. The distinct count aggregate function is used to address the fact that a given order may have more than one line item associated with it.

4. Add a calculated member to the query summing the current measure for the top five subcategories in the previous step:

```
WITH
MEMBER [Product].[Subcategory].[Top 5] AS
    Sum(
        TopCount(
            [Product].[Subcategory].[Subcategory].Members,
            5,
            ([Measures].[Reseller Sales Amount])
            ),
        ([Measures].CurrentMember)
        )
SELECT
    {
        ([Measures].[Reseller Sales Amount]),
        ([Measures].[Reseller Transaction Count]),
        ([Measures].[Reseller Order Count])
        } ON COLUMNS,
```

```
TopCount(
        [Product].[Subcategory].[Subcategory].Members,
        5,
        ([Measures].[Reseller Sales Amount])
    ) +
    {
        ([Product].[Subcategory].[Top 5]),
        ([Product].[Subcategory].[All Products])
    } ON ROWS
FROM [Step-by-Step]
```

5. Execute the query and observe the new Top 5 member located on the *ROWS* axis.

	Reseller Sales Amount	Reseller Transaction Count	Reseller Order Count
Road Bikes	$29,358,206.96	12,850	1,460
Mountain Bikes	$26,492,684.38	7,487	1,215
Touring Bikes	$10,451,490.22	4,463	478
Mountain Frames	$4,713,672.15	4,476	860
Road Frames	$3,849,853.34	4,708	1,013
Top 5	$74,865,907.05	33,984	5,026
All Products	$80,450,596.98	60,855	3,796

The new Top 5 calculated member sums the current measure for the top five product subcategories. With the additive measures Reseller Sales Amount and Reseller Transaction Count, this approach results in a value you would expect. For the non-additive Reseller Order Count measure based on the distinct count aggregate function, simple summation across the top five subcategories results in a value greater than the Reseller Order Count value across all products. This is clearly not an appropriate value because the individual distinct count values are being simply summed.

For this calculated member, what is needed instead is for each measure to be aggregated in a manner consistent with its underlying aggregate function. This is handled with the MDX *Aggregate* function.

6. Alter the query to calculate the Top 5 member using the MDX *Aggregate* function:

```
WITH
MEMBER [Product].[Subcategory].[Top 5] AS
    Aggregate(
        TopCount(
            [Product].[Subcategory].[Subcategory].Members,
            5,
            ([Measures].[Reseller Sales Amount])
            ),
        ([Measures].CurrentMember)
        )
```

```
SELECT
    {
        ([Measures].[Reseller Sales Amount]),
        ([Measures].[Reseller Transaction Count]),
        ([Measures].[Reseller Order Count])
    } ON COLUMNS,
    TopCount(
        [Product].[Subcategory].[Subcategory].Members,
        5,
        ([Measures].[Reseller Sales Amount])
        ) +
        {
            ([Product].[Subcategory].[Top 5]),
            ([Product].[Subcategory].[All Products])
        } ON ROWS
FROM [Step-by-Step]
```

7. Execute the query and observe the recalculated Top 5 member on the *ROWS* axis.

	Reseller Sales Amount	Reseller Transaction Count	Reseller Order Count
Road Bikes	$29,358,206.96	12,850	1,460
Mountain Bikes	$26,492,684.38	7,487	1,215
Touring Bikes	$10,451,490.22	4,463	478
Mountain Frames	$4,713,672.15	4,476	860
Road Frames	$3,849,853.34	4,708	1,013
Top 5	$74,865,907.05	33,984	3,445
All Products	$80,450,596.98	60,855	3,796

The Top 5 member now reflects a value for the Reseller Order Count consistent with what is expected for this non-additive measure. The additive Reseller Sales Amount and Reseller Transaction Count measures are also aggregated in a consistent manner, producing the same value as observed in the previous query.

It's important to understand that the take-home message of this exercise is not that you should use the MDX *Aggregate* function and avoid the MDX *Sum* function. Instead, you should be explicit with the type of aggregation you require for your calculations. When summation is required, employ the MDX *Sum* function. When measures should be aggregated based on their definitions, employ the MDX *Aggregate* function.

Calculating Averages

Averages are used to calculate a representative value for a set, allowing a set to be evaluated based on the size of its values and not the size of the set itself. In this way, averages facilitate cross-set comparisons. In Analysis Services, averages are calculated using both the MDX *Avg* function and custom expressions.

Calculating Averages with the *Avg* Function

You can use a number of techniques for calculating averages. Of these, the arithmetic average is the most common. With an arithmetic average, the values in a set are summed and then divided by the number of values in the set. In this manner, each value in the set is given equal weighting in terms of its contribution to the average. In MDX, this average is calculated through the *Avg* function:

```
Avg( {Set} [, Expression])
```

The syntax of the *Avg* function is very similar to that of the *Sum* and *Aggregate* functions described in the previous section. A set is specified and each tuple in that set is evaluated using the current measure or a supplied expression. These non-empty values are then averaged and that value is returned.

Define average reseller sales over a calendar year

1. If you have not already done so, open the MDX Query Editor to the MDX Step-by-Step database.

2. In the code pane, enter the following query to present monthly reseller sales:

```
SELECT
    {([Measures].[Reseller Sales Amount])} ON COLUMNS,
    {
        [Date].[Calendar].[Month].[January 2003]:
        [Date].[Calendar].[Month].[December 2003]
        } ON ROWS
FROM [Step-by-Step]
```

3. Execute the query and observe the monthly reseller sales amounts for calendar year 2003.

	Reseller Sales Amount
January 2003	$1,317,541.83
February 2003	$2,384,846.59
March 2003	$1,563,955.08
April 2003	$1,865,278.43
May 2003	$2,880,752.68
June 2003	$1,987,872.71
July 2003	$2,665,650.54
August 2003	$4,212,971.51
September 2003	$4,047,574.04
October 2003	$2,282,115.88
November 2003	$3,483,161.40
December 2003	$3,510,948.73

You can see quite a bit of variability between months. By performing an average, you can determine sales for a typical month.

4. Alter the query to calculate an average reseller sales amount over the months of calendar year 2003:

```
WITH
MEMBER [Date].[Calendar].[CY 2003 Monthly Avg Reseller Sales] AS
    Avg(
        {
            [Date].[Calendar].[Month].[January 2003]:
            [Date].[Calendar].[Month].[December 2003]
            },
        [Measures].CurrentMember
        )
SELECT
    {([Measures].[Reseller Sales Amount])} ON COLUMNS,
    {([Date].[Calendar].[CY 2003 Monthly Avg Reseller Sales])} +
        {
            [Date].[Calendar].[Month].[January 2003]:
            [Date].[Calendar].[Month].[December 2003]
            } ON ROWS
FROM [Step-by-Step]
```

5. Execute the query and compare the monthly average to an average you calculate yourself.

	Reseller Sales Amount
CY 2003 Monthly Avg Reseller Sales	$2,683,555.79
January 2003	$1,317,541.83
February 2003	$2,384,846.59
March 2003	$1,563,955.08
April 2003	$1,865,278.43
May 2003	$2,880,752.68
June 2003	$1,987,872.71
July 2003	$2,665,650.54
August 2003	$4,212,971.51
September 2003	$4,047,574.04
October 2003	$2,282,115.88
November 2003	$3,483,161.40

By summing the monthly reseller sales amounts and dividing them by the total number of months (for which reseller sales were not empty), a monthly average is calculated. Would a quarterly average return the same value?

6. Alter the query to present quarterly members along the *ROWS* axis:

```
WITH
MEMBER [Date].[Calendar].[CY 2003 Monthly Avg Reseller Sales] AS
    Avg(
        {
            [Date].[Calendar].[Month].[January 2003]:
            [Date].[Calendar].[Month].[December 2003]
            },
        [Measures].CurrentMember
        )
SELECT
    {([Measures].[Reseller Sales Amount])} ON COLUMNS,
    {([Date].[Calendar].[CY 2003 Monthly Avg Reseller Sales])} +
```

```
Hierarchize(
    {
        [Date].[Calendar].[Month].[January 2003]:
        [Date].[Calendar].[Month].[December 2003]
        } +
    {
        [Date].[Calendar].[Calendar Quarter].[Q1 CY 2003]:
        [Date].[Calendar].[Calendar Quarter].[Q4 CY 2003]
        }
    ) ON ROWS
FROM [Step-by-Step]
```

7. Alter the query to calculate a quarterly average:

```
WITH
MEMBER [Date].[Calendar].[CY 2003 Quarterly Avg Reseller Sales] AS
    Avg(
        {
            [Date].[Calendar].[Calendar Quarter].[Q1 CY 2003]:
            [Date].[Calendar].[Calendar Quarter].[Q4 CY 2003]
            },
        [Measures].CurrentMember
        )
MEMBER [Date].[Calendar].[CY 2003 Monthly Avg Reseller Sales] AS
    Avg(
        {
            [Date].[Calendar].[Month].[January 2003]:
            [Date].[Calendar].[Month].[December 2003]
            },
        [Measures].CurrentMember
        )
SELECT
    {([Measures].[Reseller Sales Amount])} ON COLUMNS,
    {
        ([Date].[Calendar].[CY 2003 Monthly Avg Reseller Sales]),
        ([Date].[Calendar].[CY 2003 Quarterly Avg Reseller Sales])
        } +
    Hierarchize(
        {
            [Date].[Calendar].[Month].[January 2003]:
            [Date].[Calendar].[Month].[December 2003]
            } +
        {
            [Date].[Calendar].[Calendar Quarter].[Q1 CY 2003]:
            [Date].[Calendar].[Calendar Quarter].[Q4 CY 2003]
            }
        ) ON ROWS
FROM [Step-by-Step]
```

8. Execute the query and compare the quarterly average to an average you calculate yourself.

> **Note** To make the manual calculation of an average easier, you can select the top, leftmost cell in the results pane to select the returned cell set and then right-click this same cell and select Copy. The results can then be pasted into Excel.

For the quarterly average, quarterly reseller sales amounts are summed and divided by the number of quarters (non-empty for quarterly sales) in the set. The calculation is very similar to that of the monthly average except the average is performed for quarterly totals. As each quarter represents multiple months, the quarterly average value is quite a bit larger than that of the monthly average.

Calculating Averages with Expressions

The *Avg* function presents an issue inherent to all the statistical functions in the MDX language. The calculation of the average value is performed across the tuples in a set. These values are typically aggregate values, and although averaging aggregate values is not necessarily inappropriate, the average value may not be what is expected.

Consider the fact table presented as Table 7-1. This simple relational fact table records six transaction-level facts: three for calendar year 2003 and three for calendar year 2004.

> **Note** Table 7-1 does not adhere to traditional fact table design principles. It is presented in this manner simply for illustrative purposes.

TABLE 7-1 Records of a Fact Table Over Which an Average Is to Be Calculated

Reseller Sales Amount	Calendar Year
$100.00	CY 2003
$100.00	CY 2003
$100.00	CY 2003
$200.00	CY 2004
$200.00	CY 2004
$200.00	CY 2004

If you were to ask most folks to calculate the average value of the Reseller Sales Amount fact measure in this table, they would calculate an average value of $150 by summing the Reseller Sales Amount values and dividing by 6.

If you were to calculate the average using the MDX *Avg* function, you would first define a set. Let's assume this set is the set of calendar years CY 2003 and CY 2004. Using this set, the aggregate values for CY 2003 ($300.00) and CY 2004 ($600.00) are returned and divided by 2 to produce an average value of $450.00.

The two averages differ significantly. Neither is wrong; they simply represent very different things. The first average represents a transaction-level average. It answers the question "What is the average reseller sales amount?" The second average represents a monthly average. It answers the question "What is the average monthly reseller sales amount?"

The transaction-level average is typical of the averages calculated in relational databases. Multidimensional databases operating on aggregates can calculate the same value but must do so using an expression employing a count measure and not the *Avg* function.

Calculate a transaction-level and monthly average for reseller sales

1. If you have not already done so, open the MDX Query Editor to the MDX Step-by-Step database.

2. In the code pane, enter the following query to retrieve reseller sales and order counts by calendar year:

```
SELECT
    {
        ([Measures].[Reseller Sales Amount]),
        ([Measures].[Reseller Order Count])
        } ON COLUMNS,
    {
        [Date].[Calendar Year].[CY 2001]:
        [Date].[Calendar Year].[CY 2004]
        } ON ROWS
FROM [Step-by-Step]
```

3. Execute the query.

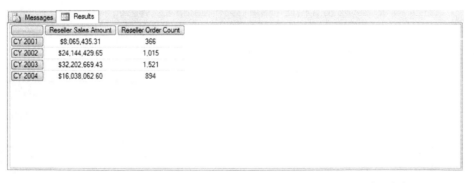

To answer the question "What were sales in a typical month in each of these years?," the *Avg* function is employed.

4. Alter the query to calculate a monthly average sales for each of the calendar years:

```
WITH
MEMBER [Measures].[Monthly Avg Reseller Sales Amount] AS
    Avg(
        EXISTING [Date].[Calendar].[Month].Members,
        [Measures].[Reseller Sales Amount]
        )
SELECT
    {
        ([Measures].[Reseller Sales Amount]),
        ([Measures].[Reseller Order Count]),
        ([Measures].[Monthly Avg Reseller Sales Amount])
        } ON COLUMNS,
    {
        [Date].[Calendar Year].[CY 2001]:
        [Date].[Calendar Year].[CY 2004]
        } ON ROWS
FROM [Step-by-Step]
```

5. Execute the query and note the differences in monthly averages between calendar years.

	Reseller Sales Amount	Reseller Order Count	Monthly Avg Reseller Sales Amount
CY 2001	$8,065,435.31	366	$1,344,239.22
CY 2002	$24,144,429.65	1,015	$2,012,035.80
CY 2003	$32,202,669.43	1,521	$2,683,555.79
CY 2004	$16,038,062.60	894	$2,673,010.43

In the calculated member, the *EXISTING* keyword forces the set of months to be considered in the current context which includes a specified calendar year. The Reseller Sales Amount measure is determined for each of those months and then averaged to produce the values returned.

> **Note** You can verify this average by dividing the yearly reseller sales value by the number of months in the year. Calendar years 2002 and 2003 each have 12 months of data, whereas calendar years 2001 and 2004 each have only 6 months of data.

This query tells you that in 2004, monthly average reseller sales exceeded those of 2003. Could this possibly be due to a higher average sales amount with each item purchased? To answer this question, you must calculate an item-level average.

6. Alter the query to include an item-level average sales amount:

```
WITH
MEMBER [Measures].[Average Reseller Sales Amount] AS
    ([Measures].[Reseller Sales Amount]) / ([Measures].[Reseller Transaction Count])
    ,FORMAT_STRING="Currency"
```

```
MEMBER [Measures].[Monthly Avg Reseller Sales Amount] AS
    Avg(
        EXISTING [Date].[Calendar].[Month].Members,
        [Measures].[Reseller Sales Amount]
        )
SELECT
    {
        ([Measures].[Reseller Sales Amount]),
        ([Measures].[Reseller Order Count]),
        ([Average Reseller Sales Amount])
        } ON COLUMNS,
    {
        [Date].[Calendar Year].[CY 2001]:
        [Date].[Calendar Year].[CY 2004]
        } ON ROWS
FROM [Step-by-Step]
```

7. Execute the query and note the newly calculated item-level average.

	Reseller Sales Amount	Reseller Order Count	Average Reseller Sales Amount
CY 2001	$8,065,435.31	366	$1,949.11
CY 2002	$24,144,429.65	1,015	$1,447.85
CY 2003	$32,202,669.43	1,521	$1,203.48
CY 2004	$16,038,062.60	894	$1,207.41

The item-level average reseller sales amount indicates that in 2004 resellers spent more per item than customers in 2003. Coupled with slightly higher number of orders, this translated to greater reseller sales in 2004 versus 2003.

Calculating Standard Deviation

The average condenses a set of values down to one representative value, shielding you from the variability in the set. Understanding the typical value of a set is important but so is understanding how widely values deviate from this value if you are to pick apart the patterns in your data. The standard deviation statistic is frequently employed to calculate the average difference between values and their average. In MDX, the calculation of standard deviations is handled through the *Stdev* function:

```
Stdev( {Set} [, Expression] )
```

The syntax of this function is the same as the *Avg* function you worked with in the previous exercises. Like the *Avg* function, the *Stdev* function calculates across a set of aggregate values.

Just as you occasionally have the need to calculate transaction-level averages, you occasionally have the need to calculate transaction-level standard deviations. By introducing a measure recording the squared values of another measure (and aggregating this squared value with the sum aggregate function), you can calculate a transaction-level standard deviation in Analysis Services, as demonstrated in the following query.

> **Note** The Squared Reseller Sales Amount measure in this query is based on a named calculation in the Step-By-Step cube's data source view employing the SQL fragment *POWER(salesamount, 2)*. The sum aggregate function is employed by the Squared Reseller Sales Amount measure.

```
WITH
MEMBER [Measures].[Average Reseller Sales Amount] AS
    ([Measures].[Reseller Sales Amount])/ ([Measures].[Reseller Transaction Count])
    ,FORMAT_STRING="Currency"
MEMBER [Measures].[Variance Reseller Sales Amount] AS
    (
        ([Measures].[Squared Reseller Sales Amount]) /
        ((([Measures].[Reseller Transaction Count])-1)
        ) -
        (([Measures].[Average Reseller Sales Amount])^2)
    ,FORMAT_STRING="Currency"
MEMBER [Measures].[StDev Reseller Sales Amount] AS
    ([Measures].[Variance Reseller Sales Amount])^(0.5)
    ,FORMAT_STRING="Currency"
SELECT
    {
        ([Measures].[Average Reseller Sales Amount]),
        ([Measures].[Variance Reseller Sales Amount]),
        ([Measures].[StDev Reseller Sales Amount])
        } ON COLUMNS,
    {
        [Date].[Calendar Year].[CY 2001]:
        [Date].[Calendar Year].[CY 2004]
        } ON ROWS
FROM [Step-by-Step]
```

	Average Reseller Sales Amount	Variance Reseller Sales Amount	StDev Reseller Sales Amount
CY 2001	$1,949.11	$9.192,654.01	$3,031.94
CY 2002	$1,447.85	$4.680,380.64	$2,163.42
CY 2003	$1,203.48	$3.909,038.58	$1,977.13
CY 2004	$1,207.41	$3,876,917.31	$1,968.99

Identifying Minimum and Maximum Values

Although statistics such as averages and standard deviations give a sense of the typical distribution of values associated with a set, the minimum and maximum values define the absolute range of values. In MDX, the calculation of minimums and maximums is supported through the MDX *Min* and *Max* functions, respectively:

```
Min( {Set} [, Expression])
Max( {Set} [, Expression])
```

The MDX *Min* and *Max* functions operate similarly to the functions described in other parts of this chapter. A set is defined and each tuple in that set is evaluated. Depending on the function employed, the maximum or minimum value from that set is then returned.

Although the use of an aggregate-level or transaction-level calculation is a big concern with the statistical functions, such as *Avg* and *Stdev*, it is less so with the MDX *Min* and *Max* functions. If you need a transaction-level maximum or minimum value, employ the MDX *Min* and *Max* functions with measures assigned a min or max aggregate function.

Determine the difference in sales for individual subcategories from a subcategory maximum

1. If you have not already done so, open the MDX Query Editor to the MDX Step-by-Step database.

2. In the code pane, enter the following query to identify product subcategory reseller sales:

```
SELECT
    {([Measures].[Reseller Sales Amount])} ON COLUMNS,
    {[Product].[Subcategory].[Subcategory].Members} ON ROWS
FROM [Step-by-Step]
```

3. Execute the query and review the sales associated with various subcategories.

	Reseller Sales Amount
Bib-Shorts	$166,739.71
Bike Racks	$197,736.16
Bike Stands	(null)
Bottles and Cages	$7,476.60
Bottom Brackets	$51,826.37
Brakes	$66,018.71
Caps	$31,541.35
Chains	$9,377.71
Cleaners	$11,188.37
Cranksets	$203,942.62
Derailleurs	$70,209.50
Fenders	(null)

The results of the query illustrate the wide variation between subcategory sales. Calculating the maximum across the range of values presented here helps you to gain some perspective on this variation.

4. Alter the query to calculate the maximum reseller sales amount across all subcategories:

```
WITH
MEMBER [Measures].[Max Sales By Subcategory] AS
    Max(
        {[Product].[Subcategory].[Subcategory].Members},
        ([Measures].[Reseller Sales Amount])
        )
SELECT
    {
        ([Measures].[Reseller Sales Amount]),
        ([Measures].[Max Sales By Subcategory])
        } ON COLUMNS,
    {[Product].[Subcategory].[Subcategory].Members} ON ROWS
FROM [Step-by-Step]
```

5. Execute the query.

	Reseller Sales Amount	Max Sales By Subcategory
Bib-Shorts	$166,739.71	$29,358,206.96
Bike Racks	$197,736.16	$29,358,206.96
Bike Stands	(null)	$29,358,206.96
Bottles and Cages	$7,476.60	$29,358,206.96
Bottom Brackets	$51,826.37	$29,358,206.96
Brakes	$66,018.71	$29,358,206.96
Caps	$31,541.35	$29,358,206.96
Chains	$9,377.71	$29,358,206.96
Cleaners	$11,188.37	$29,358,206.96
Cranksets	$203,942.62	$29,358,206.96
Derailleurs	$70,209.50	$29,358,206.96
Fenders	(null)	$29,358,206.96

Placing the subcategory sales maximum next to individual subcategory sales helps you understand each subcategory relative to this max value. It is more useful to express the individual subcategory sales as a percent of this value.

6. Calculate the percentage of individual subcategory sales relative to the subcategory maximum:

```
WITH
MEMBER [Measures].[Percent of Max] AS
    ([Measures].[Reseller Sales Amount]) /
        ([Measures].[Max Sales By Subcategory])
    ,FORMAT_STRING="Percent"
MEMBER [Measures].[Max Sales By Subcategory] AS
    Max(
        {[Product].[Subcategory].[Subcategory].Members},
        ([Measures].[Reseller Sales Amount])
        )
```

```
SELECT
    {
        ([Measures].[Reseller Sales Amount]),
        ([Measures].[Percent of Max])
        } ON COLUMNS,
    {[Product].[Subcategory].[Subcategory].Members} ON ROWS
FROM [Step-by-Step]
```

7. Execute the query and observe the newly calculated percent of maximum for each subcategory.

	Reseller Sales Amount	Percent of Max
Bib-Shorts	$166,739.71	0.57%
Bike Racks	$197,736.16	0.67%
Bike Stands	(null)	(null)
Bottles and Cages	$7,476.60	0.03%
Bottom Brackets	$51,826.37	0.18%
Brakes	$66,018.71	0.22%
Caps	$31,541.35	0.11%
Chains	$9,377.71	0.03%
Cleaners	$11,188.37	0.04%
Cranksets	$203,942.62	0.69%
Derailleurs	$70,209.50	0.24%
Fenders	(null)	(null)

Counting Tuples in Sets

As demonstrated in the previous chapter, sets can be constructed using complex criteria. Although such sets are frequently employed along query axes, occasionally such sets are constructed for no other purpose than to identify the number of tuples meeting the stated criteria. In these situations, the MDX *Count* function is frequently employed:

```
Count( {Set} [, Flag])
```

The MDX *Count* function is similar to the other MDX aggregation functions in that it operates over a set. If no flag is provided or if the *INCLUDEEMPTY* flag is specified, the function simply returns a count of the tuples in that set. With the *EXCLUDEEMPTY* flag, the set is evaluated employing the current measure and those tuples associated with a non-empty cell are counted.

Determine the number of products with Internet sales meeting or exceeding reseller sales

1. If you have not already done so, open the MDX Query Editor to the MDX Step-by-Step database.

2. In the code pane, enter the following query to review Internet and reseller sales by product:

```
SELECT
    {
        ([Measures].[Internet Sales Amount]),
        ([Measures].[Reseller Sales Amount])
    } ON COLUMNS,
    {[Product].[Product].[Product].Members} ON ROWS
FROM [Step-by-Step]
```

3. Execute the query and review the results.

	Internet Sales Amount	Reseller Sales Amount
All-Purpose Bike Stand	$39,591.00	(null)
AWC Logo Cap	(null)	$5,081.05
AWC Logo Cap	(null)	$11,698.80
AWC Logo Cap	$19,688.10	$14,761.50
Bike Wash - Dissolver	$7,218.60	$11,188.37
Cable Lock	(null)	$16,225.22
Chain	(null)	$9,377.71
Classic Vest, L	$12,382.50	$457.20
Classic Vest, M	$12,636.50	$77,614.10
Classic Vest, S	$10,668.00	$145,730.07
Fender Set - Mountain	$46,619.58	(null)
Front Brakes	(null)	$50,299.31

This query presents Internet and reseller sales amounts by product. In many situations, reseller sales exceed Internet sales. In others, Internet sales exceed reseller sales. Instead of reviewing each product's Internet and reseller sales, you can get a sense of how pervasive these patterns are by performing a count. Breaking this down by category lets you get a sense of whether this pattern varies by the general type of product. To get started, count the total number of products.

4. Replace the query with the following to count the number of products by category:

```
WITH
MEMBER [Measures].[Products By Category] AS
    Count(
        EXISTING {[Product].[Product].[Product].Members}
        )
SELECT
    {([Measures].[Products By Category])} ON COLUMNS,
    {[Product].[Category].Members} ON ROWS
FROM [Step-by-Step]
```

5. Execute the query and review the results.

	Products By Category
All Products	397
Accessories	35
Bikes	125
Clothing	48
Components	189

This query presents a simple count of the number of products by category. You can now calculate a count of products with reseller sales meeting or exceeding Internet sales and compare this to the count of all products.

6. Alter the query to count the number of products with reseller sales matching or exceeding Internet sales:

```
WITH
MEMBER [Measures].[Products] AS
    Count(
        EXISTING {[Product].[Product].[Product].Members}
        )
MEMBER [Measures].[Reseller Products] AS
    Count(
        Filter(
            EXISTING {[Product].[Product].[Product].Members},
            ([Measures].[Reseller Sales Amount]) >=
            ([Measures].[Internet Sales Amount])
            )
        )
SELECT
    {
        ([Measures].[Products]),
        ([Measures].[Reseller Products])
        } ON COLUMNS,
    {[Product].[Category].Members} ON ROWS
FROM [Step-by-Step]
```

7. Execute the query and review the results.

	Products	Reseller Products
All Products	397	363
Accessories	35	16
Bikes	125	115
Clothing	48	43
Components	189	189

The results show the number of products by category for which reseller sales match or exceed Internet sales. You may have noticed in the results of the first query that some products have no sales through either the Internet or resellers. These are showing up in the Reseller Products count as matching reseller sales. You need to exclude those products with no reseller sales. Try doing this with the *EXCLUDEEMPTY* flag.

8. Alter the query to exclude from the count those products with which empty cells are associated:

```
WITH
MEMBER [Measures].[Products] AS
    Count(
        EXISTING {[Product].[Product].[Product].Members}
        )
```

```
MEMBER [Measures].[Reseller Products] AS
    Count(
        Filter(
            EXISTING {[Product].[Product].[Product].Members},
            ([Measures].[Reseller Sales Amount]) >=
            ([Measures].[Internet Sales Amount])
            ),
            EXCLUDEEMPTY
        )
SELECT
    {
        ([Measures].[Products]),
        ([Measures].[Reseller Products])
        } ON COLUMNS,
    {[Product].[Category].Members} ON ROWS
FROM [Step-by-Step]
```

9. Execute the query and compare the results to those presented in step 7.

	Products	Reseller Products
All Products	397	363
Accessories	35	16
Bikes	125	115
Clothing	48	43
Components	189	189

Notice the values between this last query and that in step 7 are unchanged. You know that some members have no reseller sales, so why did these values not change?

The challenge with using the *EXCLUDEEMPTY* flag in this scenario is that it evaluates the tuples in the set using the current measure. What's the current measure? It's the calculated member being evaluated, which should result in an infinite recursion error as described in Chapter 5, "Working with Expressions."

Because of the way the set is evaluated, this error is not produced. Instead, Analysis Services is falling back on another measure.

Which measure is being used is less important than which measure should be used. In this scenario, the appropriate measure to evaluate on is Reseller Sales Amount. Cross-joining this measure with the set of products forces it to be used in the evaluation and gives you the desired result.

10. Alter the query to force the evaluation of the *EXCLUDEEMPTY* flag to use the Reseller Sales Amount Measure:

```
WITH
MEMBER [Measures].[Products] AS
    Count(
        EXISTING {[Product].[Product].[Product].Members}
        )
```

```
MEMBER [Measures].[Reseller Products] AS
    Count(
        Filter(
            EXISTING {[Product].[Product].[Product].Members},
            ([Measures].[Reseller Sales Amount]) >=
            ([Measures].[Internet Sales Amount])
            ) * {[Measures].[Reseller Sales Amount]},
            EXCLUDEEMPTY
        )
    )
SELECT
    {
        ([Measures].[Products]),
        ([Measures].[Reseller Products])
        } ON COLUMNS,
    {[Product].[Category].Members} ON ROWS
FROM [Step-by-Step]
```

11. Execute the query.

	Products	Reseller Products
All Products	397	316
Accessories	35	11
Bikes	125	115
Clothing	48	40
Components	189	150

With the set of products cross-joined by the Reseller Sales Amount measure, the set is forced to evaluate over this measure. The *EXCLUDEEMPTY* flag then eliminates those products for which no reseller sales are recorded.

The *DistinctCount* Function

The MDX language provides support for an alternative count function called *DistinctCount*. This function evaluates tuples, removes those associated with empty cells, removes duplicates, and then performs a count. The MDX *DistinctCount* function is functionally equivalent to the use of the MDX *Distinct* function in combination with the MDX *Count* function in the following manner:

```
Count( Distinct( {Set} ), EXCLUDEEMPTY )
```

Of course, it does this in a more compact form:

```
DistinctCount( {Set} )
```

The MDX *DistinctCount* function is frequently used when sets are being counted but you are concerned duplicates may have been introduced in the assembly of the set. When you need a count of a distinct set but do not wish to perform the tuple evaluations for the removal of empty cells, consider using *Count(Distinct({Set}))* with no flag (or the *INCLUDEEMPTY* flag) in its place.

Using the *Generate* Function to Explore Sets

The *Generate* function was introduced in Chapter 6, "Building Complex Sets," as a means of assembling a set based on iteration over another set. The *Generate* function has a second form that is useful when working with aggregations:

```
Generate( {Set}, Expression [, Delimiter] )
```

In this form, the *Generate* function iterates over the tuples of the specified set. Using an expression, properties of the tuple and its members can be extracted as strings and concatenated to each other. Using an optional delimiter, you can form a simple list that is returned as the function's value.

With the MDX aggregation functions, you are performing aggregation over what are often complex sets. Employing the *Generate* function, you can verify the contents of these sets as part of your development effort. The query is very similar to ones explored in the previous exercise and demonstrates the use of *Generate* to produce a list of products contributing to a count:

```
WITH
MEMBER [Measures].[Products] AS
    Count(
        EXISTING {[Product].[Product].[Product].Members}
        )
MEMBER [Measures].[Products List] AS
    Generate(
        EXISTING {[Product].[Product].[Product].Members},
        [Product].[Product].CurrentMember.Name,
        " | "
        )
SELECT
{
    ([Measures].[Products]),
    ([Measures].[Products List])
    } ON COLUMNS,
{[Product].[Subcategory].Members} ON ROWS
FROM [Step-by-Step]
```

Chapter 7 Quick Reference

To	Do this
Sum a set of values	Use the *Sum* function to sum the current measure or an optionally supplied expression over the tuples in the set. For example, the following query sums reseller sales for the top five products:

```
WITH
MEMBER [Product].[Subcategory].[Top 5] AS
    Sum(
        TopCount(
            [Product].[Subcategory].[Subcategory].Members,
            5,
            ([Measures].[Reseller Sales Amount])
            ),
        ([Measures].CurrentMember)
        )
SELECT
    {([Measures].[Reseller Sales Amount])} ON COLUMNS,
    {
        ([Product].[Subcategory].[Top 5]),
        ([Product].[Subcategory].[All Products])
        } ON ROWS
FROM [Step-by-Step]
```

To	Do this
Aggregate a set of values based on their underlying aggregate functions	Use the *Aggregate* function to aggregate the current measure or an optionally supplied expression over the tuples in the set. For example, the following query aggregates the reseller sales and order count for the top five products based on reseller sales. The Reseller Sales Amount measure employs a sum aggregate function whereas Reseller Order Count employs a distinct count:

```
WITH
MEMBER [Product].[Subcategory].[Top 5] AS
    Aggregate(
        TopCount(
            [Product].[Subcategory].[Subcategory].Members,
            5,
            ([Measures].[Reseller Sales Amount])
            ),
        ([Measures].CurrentMember)
        )
```

To	Do this

```
SELECT
    {
        ([Measures].[Reseller Sales Amount]),
        ([Measures].[Reseller Order Count])
    } ON COLUMNS,
    {
        ([Product].[Subcategory].[Top 5]),
        ([Product].[Subcategory].[All Products])
    } ON ROWS
FROM [Step-by-Step]
```

To	Do this
Average a set of values	Use the *Avg* function to average the current measure or an optionally supplied expression over the tuples in the set. For example, the following query calculates a monthly average sales for calendar years between 2001 and 2004:

```
WITH
MEMBER [Measures].[Monthly Avg Reseller Sales Amount] AS
    Avg(
        EXISTING [Date].[Calendar].[Month].Members,
        [Measures].[Reseller Sales Amount]
        )
SELECT
    {
        ([Measures].[Monthly Avg Reseller Sales Amount])
    } ON COLUMNS,
    {
        [Date].[Calendar Year].[CY 2001]:
        [Date].[Calendar Year].[CY 2004]
    } ON ROWS
FROM [Step-by-Step]
```

To calculate a transaction-level average, employ an expression within which the measure to average is divided by a count. The following query demonstrates the calculation of a transaction-level average for items purchased within the calendar years 2001 through 2004:

```
WITH
MEMBER [Measures].[Avg Reseller Sales Amount] AS
    ([Measures].[Reseller Sales Amount]) /
        ([Measures].[Reseller Transaction Count])
    ,FORMAT_STRING="Currency"
SELECT
    {
        ([Measures].[Avg Reseller Sales Amount])
    } ON COLUMNS,
    {
        [Date].[Calendar Year].[CY 2001]:
        [Date].[Calendar Year].[CY 2004]
    } ON ROWS
FROM [Step-by-Step]
```

To	Do this
Identify the maximum or minimum for a set of values	Use the *Max* or *Min* function to return the maximum or minimum of the current measure or an optionally supplied expression over the tuples in the set. For example, the following query returns the maximum product subcategory sales and uses that value to calculate a percentage of the maximum for each subcategory:

```
WITH
MEMBER [Measures].[Percent of Max] AS
    ([Measures].[Reseller Sales Amount]) /
      ([Measures].[Max Sales By Subcategory])
    ,FORMAT_STRING="Percent"
MEMBER [Measures].[Max Sales By Subcategory] AS
    Max(
        {[Product].[Subcategory].[Subcategory].Members},
        ([Measures].[Reseller Sales Amount])
        )
SELECT
    {
        ([Measures].[Reseller Sales Amount]),
        ([Measures].[Percent of Max])
        } ON COLUMNS,
    {[Product].[Subcategory].[Subcategory].Members} ON ROWS
FROM [Step-by-Step]
```

To	Do this
Count the tuples in a set	Use the *Count* function to count the tuples in the set. Specify the *EXCLUDEEMPTY* flag to eliminate tuples empty for the current measure. Specify the *INCLUDEEMPTY* flag (or no flag) to count all tuples in the set. For example, the following query returns the count of products by category:

```
WITH
MEMBER [Measures].[Products By Category] AS
    Count(
        EXISTING {[Product].[Product].[Product].Members}
        )
SELECT
    {([Measures].[Products By Category])} ON COLUMNS,
    {[Product].[Category].Members} ON ROWS
FROM [Step-by-Step]
```

Chapter 8
Navigating Hierarchies

After completing this chapter, you will be able to:

- Explain the use of the various navigational MDX functions
- Use the navigational functions to locate members within a hierarchy
- Evaluate a given member's position within a hierarchy

A defining feature of Analysis Services is the organization of members within hierarchies. For a given hierarchy—whether an attribute- or user-hierarchy—a member resides at a precise location within a specific level. Its position is determined by its relationship to members in higher levels and the ordering of the members within its own level.

The deterministic nature of a member's position within a hierarchy allows members to be located relative to one another. This is referred to as *navigation* and is facilitated by a myriad of MDX functions. The purpose of this chapter is to introduce you to these functions and expose you to some of their potential applications.

Accessing Immediate Relatives

Relationships between the members of a hierarchy are often described in familial terms. For a given member, the member in the level above it to which it has a direct relationship is referred to as its *parent*. This makes the given member its parent's *child*. The parent member may have multiple *children*, each of which is a *sibling* of the others. These immediate relatives of a given member are illustrated in Figure 8-1.

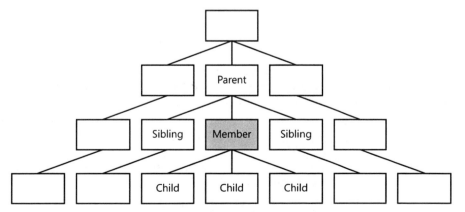

FIGURE 8-1 The immediate relatives of a given member in a hierarchy (shaded)

This way of describing the immediate relatives of a given member goes beyond simple terminology. As summarized in Table 8-1, a number of MDX functions are made available employing these same descriptive names to identify the immediate relatives of a given member.

TABLE 8-1 Navigation Functions Accessing Immediate Relatives

Function	Description
member.Parent	Returns a member's parent member
member.Children	Returns a set containing a member's children
member.FirstChild	Returns a member's first child member
member.LastChild	Returns a member's last child member
member.Siblings	Returns a set containing a member's siblings, including the member itself
member.FirstSibling	Returns the first child member of a member's parent
member.LastSibling	Returns the last child member of a member's parent

Each of these is used by appending the function to a member. In this example, the *Parent* function is appended to the explicitly referenced Road Bikes member to identify its parent member:

```
[Product].[Product Categories].[Subcategory].[Road Bikes].Parent
```

Because the *Parent* function itself returns a member, additional navigation functions can be appended to identify other members. In this example, the *Children* function is used to return the set of the Road Bikes member's parent member's children:

```
[Product].[Product Categories].[Subcategory].[Road Bikes].Parent.Children
```

You may recognize the set returned by the example above as functionally equivalent to the set of the Road Bikes member's siblings. Using the *Siblings* function, you can return this same set in a more concise manner:

```
[Product].[Product Categories].[Subcategory].[Road Bikes].Siblings
```

This last example demonstrates an important point about the MDX navigation functions. Quite often, you can use these functions to locate a member or set of members a number of different ways. The right way is often the simplest combination of functions that produces the correct result across the range of potential (given) members. Careful testing of your expressions is critical to your success with the navigational functions.

In the following exercises, you explore some of the navigational functions in Table 8-1 to perform a percent-of-parent calculation and to compare a given member to its siblings.

Calculate a member's percent contribution to its parent's total

1. Open the MDX Query Editor to the MDX Step-by-Step database.

2. In the code pane, enter the following query to retrieve reseller sales for each member of the Product Categories hierarchy:

```
SELECT
    {([Measures].[Reseller Sales Amount])} ON COLUMNS,
    {[Product].[Product Categories].Members} ON ROWS
FROM [Step-by-Step]
```

3. Execute the query and review the results.

	Reseller Sales Amount
All Products	$80,450,596.98
Accessories	$571,297.93
Bike Racks	$197,736.16
Hitch Rack - 4-Bike	$197,736.16
Bike Stands	(null)
All-Purpose Bike Stand	(null)
Bottles and Cages	$7,476.60
Mountain Bottle Cage	(null)
Road Bottle Cage	(null)
Water Bottle - 30 oz.	$7,476.60
Cleaners	$11,188.37
Bike Wash - Dissolver	$11,188.37

This query is very simple, with reseller sales presented for each member of the Product Categories hierarchy. The hierarchy members presented along the *ROWS* axis are retrieved from multiple levels of the Product Categories hierarchy. Significant variations in sales amounts are visible across these levels and even within the levels.

To help better understand the significance of the values associated with various products, subcategories, and categories, it might be interesting to look at each member's contribution to its parent's total. In other words, you might calculate the ratio of a given product's sales to that of its parent subcategory. You might then calculate the ratio of that Subcategory member's sales to those of its parent category and that parent category's sales to that of all sales. This is referred to as a *percent-of-parent* calculation, and it is easily assembled using the *Parent* function.

As a first step towards the percent-of-parent calculation, use the *Parent* function to identify the parent of each member by name. This will help you later with the validation of your results.

4. Alter the query to identify each Product Categories member's parent member:

```
WITH
MEMBER [Measures].[Parent Member] AS
    [Product].[Product Categories].CurrentMember.Parent.Name
SELECT
    {
        ([Measures].[Reseller Sales Amount]),
```

```
            ([Measures].[Parent Member])
        } ON COLUMNS,
    {[Product].[Product Categories].Members} ON ROWS
FROM [Step-by-Step]
```

5. Execute the query and review the results.

	Reseller Sales Amount	Parent Member
All Products	$80,450,596.98	(null)
Accessories	$571,297.93	All Products
Bike Racks	$197,736.16	Accessories
Hitch Rack - 4-Bike	$197,736.16	Bike Racks
Bike Stands	(null)	Accessories
All-Purpose Bike Stand	(null)	Bike Stands
Bottles and Cages	$7,476.60	Accessories
Mountain Bottle Cage	(null)	Bottles and Cages
Road Bottle Cage	(null)	Bottles and Cages
Water Bottle - 30 oz	$7,476.60	Bottles and Cages
Cleaners	$11,188.37	Accessories
Bike Wash - Dissolver	$11,188.37	Cleaners

Now that the parent member is clearly identified, employ the *Parent* function in a percent-of-parent calculation.

6. Alter the query to calculate a percent-of-parent value for sales:

```
WITH
MEMBER [Measures].[Parent Member] AS
    [Product].[Product Categories].CurrentMember.Parent.Name
MEMBER [Measures].[Percent of Parent] AS
    ([Measures].[Reseller Sales Amount])/
        (
            [Product].[Product Categories].CurrentMember.Parent,
            [Measures].[Reseller Sales Amount]
        )
    ,FORMAT="Percent"
SELECT
    {
        ([Measures].[Reseller Sales Amount]),
        ([Measures].[Parent Member]),
        ([Measures].[Percent of Parent])
        } ON COLUMNS,
    {[Product].[Product Categories].Members} ON ROWS
FROM [Step-by-Step]
```

7. Execute the query and review the results.

	Reseller Sales Amount	Parent Member	Percent of Parent
All Products	$80,450,596.98	(null)	1.#INF
Accessories	$571,297.93	All Products	0.71%
Bike Racks	$197,736.16	Accessories	34.61%
Hitch Rack - 4-Bike	$197,736.16	Bike Racks	100.00%
Bike Stands	(null)	Accessories	(null)
All-Purpose Bike Stand	(null)	Bike Stands	(null)
Bottles and Cages	$7,476.60	Accessories	1.31%
Mountain Bottle Cage	(null)	Bottles and Cages	(null)
Road Bottle Cage	(null)	Bottles and Cages	(null)
Water Bottle - 30 oz	$7,476.60	Bottles and Cages	100.00%
Cleaners	$11,188.37	Accessories	1.96%
Bike Wash - Dissolver	$11,188.37	Cleaners	100.00%

In the expression for the Percent of Parent calculated member, the *Parent* function is used to identify the current Product Categories hierarchy member's parent. This member is then employed within a tuple to access the parent member's sales. This value serves as the denominator of the ratio comparing the current member's sales to that of its parent. The calculated value is formatted as a percentage and presented in the results. Using the name of the current member's parent, as identified by the Parent Member calculated member, and then locating that member's sales in the query results, you can verify the values returned with the Percent of Parent member for yourself.

The *1.#INF* value returned by the Percent of Parent calculated member for All Products indicates that a division-by-zero error is occurring in the expression. As the *(null)* value associated with Parent Member makes clear, the All Products member (the root member of the Product Categories hierarchy) has no parent. As a result, it has no parent sales, and because Analysis Services substitutes a zero value in place of the null, the expression attempts to divide the All Products member's sales by zero.

For a member with no parent, such as the All Products member, you want to bypass the calculation of the ratio to avoid this error. Although you can do this in a number of ways, one of most direct is simply to test for the presence of a parent member.

8. Add logic to determine whether the current member has a parent. If it has no parent, substitute an appropriate value in place of the ratio calculation:

```
WITH
MEMBER [Measures].[Parent Member] AS
    [Product].[Product Categories].CurrentMember.Parent.Name
MEMBER [Measures].[Percent of Parent] AS
    IIF(
        [Product].[Product Categories].CurrentMember.Parent Is Null,
        Null,
        ([Measures].[Reseller Sales Amount])/
            (
                [Product].[Product Categories].CurrentMember.Parent,
                [Measures].[Reseller Sales Amount]
                )
        )
    ,FORMAT="Percent"
SELECT
    {
        ([Measures].[Reseller Sales Amount]),
        ([Measures].[Parent Member]),
        ([Measures].[Percent of Parent])
        } ON COLUMNS,
    {
        [Product].[Product Categories].Members
        } ON ROWS
FROM [Step-by-Step]
```

9. Execute the query and review the results.

	Reseller Sales Amount	Parent Member	Percent of Parent
All Products	$80,450,596.98	(null)	(null)
Accessories	$571,297.93	All Products	0.71%
Bike Racks	$197,736.16	Accessories	34.61%
Hitch Rack - 4-Bike	$197,736.16	Bike Racks	100.00%
Bike Stands	(null)	Accessories	(null)
All-Purpose Bike Stand	(null)	Bike Stands	(null)
Bottles and Cages	$7,476.60	Accessories	1.31%
Mountain Bottle Cage	(null)	Bottles and Cages	(null)
Road Bottle Cage	(null)	Bottles and Cages	(null)
Water Bottle - 30 oz.	$7,476.60	Bottles and Cages	100.00%
Cleaners	$11,188.37	Accessories	1.96%
Bike Wash - Dissolver	$11,188.37	Cleaners	100.00%

With the addition of conditional logic, a Null value is returned for those members with no parent. For all other members, the percent-of-parent calculation is performed as before.

The *Rank* Function

In the previous exercise, each member of a hierarchy's contribution to its parent's total is calculated. The percent-of-parent calculation can be quite insightful but often is used as a subtle means to compare siblings to one another.

An alternative technique for sibling comparison is to simply rank siblings against each other. This can be done by combining the navigational functions with the MDX *Rank* function:

```
Rank( Tuple, {Set} [, Expression] )
```

The *Rank* function identifies the position of a tuple within a set of tuples. Respectively, these serve as the function's first and second arguments. A third, optional argument supplies an expression by which the specified set is sorted (in descending order) prior to performing the search.

If the specified tuple is found in the set, the *Rank* function returns its one-based, ordinal position within that set. If the tuple is not found, a value of 0 is returned.

If the set of tuples is sorted using an optional expression and more than one tuple evaluate to the same expression value, those tuples identified as tied for a position within the set return the same rank values. Subsequent tuples in the set return a rank value accounting for the number of tied tuples preceding them. This may lead to the presence of duplicates and gaps in the values returned by the *Rank* function.

Armed with this knowledge, you are now ready to take on the next exercise.

Rank members of a hierarchy relative to their siblings

1. If you have not already done so, open the MDX Query Editor to the MDX Step-by-Step database.

2. In the code pane, enter the following query retrieving reseller sales for each member of the Product Categories hierarchy:

```
SELECT
    {([Measures].[Reseller Sales Amount])} ON COLUMNS,
    {[Product].[Product Categories].Members} ON ROWS
FROM [Step-by-Step]
```

3. Execute the query and review the results.

	Reseller Sales Amount
All Products	$80,450,596.98
Accessories	$571,297.93
Bike Racks	$197,736.16
Hitch Rack - 4-Bike	$197,736.16
Bike Stands	(null)
All-Purpose Bike Stand	(null)
Bottles and Cages	$7,476.60
Mountain Bottle Cage	(null)
Road Bottle Cage	(null)
Water Bottle - 30 oz	$7,476.60
Cleaners	$11,188.37
Bike Wash - Dissolver	$11,188.37

As before, this query returns reseller sales for the members of each level of the Product Categories hierarchy. To assist in evaluating the contribution of each member relative to its siblings, you can use the *Rank* function to rank each member from highest to lowest based on sales.

4. Alter the query to rank each Product Categories member relative to its siblings:

```
WITH
MEMBER [Measures].[Sibling Rank] AS
    Rank(
        [Product].[Product Categories].CurrentMember,
        [Product].[Product Categories].CurrentMember.Siblings,
        ([Measures].[Reseller Sales Amount])
        )
SELECT
    {
        ([Measures].[Reseller Sales Amount]),
        ([Measures].[Sibling Rank])
        } ON COLUMNS,
    {[Product].[Product Categories].Members} ON ROWS
FROM [Step-by-Step]
```

5. Execute the query and review the results.

	Reseller Sales Amount	Sibling Rank
All Products	$80,450,596.98	1
Accessories	$571,297.93	4
Bike Racks	$197,736.16	2
Hitch Rack - 4-Bike	$197,736.16	1
Bike Stands	(null)	9
All-Purpose Bike Stand	(null)	1
Bottles and Cages	$7,476.60	7
Mountain Bottle Cage	(null)	2
Road Bottle Cage	(null)	2
Water Bottle - 30 oz.	$7,476.60	1
Cleaners	$11,188.37	6
Bike Wash - Dissolver	$11,188.37	1

The *Rank* function is used to return the position of the current Product Categories member in the set of that member's siblings as identified using the *Siblings* function. (It is important to remember that the *Siblings* function includes the specified member.) Before the set is searched, Analysis Services sorts the set of siblings in descending order based on the Reseller Sales Amount value associated with each member as instructed through the *Rank* function's third argument.

The results of the query are very interesting but a little difficult to review given the current sort order of the results. Sorting the members along the *ROWS* axis from highest to lowest rank relative to their parent member makes the results a bit easier to interpret. You should recognize this as a hierarchical ascending sort, as described in Chapter 6, "Building Complex Sets."

6. Alter the query to order the Product Category members by rank relative to their parent:

```
WITH
MEMBER [Measures].[Sibling Rank] AS
    Rank(
        [Product].[Product Categories].CurrentMember,
        [Product].[Product Categories].CurrentMember.Siblings,
        ([Measures].[Reseller Sales Amount])
        )
SELECT
    {
        ([Measures].[Reseller Sales Amount]),
        ([Measures].[Sibling Rank])
        } ON COLUMNS,
    {
        Order(
            {[Product].[Product Categories].Members},
            ([Measures].[Sibling Rank]),
            ASC
            )
        } ON ROWS
FROM [Step-by-Step]
```

7. Execute the query and review the results.

	Reseller Sales Amount	Sibling Rank
All Products	$80,450,596.98	1
Bikes	$66,302,381.56	1
Road Bikes	$29,358,206.96	1
Road-350-W Yellow, 48	$1,380,253.88	1
Road-350-W Yellow, 40	$1,230,754.64	2
Road-250 Red, 44	$1,096,280.08	3
Road-250 Black, 44	$975,155.82	4
Road-250 Red, 48	$947,659.16	5
Road-250 Black, 44	$913,324.23	6
Road-250 Black, 48	$842,197.44	7
Road-250 Black, 48	$814,252.25	8
Road-150 Red, 56	$792,228.98	9

From the results, you can see the All Products member is ranked number 1 against its siblings, which includes only itself. More meaningfully, you can see across the Categories level that Bikes is ranked number 1 relative to other categories. Of the subcategories under the Bikes category, Road Bikes is ranked number 1 relative to its siblings, Mountain Bikes and Touring Bikes. Within the Road Bikes subcategory, Road-350-W Yellow, 48 is the top selling product followed by Road-350-W Yellow, 40 and the other Road Bikes products.

You should explore the other rankings returned by this query. For each, keep in mind that each member is ranked relative to its siblings (its parent's children).

Accessing Extended Relatives

Navigation is not limited to immediate relatives. Analysis Services expands the familial analogy to provide access to extended relatives from across the hierarchy. A given member's parent is one of its many *ancestors* extending up the levels of the hierarchy back to the root member. Relative to its ancestors, the given member is a *descendant* and may have descendants of its own. Two descendants of divergent lineages are each other's *cousins*. These extended relationships relative to a given member are illustrated in Figure 8-2.

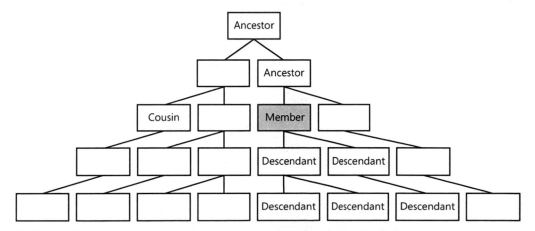

FIGURE 8-2 The extended relatives of a given member within a hierarchy (shaded)

As you would expect, these relations are made accessible through a number of MDX functions. These are identified in Table 8-2.

TABLE 8-2 Navigation Functions for Accessing Extended Relatives

Function	Description
`Ancestor( Member, Level | Distance )`	Returns a member's ancestor from a given level
`Ancestors( Member, Level | Distance )`	Returns a member's ancestor from a given level as a single-member set
`Ascendants( Member )`	Returns the complete set of a member's ancestors, including the given member itself

`Descendants(`
`    Member | {Set}`
`    [, Level | Distance [, Flag ]]`
`    )`
	Returns the descendants of a member(s) from a given level as modified by one of eight optional flags

`Cousin( Member1, Member2 )`	Returns the member in the same relative position as the (first) specified member but under the (second) member of a higher level

Because of their greater navigational flexibility, these functions are a bit more complex than those introduced earlier in this chapter. As such, they require a bit more explanation.

The *Ancestor* and *Ancestors* functions are nearly identical. Each identifies the ancestor member of a specified member from a given level. This level can either be identified by reference or by the number of levels, the distance, between it and the given member. These two functions differ in that the *Ancestor* function returns a reference to the ancestor member, whereas the *Ancestors* function returns the ancestor member as a single-member set. The type of object you require determines which of these two functions you employ.

The *Ascendants* function is closely related to the *Ancestor* and *Ancestors* functions in that it traverses a specified member's lineage. It differs in that instead of returning a single member from an identified level, it returns all the member's ancestors and the specified member itself as a set. This function is commonly employed in reporting applications.

The *Descendants* function returns the descendants of a given member (or members) as a set. As with other navigational functions, the level from which the descendants should be retrieved can be identified by reference or by distance from the specified member(s). If no level is specified, the level(s) of the specified member(s) is assumed.

The member and level arguments serve as the starting point for the generation of the returned set. Flags are then employed to determine the set returned. If no flag is specified, the descendant members of the identified level are returned. This is functionally equivalent to specifying the *SELF* flag.

This and the other seven flags supported with the Descendants function are explained in Table 8-3. The basic flags—*SELF*, *AFTER*, and *BEFORE*—serve as the foundation of the compounded flags *SELF_AND_AFTER*, *SELF_AND_BEFORE*, *BEFORE_AND_AFTER*, and *SELF_BEFORE_AFTER*, and are illustrated in Figure 8-3. The *LEAVES* flag specifies that only leaf-level members should be returned. Because of its incredible flexibility, the *Descendants* function is a mainstay of MDX developers.

TABLE 8-3 Flags Available for Use with the *Descendants* Function

Flag	Description
SELF	Instructs the function to return the descendant members of the identified level
AFTER	Instructs the function to return the descendant members in the levels below the identified level
BEFORE	Instructs the function to return the descendant members in the levels prior to the specified level and including the specified member
SELF_AND_AFTER	Instructs the function to return the set representing the combination of those returned by the *SELF* and *AFTER* flags
SELF_AND_BEFORE	Instructs the function to return the set representing the combination of those returned by the *SELF* and *BEFORE* flags
SELF_BEFORE_AFTER	Instructs the function to return the set representing the combination of those returned by the *SELF*, *BEFORE*, and *AFTER* flags. The set returned is the complete set of descendants of the specified member.
BEFORE_AND_AFTER	Instructs the function to return the set representing the combination of those returned by the *BEFORE* and *AFTER* flags. This set returns the complete set of descendants of the specified member excluding the members of the identified level.
LEAVES	Instructs the function to return the leaf-level descendants of the specified member between the specified member and the identified level

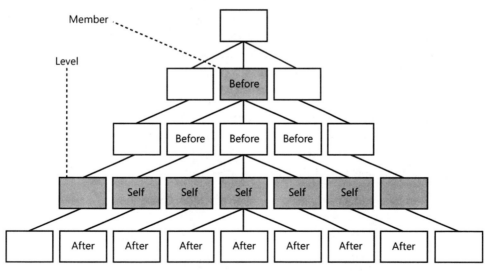

FIGURE 8-3 The members accessed with the basic flags of the *Descendants* function given a specified member and level (shaded)

Finally, the *Cousin* function returns the member in the same relative position as the first specified member but under a second member residing at a higher level in the hierarchy. That's quite a bit to absorb in one sentence. To understand what the *Cousin* function returns, it is helpful to think of its navigation as a two-step process:

1. Analysis Services determines the position of the first specified member relative to its ancestor in the same level as the second specified member.

2. The member under the second specified member in the same relative position as the first is then returned.

At this point you are probably asking yourself how the *Cousin* function could possibly be useful outside an academic discussion of hierarchical navigation. Before exploring its practical applications, it is important to address a deeper concern related to all the navigation functions.

Throughout this chapter, the navigation functions have been employed under the assumption that relationships between the members of a hierarchy, whether between levels or within a level, are meaningful in a business sense. This is not always the case.

For example, the Calendar-to-Fiscal Year hierarchy explored in Chapter 3, "Understanding Tuples," exists for no purpose other than to illustrate a concept. In real-world databases, other hierarchies may exist for similarly arbitrary purposes, such as to support a report.

It is important that you, as the MDX developer, challenge the significance of relationships between the members of a hierarchy both within and between levels before employing the navigation functions to ensure that you are deriving meaningful information.

Returning to the question of the relevance of the *Cousin* function, this function is useful in hierarchies that are organized both horizontally and vertically in a meaningful manner. Such hierarchies are often found in dimensions representing time. In a time-based hierarchy the *Cousin* function might be used to identify something such as the fifth day of the month in a prior quarter or the fourth quarter of a prior year. These are two examples of a parallel period, a concept you explore in the next chapter, "Working with Time."

In the exercises that follow, you use the *Ancestor* and *Ascendants* navigation functions to calculate a member's percent contribution to its ancestors and explore the *Descendants* function.

Calculate percent contribution to ancestors

1. If you have not already done so, open the MDX Query Editor to the MDX Step-by-Step database.

2. In the code pane, enter the following query calculating a member's percent contribution to its parent's total:

```
WITH
MEMBER [Measures].[Percent of Parent] AS
    IIF(
        [Product].[Product Categories].CurrentMember.Parent Is Null,
        Null,
        ([Measures].[Reseller Sales Amount])/
            (
                [Product].[Product Categories].CurrentMember.Parent,
                [Measures].[Reseller Sales Amount]
                )
        )
    ,FORMAT="Percent"
SELECT
    {
        ([Measures].[Reseller Sales Amount]),
        ([Measures].[Percent of Parent])
        } ON COLUMNS,
    {
        [Product].[Product Categories].Members
        } ON ROWS
FROM [Step-by-Step]
```

3. Execute the query and review the results.

	Reseller Sales Amount	Percent of Parent
All Products	$80,450,596.98	(null)
Accessories	$571,297.93	0.71%
Bike Racks	$197,736.16	34.61%
Hitch Rack - 4-Bike	$197,736.16	100.00%
Bike Stands	(null)	(null)
All-Purpose Bike Stand	(null)	(null)
Bottles and Cages	$7,476.60	1.31%
Mountain Bottle Cage	(null)	(null)
Road Bottle Cage	(null)	(null)
Water Bottle - 30 oz	$7,476.60	100.00%
Cleaners	$11,188.37	1.96%
Bike Wash - Dissolver	$11,188.37	100.00%

This query is very similar to the one you implemented in a previous exercise. The percent-of-parent calculation is useful for particular forms of analysis, but the ratio's frequently changing denominator, sales for the parent of the current member, can make the calculated value challenging to interpret. Fixing the denominator to an ancestor at a particular level within the hierarchy, such as the current member's Category-level ancestor, adds a bit more consistency to the values returned.

4. Alter the query to calculate the percent contribution of each member to its Category ancestor:

```
WITH
MEMBER [Measures].[Percent of Parent] AS
    IIF(
        [Product].[Product Categories].CurrentMember.Parent Is Null,
        Null,
        ([Measures].[Reseller Sales Amount])/
            (
                [Product].[Product Categories].CurrentMember.Parent,
                [Measures].[Reseller Sales Amount]
                )
        )
    ,FORMAT="Percent"
MEMBER [Measures].[Percent of Category] AS
    ([Measures].[Reseller Sales Amount])/
        (
            Ancestor(
                [Product].[Product Categories].CurrentMember,
                [Product].[Product Categories].[Category]
                ),
            [Measures].[Reseller Sales Amount]
                )
    ,FORMAT="Percent"
SELECT
    {
        ([Measures].[Reseller Sales Amount]),
        ([Measures].[Percent of Parent]),
        ([Measures].[Percent of Category])
        } ON COLUMNS,
    {[Product].[Product Categories].Members} ON ROWS
FROM [Step-by-Step]
```

5. Execute the query and review the results.

	Reseller Sales Amount	Percent of Parent	Percent of Category
All Products	$80,450,596.98	(null)	1.#INF
Accessories	$571,297.93	0.71%	100.00%
Bike Racks	$197,736.16	34.61%	34.61%
Hitch Rack - 4-Bike	$197,736.16	100.00%	34.61%
Bike Stands	(null)	(null)	(null)
All-Purpose Bike Stand	(null)	(null)	(null)
Bottles and Cages	$7,476.60	1.31%	1.31%
Mountain Bottle Cage	(null)	(null)	(null)
Road Bottle Cage	(null)	(null)	(null)
Water Bottle - 30 oz.	$7,476.60	100.00%	1.31%
Cleaners	$11,188.37	1.96%	1.96%
Bike Wash - Dissolver	$11,188.37	100.00%	1.96%

Using the *Ancestor* function, sales for each member's Category-level ancestor are retrieved and then used in the percent-of-category calculation. This provides a bit more consistency to the numbers within a particular category, which may be more appropriate for intra-category analysis than a percent-of-parent calculation.

As with the percent-of-parent calculation, the percent-of-category results indicate a division-by-zero error is occurring with the All Products member. This member exists in a level above the Category level and therefore cannot have a Category-level ancestor. This results in a Null value in the ratio's denominator, which because of substitution generates a division-by-zero error. As with the Percent of Parent calculated member, this problem is addressed with the addition of conditional logic.

6. Alter the calculated member to avoid division-by-zero errors resulting from empty values in the denominator:

```
WITH
MEMBER [Measures].[Percent of Parent] AS
    IIF(
        [Product].[Product Categories].CurrentMember.Parent Is Null,
        Null,
        ([Measures].[Reseller Sales Amount])/
            (
                [Product].[Product Categories].CurrentMember.Parent,
                [Measures].[Reseller Sales Amount]
                )
        )
    ,FORMAT="Percent"
MEMBER [Measures].[Percent of Category] AS
    IIF(
        Ancestor(
                    [Product].[Product Categories].CurrentMember,
                    [Product].[Product Categories].[Category]
                    ) Is Null,
        Null,
        ([Measures].[Reseller Sales Amount])/
            (
                Ancestor(
                    [Product].[Product Categories].CurrentMember,
                    [Product].[Product Categories].[Category]
                    ),
                [Measures].[Reseller Sales Amount]
                )
        )
    ,FORMAT="Percent"
SELECT
    {
        ([Measures].[Reseller Sales Amount]),
        ([Measures].[Percent of Parent]),
        ([Measures].[Percent of Category])
        } ON COLUMNS,
    {[Product].[Product Categories].Members} ON ROWS
FROM [Step-by-Step]
```

7. Execute the query and review the results.

	Reseller Sales Amount	Percent of Parent	Percent of Category
All Products	$80,450,596.98	(null)	(null)
Accessories	$571,297.93	0.71%	100.00%
Bike Racks	$197,736.16	34.61%	34.61%
Hitch Rack - 4-Bike	$197,736.16	100.00%	34.61%
Bike Stands	(null)	(null)	(null)
All-Purpose Bike Stand	(null)	(null)	(null)
Bottles and Cages	$7,476.60	1.31%	1.31%
Mountain Bottle Cage	(null)	(null)	(null)
Road Bottle Cage	(null)	(null)	(null)
Water Bottle - 30 oz.	$7,476.60	100.00%	1.31%
Cleaners	$11,188.37	1.96%	1.96%
Bike Wash - Dissolver	$11,188.37	100.00%	1.96%

With the addition of the conditional logic, a Null value is returned for any member that does not have a Category ancestor. This avoids the division-by-zero error for the All Products member.

Calculate a product's percent contribution across its lineage

1. If you have not already done so, open the MDX Query Editor to the MDX Step-by-Step database.

2. In the code pane, enter the following query to retrieve reseller sales for the product Mountain-200 Black, 42:

```
SELECT
    {([Measures].[Reseller Sales Amount])} ON COLUMNS,
    {([Product].[Product Categories].[Product].[Mountain-200 Black, 42])} ON ROWS
FROM [Step-by-Step]
```

3. Execute the query and review the results.

	Reseller Sales Amount
Mountain-200 Black, 42	$1,285,524.65

The query shows reseller sales focused on an individual product–AdventureWorks Cycle's black, 42-inch, 200 Series mountain bike. Although simplistic, a query such as this (focused on a single product) is typical of one you might find in a product-specific report.

On such a report, it may be interesting to not only show sales for this product but also to present the sales value next to those of the product's subcategory, category, and all products available through the company. The *Ascendants* function allows you to assemble this set of the product's ancestors with ease.

4. Alter the query to display the Mountain-200 Black, 42 product along with all of its ancestors in the Product Categories hierarchy:

```
SELECT
    {([Measures].[Reseller Sales Amount])} ON COLUMNS,
    {
        Ascendants(
            [Product].[Product Categories].[Product].[Mountain-200 Black, 42]
            )
        } ON ROWS
FROM [Step-by-Step]
```

5. Execute the query and review the results.

	Reseller Sales Amount
Mountain-200 Black, 42	$1,285,524.65
Mountain Bikes	$26,492,684.38
Bikes	$66,302,381.56
All Products	$80,450,596.98

The *Ascendants* function returns the members forming the product's lineage as a set. Notice that the set is sorted in reverse order by level, with the lowest-level member at the top and the highest-level member at the bottom. To reverse this, you can use the *Hierarchize* function as described in Chapter 6.

6. Alter the query to sort the members of the product's lineage in hierarchical order:

```
SELECT
    {([Measures].[Reseller Sales Amount])} ON COLUMNS,
    Hierarchize(
        {
            Ascendants(
                [Product].[Product Categories].[Product].[Mountain-200 Black, 42]
                )
            }
        ) ON ROWS
FROM [Step-by-Step]
```

7. Execute the query and review the results.

	Reseller Sales Amount
All Products	$80,450,596.98
Bikes	$66,302,381.56
Mountain Bikes	$26,492,684.38
Mountain-200 Black, 42	$1,285,524.65

To assist with the interpretation of these results, you might perform a percent contribution calculation similar to what you did in earlier exercises.

8. Alter the query to calculate the product's percent contribution to each member in its lineage:

```
WITH
MEMBER [Measures].[Percent Contribution Reseller Sales] AS
    (
        [Product].[Product Categories].[Product].[Mountain-200 Black, 42],
        [Measures].[Reseller Sales Amount]
        ) /
    ([Measures].[Reseller Sales Amount])
    ,FORMAT="Percent"
SELECT
    {
        ([Measures].[Reseller Sales Amount]),
        ([Measures].[Percent Contribution Reseller Sales])
        } ON COLUMNS,
    Hierarchize(
        {
            Ascendants(
                [Product].[Product Categories].[Product].[Mountain-200 Black, 42]
                )
            }
        ) ON ROWS
FROM [Step-by-Step]
```

9. Execute the query and review the results.

	Reseller Sales Amount	Percent Contribution Reseller Sales
All Products	$80,450,596.98	1.60%
Bikes	$66,302,381.56	1.94%
Mountain Bikes	$26,492,684.38	4.85%
Mountain-200 Black, 42	$1,285,524.65	100.00%

Using the *Ascendants* function, sales for the Mountain-200 Black, 42 product is shown in relation to those for each of its ancestors. On a product-specific report, information presented this way can help you more quickly assess the importance of a product to your business.

Assemble the set of descendants for a given category

1. If you have not already done so, open the MDX Query Editor to the MDX Step-by-Step database.

2. In the code pane, enter the following query to retrieve sales for the Category member Bikes:

```
SELECT
    {([Measures].[Reseller Sales Amount])} ON COLUMNS,
    {[Product].[Product Categories].[Category].[Bikes]} ON ROWS
FROM [Step-by-Step]
```

3. Execute the query and review the results.

This query serves as a starting point for the retrieval of the descendants of the Bikes category using the appropriately named *Descendants* function. One of the most straightforward applications of the function is the retrieval of descendants from a specified level of a hierarchy.

4. Alter the query to retrieve the descendants of the Bikes category from the Subcategory level of the hierarchy:

```
SELECT
    {([Measures].[Reseller Sales Amount])} ON COLUMNS,
    Descendants(
        {[Product].[Product Categories].[Category].[Bikes]},
        [Product].[Product Categories].[Subcategory]
        ) ON ROWS
FROM [Step-by-Step]
```

5. Execute the query and review the results.

	Reseller Sales Amount
Mountain Bikes	$26,492,684.38
Road Bikes	$29,358,206.96
Touring Bikes	$10,451,490.22

Without a specified flag, the *Descendants* function returns the members of the identified level descendant from the specified member. This is the equivalent to using the *SELF* flag. (You can test this by altering the previous query to include *SELF* as the *Descendants* function's third argument.)

You may recognize the members retrieved in the previous query as the Bikes member's children. This same set can therefore be assembled using the *Children* function presented earlier in this chapter. You can use still other techniques for assembling this same set, such as using the *Exists* function to limit the set of Subcategory-level members to those associated with Bikes.

Although a particular set may be assembled using a variety of functions, no other function matches the versatility of the *Descendants* function in assembling complex sets of descendant members. This versatility is provided through the use of flags.

6. Employ the *AFTER* flag to retrieve the set of descendants below the Subcategory level:

```
SELECT
    {([Measures].[Reseller Sales Amount])} ON COLUMNS,
    Descendants(
        {[Product].[Product Categories].[Category].[Bikes]},
        [Product].[Product Categories].[Subcategory],
        AFTER
    ) ON ROWS
FROM [Step-by-Step]
```

7. Execute the query and review the results.

	Reseller Sales Amount
Mountain-100 Black, 38	$1,174,622.74
Mountain-100 Black, 42	$1,102,848.18
Mountain-100 Black, 44	$1,163,352.98
Mountain-100 Black, 48	$1,041,901.60
Mountain-100 Silver, 38	$1,094,669.28
Mountain-100 Silver, 42	$1,043,695.27
Mountain-100 Silver, 44	$1,050,610.85
Mountain-100 Silver, 48	$897,257.36
Mountain-200 Black, 38	$1,471,078.72
Mountain-200 Black, 38	$1,634,647.94
Mountain-200 Black, 42	$1,360,828.02
Mountain-200 Black, 42	$1,285,524.65

Using the *AFTER* flag, the query now presents the descendants of the Bikes category member along the levels below the specified Subcategory level. Because the Product level is the only level below the Subcategory level in this hierarchy, the members returned are all products. Had the hierarchy employed other levels, the members of these levels would be returned as well.

To include the members of the identified Subcategory level along with the members of those levels below it, use the *SELF_AND_AFTER* flag, which combines the functionality of the *SELF* and *AFTER* flags.

8. Employ the *SELF_AND_AFTER* flag to retrieve the set of descendants below and including the Subcategory level:

```
SELECT
     {([Measures].[Reseller Sales Amount])} ON COLUMNS,
     Descendants(
          {[Product].[Product Categories].[Category].[Bikes]},
          [Product].[Product Categories].[Subcategory],
          SELF_AND_AFTER
          ) ON ROWS
FROM [Step-by-Step]
```

9. Execute the query and review the results.

	Reseller Sales Amount
Mountain Bikes	$26,492,684.38
Mountain-100 Black, 38	$1,174,622.74
Mountain-100 Black, 42	$1,102,848.18
Mountain-100 Black, 44	$1,163,352.98
Mountain-100 Black, 48	$1,041,901.60
Mountain-100 Silver, 38	$1,094,669.28
Mountain-100 Silver, 42	$1,043,695.27
Mountain-100 Silver, 44	$1,050,610.85
Mountain-100 Silver, 48	$897,257.36
Mountain-200 Black, 38	$1,471,078.72
Mountain-200 Black, 38	$1,634,647.94
Mountain-200 Black, 42	$1,360,828.02

To include the members in levels prior to the specified Subcategory level, you specify the *BEFORE* flag. To combine these members with those identified with the *AFTER* flag, use *BEFORE_AND_AFTER*. (The *BEFORE_AND_AFTER* flag returns the complete set of a member's descendants excluding those of the specified level.)

10. Employ the *BEFORE_AND_AFTER* flag to retrieve the set of descendants of the specified Bikes category member excluding members of the specified Subcategory level:

```
SELECT
     {([Measures].[Reseller Sales Amount])} ON COLUMNS,
     Descendants(
          {[Product].[Product Categories].[Category].[Bikes]},
          [Product].[Product Categories].[Subcategory],
          BEFORE_AND_AFTER
          ) ON ROWS
FROM [Step-by-Step]
```

11. Execute the query and review the results.

You could (and should) go on like this evaluating the effect of the other available flags on the returned set. Although you can employ other functions and techniques to retrieve many of the same sets retrievable through the *Descendants* function, none is as flexible, making the *Descendants* function an indispensible tool to you, the MDX developer.

Investigating Members in a Hierarchy

When navigating hierarchies, you may need to apply logic based on a particular member's position within the hierarchy. To assist with this, the MDX language makes available the functions *IsAncestor*, *IsSibling*, and *IsLeaf*, summarized in Table 8-4.

TABLE 8-4 Functions for Evaluating a Member's Position within a Hierarchy

Function	Description
IsAncestor(Member1, Member2)	Returns True if the first specified member is an ancestor of the second specified member. Otherwise, the function returns False. For the purposes of this function, a member is not considered to be its own ancestor.
IsSibling(Member1, Member2)	Returns True if the first specified member is a sibling of the second specified member. Otherwise, the function returns False. For the purposes of this function, a member is considered to be its own sibling.
IsLeaf(Member)	Returns True if the specified member is a leaf-level member of its hierarchy. Otherwise, the function returns False.

To demonstrate how these functions might be used in an expression, the following query employs the *IsLeaf* function to determine whether the current member of a hierarchy is a leaf-level member. Because leaf-level members have no children, the calculation of the number of children for these members may be considered not applicable:

```
WITH
MEMBER [Measures].[Number of Children] AS
    IIF(
        IsLeaf([Product].[Product Categories].CurrentMember),
        "N/A",
        COUNT(
            [Product].[Product Categories].CurrentMember.Children
            )
        )
SELECT
    {[Measures].[Number of Children]} ON COLUMNS,
    {[Product].[Product Categories].Members} ON ROWS
FROM [Step-by-Step]
```

	Number of Children
All Products	4
Accessories	12
Bike Racks	1
Hitch Rack - 4-Bike	N/A
Bike Stands	1
All-Purpose Bike Stand	N/A
Bottles and Cages	3
Mountain Bottle Cage	N/A
Road Bottle Cage	N/A
Water Bottle - 30 oz.	N/A
Cleaners	1
Bike Wash - Dissolver	N/A

Navigating within a Level

Navigation, as explored so far, has been heavily focused on the relationships between members of differing levels. Ancestor and descendant relatives are obvious examples of this, but even cousins and siblings are identified based on their position relative to a member in a higher level of the hierarchy.

When the order of the members within a level of a hierarchy is meaningful without regard to relationships with the members of higher levels, you can navigate the members of a level without regard for their positions relative to members of higher levels. This is loosely referred to as *horizontal navigation* (as opposed to *vertical navigation*, which implies movement between levels).

Table 8-5 identifies the horizontal navigation functions. Each of these functions, *PrevMember*, *NextMember*, *Lag*, and *Lead*, identifies members relative to a given member and within the same level without regard to relationships with higher-level members.

TABLE 8-5 **Navigation Functions for Accessing Members within a Level**

Function	Description
member.PrevMember	Returns the previous member within the given member's level
member.NextMember	Returns the next member within the given member's level
member.Lag(n)	Returns the member *n* number of positions prior to a given member
member.Lead(n)	Returns the member *n* number of positions following a given member

As mentioned in the previous section, meaningful horizontal relationships between members are often limited to members in time-based hierarchies. As such, the following exercise uses *PrevMember* to calculate a percent change in sales between months. This provides a useful demonstration of this class of navigation functions and serves as an interesting starting point for the exploration of time, continued in the next chapter.

Calculate the percent change in sales between months

1. If you have not already done so, open the MDX Query Editor to the MDX Step-by-Step database.

2. In the code pane, enter the following query presenting monthly reseller sales:

```
SELECT
    {([Measures].[Reseller Sales Amount])} ON COLUMNS,
    {[Date].[Calendar].[Month].Members} ON ROWS
FROM [Step-by-Step]
```

3. Execute the query and review the results.

	Reseller Sales Amount
July 2001	$489,328.58
August 2001	$1,538,408.31
September 2001	$1,165,897.08
October 2001	$844,721.00
November 2001	$2,324,135.80
December 2001	$1,702,944.54
January 2002	$713,116.69
February 2002	$1,900,788.93
March 2002	$1,455,280.41
April 2002	$882,899.94
May 2002	$2,269,116.71
June 2002	$1,001,803.77

The results show considerable variability between monthly sales. To present this variability in relative terms, you might calculate a monthly percent change in sales. The first step in this calculation is to identify the prior month's sales. Because months are presented in chronological order, you can locate the month prior to the current month member using the *PrevMember* function.

4. Alter the query to determine prior month sales for each month along the *ROWS* axis:

```
WITH
MEMBER [Measures].[Prior Period Reseller Sales] AS
    (
        [Date].[Calendar].CurrentMember.PrevMember,
        [Measures].[Reseller Sales Amount]
        )
    ,FORMAT="Currency"
SELECT
    {
        ([Measures].[Reseller Sales Amount]),
        ([Measures].[Prior Period Reseller Sales])
        } ON COLUMNS,
    {[Date].[Calendar].[Month].Members} ON ROWS
FROM [Step-by-Step]
```

5. Execute the query and review the results.

	Reseller Sales Amount	Prior Period Reseller Sales
July 2001	$489,328.58	(null)
August 2001	$1,538,408.31	$489,328.58
September 2001	$1,165,897.08	$1,538,408.31
October 2001	$844,721.00	$1,165,897.08
November 2001	$2,324,135.80	$844,721.00
December 2001	$1,702,944.54	$2,324,135.80
January 2002	$713,116.69	$1,702,944.54
February 2002	$1,900,788.93	$713,116.69
March 2002	$1,455,280.41	$1,900,788.93
April 2002	$882,899.94	$1,455,280.41
May 2002	$2,269,116.71	$882,899.94
June 2002	$1,001,803.77	$2,269,116.71

For each month, the *PrevMember* function is used to locate the Month member preceding it. (You could also have used the *Lag* function with a value of 1 to identify this same member.) The member returned is then used within a tuple to retrieve reseller sales for the period. With both current month and prior month sales displayed in the query results for multiple months, you can easily verify the calculated value.

With the previous month's sales now identified, you can calculate the change in sales between the current and prior month.

6. Alter the query to calculate the change in sales from the current month and the prior month:

```
WITH
MEMBER [Measures].[Prior Period Reseller Sales] AS
    (
        [Date].[Calendar].CurrentMember.PrevMember,
        [Measures].[Reseller Sales Amount]
        )
    ,FORMAT="Currency"
MEMBER [Measures].[Change in Reseller Sales] AS
    ([Measures].[Reseller Sales Amount]) - ([Measures].[Prior Period Reseller Sales])
    ,FORMAT="Currency"
```

```
SELECT
    {
        ([Measures].[Reseller Sales Amount]),
        ([Measures].[Prior Period Reseller Sales]),
        ([Measures].[Change in Reseller Sales])
        } ON COLUMNS,
    {[Date].[Calendar].[Month].Members} ON ROWS
FROM [Step-by-Step]
```

7. Execute the query and review the results.

	Reseller Sales Amount	Prior Period Reseller Sales	Change in Reseller Sales
July 2001	$489,328.58	(null)	$489,328.58
August 2001	$1,538,408.31	$489,328.58	$1,049,079.73
September 2001	$1,165,897.08	$1,538,408.31	($372,511.23)
October 2001	$844,721.00	$1,165,897.08	($321,176.08)
November 2001	$2,324,135.80	$844,721.00	$1,479,414.80
December 2001	$1,702,944.54	$2,324,135.80	($621,191.25)
January 2002	$713,116.69	$1,702,944.54	($989,827.85)
February 2002	$1,900,788.93	$713,116.69	$1,187,672.24
March 2002	$1,455,280.41	$1,900,788.93	($445,508.52)
April 2002	$882,899.94	$1,455,280.41	($572,380.47)
May 2002	$2,269,116.71	$882,899.94	$1,386,216.77
June 2002	$1,001,803.77	$2,269,116.71	($1,267,312.94)

Because of the magnitude of the sales values, the significance of the change between months can be difficult to immediately interpret. Presenting the change in sales as a percentage of the prior month's sales may make the significance of the changes easier to understand.

8. Alter the query to calculate the percent change in sales:

```
WITH
MEMBER [Measures].[Prior Period Reseller Sales] AS
    (
        [Date].[Calendar].CurrentMember.PrevMember,
        [Measures].[Reseller Sales Amount]
        )
    ,FORMAT="Currency"
MEMBER [Measures].[Change in Reseller Sales] AS
    ([Measures].[Reseller Sales Amount]) - ([Measures].[Prior Period Reseller Sales])
    ,FORMAT="Currency"
MEMBER [Measures].[Percent Change in Reseller Sales] AS
    ([Measures].[Change in Reseller Sales])/
        ([Measures].[Prior Period Reseller Sales])
    ,FORMAT="Percent"
SELECT
    {
        ([Measures].[Reseller Sales Amount]),
        ([Measures].[Prior Period Reseller Sales]),
        ([Measures].[Change in Reseller Sales]),
        ([Measures].[Percent Change in Reseller Sales])
        } ON COLUMNS,
    {[Date].[Calendar].[Month].Members} ON ROWS
FROM [Step-by-Step]
```

9. Execute the query and review the results.

	Reseller Sales Amount	Prior Period Reseller Sales	Change in Reseller Sales	Percent Change in Reseller Sales
July 2001	$489,328.58	(null)	$489,328.58	1.#INF
August 2001	$1,538,408.31	$489,328.58	$1,049,079.73	214.39%
September 2001	$1,165,897.08	$1,538,408.31	($372,511.23)	-24.21%
October 2001	$844,721.00	$1,165,897.08	($321,176.08)	27.55%
November 2001	$2,324,135.80	$844,721.00	$1,479,414.80	175.14%
December 2001	$1,702,944.54	$2,324,135.80	($621,191.25)	-26.73%
January 2002	$713,116.69	$1,702,944.54	($989,827.85)	-58.12%
February 2002	$1,900,788.93	$713,116.69	$1,187,672.24	166.55%
March 2002	$1,455,280.41	$1,900,788.93	($445,508.52)	-23.44%
April 2002	$882,899.94	$1,455,280.41	($572,380.47)	-39.33%
May 2002	$2,269,116.71	$882,899.94	$1,386,216.77	157.01%
June 2002	$1,001,803.77	$2,269,116.71	($1,267,312.94)	-55.85%

The results indicate that a division-by-zero error has occurred with the first member of the level, which has no previous member from which to calculate a percent change in sales. Applying logic similar to that employed before, you can bypass the division operation and substitute an appropriate value in its place.

10. Alter the calculated member to avoid division-by-zero errors resulting from empty values in the denominator:

```
WITH
MEMBER [Measures].[Prior Period Reseller Sales] AS
    (
        [Date].[Calendar].CurrentMember.PrevMember,
        [Measures].[Reseller Sales Amount]
        )
    ,FORMAT="Currency"
MEMBER [Measures].[Change in Reseller Sales] AS
    ([Measures].[Reseller Sales Amount]) - ([Measures].[Prior Period Reseller Sales])
    ,FORMAT="Currency"
MEMBER [Measures].[Percent Change in Reseller Sales] AS
    IIF(
        [Date].[Calendar].CurrentMember.PrevMember Is Null,
        Null,
        ([Measures].[Change in Reseller Sales])/
            ([Measures].[Prior Period Reseller Sales])
        )
    ,FORMAT="Percent"
SELECT
    {
        ([Measures].[Reseller Sales Amount]),
        ([Measures].[Prior Period Reseller Sales]),
        ([Measures].[Change in Reseller Sales]),
        ([Measures].[Percent Change in Reseller Sales])
        } ON COLUMNS,
    {[Date].[Calendar].[Month].Members} ON ROWS
FROM [Step-by-Step]
```

11. Execute the query and review the results.

	Reseller Sales Amount	Prior Period Reseller Sales	Change in Reseller Sales	Percent Change in Reseller Sales
July 2001	$489,328.58	(null)	$489,328.58	(null)
August 2001	$1,538,408.31	$489,328.58	$1,049,079.73	214.39%
September 2001	$1,165,897.08	$1,538,408.31	($372,511.23)	-24.21%
October 2001	$844,721.00	$1,165,897.08	($321,176.08)	-27.55%
November 2001	$2,324,135.80	$844,721.00	$1,479,414.80	175.14%
December 2001	$1,702,944.54	$2,324,135.80	($621,191.25)	-26.73%
January 2002	$713,116.69	$1,702,944.54	($989,827.85)	-58.12%
February 2002	$1,900,788.93	$713,116.69	$1,187,672.24	166.55%
March 2002	$1,455,280.41	$1,900,788.93	($445,508.52)	-23.44%
April 2002	$882,899.94	$1,455,280.41	($572,380.47)	-39.33%
May 2002	$2,269,116.71	$882,899.94	$1,386,216.77	157.01%
June 2002	$1,001,803.77	$2,269,116.71	($1,267,312.94)	-55.85%

With the addition of the conditional logic, a Null value is returned for any member that does not have a previous member. This avoids the division-by-zero error for the first member in the Months level.

Chapter 8 Quick Reference

To	Do this

Return a member's parent member	Use the *Parent* function. For example, the following query uses the *Parent* function to identify the parent of the current member of the Product Categories hierarchy to calculate a percent-of-parent value:
	
	`WITH`
	`MEMBER [Measures].[Percent of Parent] AS`
	`  ([Measures].[Reseller Sales Amount])/`
	`    (`
	`      [Product].[Product Categories].CurrentMember.Parent,`
	`      [Measures].[Reseller Sales Amount]`
	`      )`
	`    ,FORMAT="Percent"`
	`SELECT`
	`  {`
	`    ([Measures].[Reseller Sales Amount]),`
	`    ([Measures].[Percent of Parent])`
	`    } ON COLUMNS,`
	`  {[Product].[Product Categories].Members} ON ROWS`
	`FROM [Step-by-Step]`

Return a set of the member's child members	Use the *Children* function. For example, the following query uses the *Children* function to count the child members associated with a given product category:
	
	`WITH`
	`MEMBER [Measures].[Number of Children] AS`
	`  Count(`
	`    [Product].[Product Categories].CurrentMember.Children`
	`    )`
	`SELECT`
	`  {([Measures].[Number of Children])} ON COLUMNS,`
	`  {[Product].[Product Categories].[Category].Members} ON ROWS`
	`FROM [Step-by-Step]`

To	Do this
Return the set of a member's siblings including the member itself	Use the member's *Siblings* function. For example, the following query uses the *Siblings* function to return the set of siblings for each Category member to determine its rank:

```
WITH
MEMBER [Measures].[Sibling Rank] AS
   Rank(
      [Product].[Category].CurrentMember,
      [Product].[Category].CurrentMember.Siblings,
      ([Measures].[Reseller Sales Amount])
      )
SELECT
   {
      ([Measures].[Reseller Sales Amount]),
      ([Measures].[Sibling Rank])
      } ON COLUMNS,
   {[Product].[Category].[Category].Members} ON ROWS
FROM [Step-by-Step]
```

To	Do this
Return a member's ancestor member from a level	Use the *Ancestor* function identifying the member and the level from which its ancestor should be retrieved. For example, the following query uses the *Ancestor* function to identify the Category-level ancestor for the current member of the Product Categories hierarchy as part of the Percent of Category calculation:

```
WITH
MEMBER [Measures].[Percent of Category] AS
   ([Measures].[Reseller Sales Amount])/
      (
         Ancestor(
            [Product].[Product Categories].CurrentMember,
            [Product].[Product Categories].[Category]
            ),
         [Measures].[Reseller Sales Amount]
         )
   ,FORMAT="Percent"
SELECT
   {
      ([Measures].[Reseller Sales Amount]),
      ([Measures].[Percent of Category])
      } ON COLUMNS,
   {[Product].[Product Categories].[Product].Members} ON ROWS
FROM [Step-by-Step]
```

To	Do this
Return the set of members forming the lineage of the specified member including the specified member itself	Use the *Ascendants* function. For example, the following query uses the *Ascendants* function to return the set of members forming the lineage of the product named Mountain-200 Black, 42:

```
SELECT
   {([Measures].[Reseller Sales Amount])} ON COLUMNS,
   {
   Ascendants(
      [Product].[Product Categories].[Mountain-200 Black, 42]
      )
   } ON ROWS
FROM [Step-by-Step]
```

To	Do this
| Return the descendants of a member or set of members from a level as modified by one of eight flags | Use the *Descendants* function with the appropriate flag. For example, the following query uses the *Descendants* function with the *SELF_AND_AFTER* flag to retrieve the Subcategory and lower-level descendants of the Category-level Bikes member:<br><br>```
SELECT
    {([Measures].[Reseller Sales Amount])} ON COLUMNS,
    Descendants(
        {[Product].[Product Categories].[Category].[Bikes]},
        [Product].[Product Categories].[Subcategory],
        SELF_AND_AFTER
        ) ON ROWS
FROM [Step-by-Step]
``` |
| Return the previous member within the given member's level | Use the *PrevMember* function. For example, the following query uses the *PrevMember* function to return reseller sales for the previous Month-level member:<br><br>```
WITH
MEMBER [Measures].[Prior Period Reseller Sales] AS
    (
        [Date].[Calendar].CurrentMember.PrevMember,
        [Measures].[Reseller Sales Amount]
        )
    ,FORMAT="Currency"
SELECT
    {
        ([Measures].[Reseller Sales Amount]),
        ([Measures].[Prior Period Reseller Sales])
        } ON COLUMNS,
    {[Date].[Calendar].[Month].Members} ON ROWS
FROM [Step-by-Step]
``` |
| Return the member *n* number of positions prior to a given member | Use the member's *Lag* function, indicating the number of prior positions from which to retrieve the member. For example, the following query uses the *Lag* function with a value of 1 to return reseller sales for the previous Month-level member. Using *Lag* with a value of 1 is equivalent to using the *PrevMember* function:<br><br>```
WITH
MEMBER [Measures].[Prior Period Reseller Sales] AS
    (
        [Date].[Calendar].CurrentMember.Lag(1),
        [Measures].[Reseller Sales Amount]
        )
    ,FORMAT="Currency"
SELECT
    {
        ([Measures].[Reseller Sales Amount]),
        ([Measures].[Prior Period Reseller Sales])
        } ON COLUMNS,
    {[Date].[Calendar].[Month].Members} ON ROWS
FROM [Step-by-Step]
``` |
```

Chapter 9
Working with Time

After completing this chapter, you will be able to:

- Explain the requirements for effective time-based analysis in Analysis Services
- Employ MDX functions to calculate common time-based metrics
- Combine time-based expressions to assemble complex metrics

Time is a critical component of business analysis. Analysts interpret the state of the business now, often in relation to what it was in the past, with the goal of understanding what it might be in the future.

To support this, Analysis Services provides a number of time-based MDX functions. Using these functions, powerful metrics can be assembled. In this chapter, you learn how to employ the time-based MDX functions to calculate some of the more frequently requested of these metrics.

Understanding the Time Dimension

Analysis Services has no inherent awareness of the concept of time. Although at first glance this may seem like a shortcoming of the tool, it actually affords you the flexibility to define your time dimension in a way that reflects how time is managed in your specific organization.

At the heart of the time dimension is one or more user-hierarchies referred to as *calendars*. Calendars allow you to drill down in time from higher levels of granularity, such as years, into lower levels of granularity, such as quarters, months, and days. Figure 9-1 illustrates one such calendar hierarchy based on the standard calendar we employ in everyday life.

When employed against calendar hierarchies, the time-based MDX functions give the appearance of time awareness. However, most time-based functions are simply exploiting the basic structure of the hierarchy to return the set or member required. In fact, SQL Server Books Online goes so far as to provide the navigational equivalents of each of the time-based functions. If you require slightly different functionality, you can use the navigational functions to implement it yourself.

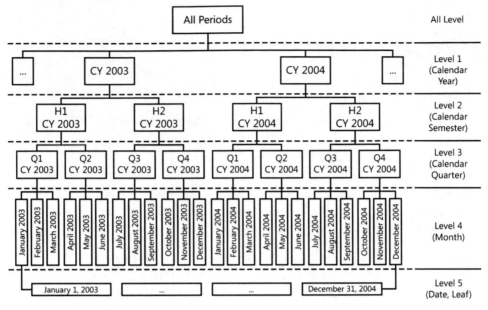

FIGURE 9-1 A user-hierarchy based on the standard calendar

The reliance on the calendar hierarchies for time-based functionality imposes two critical constraints on the attributes of the time dimension. First, the members of the attributes comprising the calendar hierarchies must be ordered in time-based sequence from the past to the present because many time-based functions assume this order. Second, complete sets of members for each attribute should be provided because missing members throw off position-based navigation.

Each of these issues is addressed through cube and ETL-layer design. As an MDX developer, you may not have the responsibility or the access required to ensure that these are addressed in a manner appropriate to your needs. However, if you intend to successfully make use of the time-based functions, you must make sure those responsible for assembling the time dimension are aware of these issues.

Determining the Current Value

A very common request is to return the current value of a metric. Although determining the current value is a seemingly simple request, it can be quite challenging.

First, you need to determine the granularity of the request. We often think of time as continuous, but in Analysis Services time is recorded as discrete members representing ranges of time. Between attributes, these members overlap so that the current date member of one attribute is associated with the current month member of another and the current quarter and year members of still others. Each of these represents quite different ranges of time, but each represents the current time.

Once you know the grain, the next challenge is to determine which member represents the current time. A key characteristic of any data warehouse is latency. The time it takes for changes to data in source systems to be reflected in the data warehouse varies from implementation to implementation, but some degree of latency is always present. Because of this, the data warehouse is only current as of some point in the past. Knowing this simply shifts the challenge from identifying the member associated with the current time to identifying the member associated with the time at which the data is current.

One technique for identifying the time at which the data is current is to employ the VBA time functions *Date*, *Time*, or *Now* to retrieve the current time, and then use the VBA date math functions *DateAdd* or *DateDiff* to adjust the time for latency. You can then use the adjusted value or parts of it extracted by using the VBA *DatePart* function to locate the current time member.

Although effective, this technique requires certainty in the amount of latency in the data. Try as you might, you may not be able to always accurately reflect this in the calculation. Considering the potential complexity of the expression logic as well, other alternatives should be explored.

A preferred alternative is to incorporate a property or attribute within the time dimension identifying a member at an appropriately low level of granularity as current. Relationships between attributes can then be employed to identify current time members at higher levels of granularity. The particulars of this design-time solution to the problem of identifying the current time member vary with the circumstances of your data warehouse, but the approach allows the data warehouse to tell you how up to date it is rather than you telling it how up to date it should be.

Calculating an Accumulating Total

In business, metrics are quite frequently reported as accumulating totals. For example, consider reseller sales in the month of October. Although sales in this month alone are interesting and important, the accumulation of sales over the months of the year up to and including October may be more interesting, especially if you are tracking sales against an annual target.

To calculate accumulating totals, you must determine the set of time members over which a value is to be aggregated. This is done using the *PeriodsToDate* function:

```
PeriodsToDate( [Level , [Member]] )
```

The *PeriodsToDate* function returns the set of members from the start of a given period up to and including a specified member. The *Level* argument identifies the level of the hierarchy representing the period over which the returned set should span, whereas the *Member* argument identifies the set's ending member. You can think of Analysis Services as starting with the specified member, navigating up to its ancestor in the specified level and then back down to the first sibling of the specified member under this shared ancestor. The set returned represents the range of members between and including these two members.

If the *Member* argument is not specified but the *Level* argument is, Analysis Services infers the current member of the hierarchy for the *Member* argument. If neither the *Member* nor the *Level* argument is specified, Analysis Services infers the current member of a hierarchy in a time dimension for the *Member* argument and the parent level of this member for the *Level* argument. For most applications of the *PeriodsToDate* function, you are encouraged to supply both arguments to ensure clarity.

Calculate year-to-date reseller sales

1. Open the MDX Query Editor to the MDX Step-by-Step database.

2. In the code pane, enter the following query to retrieve reseller sales for the periods to date for the month of April 2002:

```
SELECT
    {([Measures].[Reseller Sales Amount])} ON COLUMNS,
    {
        PeriodsToDate(
            [Date].[Calendar].[Calendar Year],
            [Date].[Calendar].[Month].[April 2002]
            )
        } ON ROWS
FROM [Step-by-Step]
```

3. Execute the query and review the results.

In the preceding query, you use the *PeriodsToDate* function to retrieve all months in the year 2002 prior to and including the month of April. By specifying the Calendar Year level of the Calendar hierarchy, Analysis Services moves from the member April 2002 to its ancestor along this level, CY 2002. It then selects the CY 2002 member's first descendant within the Month level—the level occupied by the specified member April 2002. This first descendant, January 2002, and the specified member, April 2002, then are used to form a range, [Date].[Calendar].[Month].[January 2002]:[Date].[Calendar].[Month].[April 2002], which resolves to the set presented along the *ROWS* axis.

This query demonstrates the basic functionality of the *PeriodsToDate* function, but your goal is to calculate a year-to-date total for reseller sales. Instead of using *PeriodsToDate* to define a set along an axis, you can use the function to define the set over which you aggregate values in a calculated member. As a starting point towards this goal, re-factor the query to return all months along the *ROWS* axis.

4. Modify the query to retrieve reseller sales for each month:

```
SELECT
    {([Measures].[Reseller Sales Amount])} ON COLUMNS,
    {[Date].[Calendar].[Month].Members} ON ROWS
FROM [Step-by-Step]
```

5. Execute the query and review the results.

	Reseller Sales Amount
July 2001	$489,328.58
August 2001	$1,538,408.31
September 2001	$1,165,897.08
October 2001	$844,721.00
November 2001	$2,324,135.80
December 2001	$1,702,944.54
January 2002	$713,116.69
February 2002	$1,900,788.93
March 2002	$1,455,280.41
April 2002	$882,899.94
May 2002	$2,269,116.71
June 2002	$1,001,803.77

6. Modify the query to calculate the year-to-date cumulative reseller sales for each member along the *ROWS* axis:

```
WITH
MEMBER [Measures].[Year to Date Reseller Sales] AS
    Aggregate(
        PeriodsToDate(
            [Date].[Calendar].[Calendar Year],
            [Date].[Calendar].CurrentMember
            ),
        ([Measures].[Reseller Sales Amount])
        )
SELECT
    {
        ([Measures].[Reseller Sales Amount]),
        ([Measures].[Year to Date Reseller Sales])
        } ON COLUMNS,
    {[Date].[Calendar].[Month].Members} ON ROWS
FROM [Step-by-Step]
```

7. Execute the query and review the results.

	Reseller Sales Amount	Year to Date Reseller Sales
July 2001	$489,328.58	$489,328.58
August 2001	$1,538,408.31	$2,027,736.89
September 2001	$1,165,897.08	$3,193,633.97
October 2001	$844,721.00	$4,038,354.97
November 2001	$2,324,135.80	$6,362,490.76
December 2001	$1,702,944.54	$8,065,435.31
January 2002	$713,116.69	$713,116.69
February 2002	$1,900,788.93	$2,613,905.62
March 2002	$1,455,280.41	$4,069,186.04
April 2002	$882,899.94	$4,952,085.98
May 2002	$2,269,116.71	$7,221,202.69
June 2002	$1,001,803.77	$8,223,006.46

For each member along the *ROWS* axis, the *PeriodsToDate* function returns the set of members from the start of its calendar year up to and including this member. Over this set, the current measure, Reseller Sales Amount, is aggregated to calculate year-to-date sales. Comparing the year-to-date totals to the monthly sales values for previous months, you can verify this logic.

> **Note** The preceding calculation employs the *Aggregate* function to calculate a running total. For more information on this and the other MDX aggregation functions, see Chapter 7, "Performing Aggregation."

As you review these results, notice between December 2001 and January 2002 the value of the accumulating total "resets." This is because these two members have differing ancestor members within the Calendar Year level. This pattern of accumulation and reset is observed whenever transitions between ancestors occur, as demonstrated in the following calculations of quarter-to-date totals.

8. Add a quarter-to-date total for reseller sales to the query:

```
WITH
MEMBER [Measures].[Year to Date Reseller Sales] AS
    Aggregate(
        PeriodsToDate(
            [Date].[Calendar].[Calendar Year],
            [Date].[Calendar].CurrentMember
            ),
        ([Measures].[Reseller Sales Amount])
        )
MEMBER [Measures].[Quarter to Date Reseller Sales] AS
    Aggregate(
        PeriodsToDate(
            [Date].[Calendar].[Calendar Quarter],
            [Date].[Calendar].CurrentMember
            ),
        ([Measures].[Reseller Sales Amount])
        )
```

```
SELECT
    {
        ([Measures].[Reseller Sales Amount]),
        ([Measures].[Year to Date Reseller Sales]),
        ([Measures].[Quarter to Date Reseller Sales])
        } ON COLUMNS,
    {[Date].[Calendar].[Month].Members} ON ROWS
FROM [Step-by-Step]
```

9. Execute the query and review the new Quarter To Date Reseller Sales values.

	Reseller Sales Amount	Year to Date Reseller Sales	Quarter to Date Reseller Sales
July 2001	$489,328.58	$489,328.58	$489,328.58
August 2001	$1,538,408.31	$2,027,736.89	$2,027,736.89
September 2001	$1,165,897.08	$3,193,633.97	$3,193,633.97
October 2001	$844,721.00	$4,038,354.97	$844,721.00
November 2001	$2,324,135.80	$6,362,490.76	$3,168,856.79
December 2001	$1,702,944.54	$8,065,435.31	$4,871,801.34
January 2002	$713,116.69	$713,116.69	$713,116.69
February 2002	$1,900,788.93	$2,613,905.62	$2,613,905.62
March 2002	$1,455,280.41	$4,069,186.04	$4,069,186.04
April 2002	$882,899.94	$4,952,085.98	$882,899.94
May 2002	$2,269,116.71	$7,221,202.69	$3,152,016.65
June 2002	$1,001,803.77	$8,223,006.46	$4,153,820.42

Reviewing the results, you can see the same pattern of accumulation and reset with the Quarter To Date Reseller Sales calculated measure as you do with the Year To Date Reseller Sales calculated measure. The only difference is that the pattern is based on a quarterly cycle as opposed to an annual one.

Simplifying Periods-to-Date Calculations

Many of the attributes in a time dimension are assigned *Type* property values at design time, identifying the attributes as representing years, quarters, months, or weeks. Analysis Services can return period-to-date sets based on these type assignments without the identification of a level by name. This functionality is provided through the specialized *Ytd*, *Qtd*, *Mtd*, and *Wtd* functions returning year-to-date, quarter-to-date, month-to-date, and week-to-date sets, respectively:

```
Ytd( [Member] )
Qtd( [Member] )
Mtd( [Member] )
Wtd( [Member] )
```

These functions, collectively referred to as the *xTD* functions, are logically equivalent to the *PeriodsToDate* function with hard-coded level arguments. Their reliance on the proper assignment of *Type* property values at design time makes them more succinct but also makes them dependent on settings into which you may have little insight. If you use the *xTD* functions, it is important for you to verify the set returned.

To demonstrate the use of the *xTD* functions, the last query of the previous exercise is rewritten using *Ytd* and *Qtd* to derive the year-to-date and quarter-to-date sets, respectively:

```
WITH
MEMBER [Measures].[Year to Date Reseller Sales] AS
    Aggregate(
        Ytd([Date].[Calendar].CurrentMember),
        ([Measures].[Reseller Sales Amount])
        )
MEMBER [Measures].[Quarter to Date Reseller Sales] AS
    Aggregate(
        Qtd([Date].[Calendar].CurrentMember),
        ([Measures].[Reseller Sales Amount])
        )
SELECT
    {
        ([Measures].[Reseller Sales Amount]),
        ([Measures].[Year to Date Reseller Sales]),
        ([Measures].[Quarter to Date Reseller Sales])
        } ON COLUMNS,
    {[Date].[Calendar].[Month].Members} ON ROWS
FROM [Step-by-Step]
```

Messages	Results		
	Reseller Sales Amount	Year to Date Reseller Sales	Quarter to Date Reseller Sales
July 2001	$489,328.58	$489,328.58	$489,328.58
August 2001	$1,538,408.31	$2,027,736.89	$2,027,736.89
September 2001	$1,165,897.08	$3,193,633.97	$3,193,633.97
October 2001	$844,721.00	$4,038,354.97	$844,721.00
November 2001	$2,324,135.80	$6,362,490.76	$3,168,856.79
December 2001	$1,702,944.54	$8,065,435.31	$4,871,801.34
January 2002	$713,116.69	$713,116.69	$713,116.69
February 2002	$1,900,788.93	$2,613,905.62	$2,613,905.62
March 2002	$1,455,280.41	$4,069,186.04	$4,069,186.04
April 2002	$882,899.94	$4,952,085.98	$882,899.94
May 2002	$2,269,116.71	$7,221,202.69	$3,152,016.65
June 2002	$1,001,803.77	$8,223,006.46	$4,153,820.42

Calculating Inception-to-Date

The period-to-date calculations return a value based on a range that is restricted to a particular period, such as a quarter or year. Occasionally, you may wish to calculate an accumulating value across all periods for which data is recorded. This is referred to as an *inception-to-date* value.

You can retrieve the inception-to-date range using the *PeriodsToDate* function with the calendar's (All) member's level as the period identifier, as demonstrated in the following expression:

```
PeriodsToDate(
    [Date].[Calendar].[(All)],
    [Date].[Calendar].CurrentMember
    )
```

Although this expression is perfectly valid, many MDX developers typically calculate inception-to-date sets employing a range-based shortcut:

```
Null: [Date].[Calendar].CurrentMember
```

The Null member reference forces Analysis Services to evaluate the range from a position just prior to the first member of the level on which the current time member resides. The result is the same set returned by the previous expression that employed the *PeriodsToDate* function.

Whichever technique you employ, measures are aggregated over the set just as with other period-to-date calculations, as demonstrated in the following example:

```
WITH
MEMBER [Measures].[Inception to Date Reseller Sales - PTD] AS
    Aggregate(
        PeriodsToDate(
            [Date].[Calendar].[(All)],
            [Date].[Calendar].CurrentMember
            ),
        ([Measures].[Reseller Sales Amount])
        )
MEMBER [Measures].[Inception to Date Reseller Sales - Range] AS
    Aggregate(
        NULL:[Date].[Calendar].CurrentMember,
        ([Measures].[Reseller Sales Amount])
        )
SELECT
    {
        ([Measures].[Reseller Sales Amount]),
        ([Measures].[Inception to Date Reseller Sales - PTD]),
        ([Measures].[Inception to Date Reseller Sales - Range])
        } ON COLUMNS,
    {[Date].[Calendar].[Month].Members} ON ROWS
FROM [Step-by-Step]
```

	Reseller Sales Amount	Inception to Date Reseller Sales - PTD	Inception to Date Reseller Sales - Range
July 2001	$489,328.58	$489,328.58	$489,328.58
August 2001	$1,538,408.31	$2,027,736.89	$2,027,736.89
September 2001	$1,165,897.08	$3,193,633.97	$3,193,633.97
October 2001	$844,721.00	$4,038,354.97	$4,038,354.97
November 2001	$2,324,135.80	$6,362,490.76	$6,362,490.76
December 2001	$1,702,944.54	$8,065,435.31	$8,065,435.31
January 2002	$713,116.69	$8,778,552.00	$8,778,552.00
February 2002	$1,900,788.93	$10,679,340.93	$10,679,340.93
March 2002	$1,455,280.41	$12,134,621.34	$12,134,621.34
April 2002	$882,899.94	$13,017,521.29	$13,017,521.29
May 2002	$2,269,116.71	$15,286,638.00	$15,286,638.00
June 2002	$1,001,803.77	$16,288,441.77	$16,288,441.77

Calculating Rolling Averages

Analysts often look for changes in values over time. Natural variability in most data can make it difficult to identify meaningful changes. Rolling averages are frequently employed to *smooth out* some of this variation, allowing more significant or longer-term changes to be more readily identified.

A rolling average is calculated as the average of values for some number of periods before or after (and including) the period of interest. For example, the three-month rolling average of sales for the month of February might be determined as the average of sales for February, January, and December. A three-month rolling average calculated in this manner is common in business analysis.

The heart of the rolling average calculation is the determination of the set of periods over which values will be averaged. To support the retrieval of this set, the MDX function *LastPeriods* is provided:

```
LastPeriods( n [, Member] )
```

The *LastPeriods* function returns a set of *n* members before or after (and including) a specified member of a time hierarchy. If a positive *n* value is provided, the set returned includes the members preceding the member of interest. If a negative *n* value is provided, the set returned includes the members following the member of interest.

The function's second argument is optional. If the second argument is not supplied, Analysis Services assumes the current member of a hierarchy in a time dimension. For most applications of the *LastPeriods* function, you are encouraged to employ the *Member* argument to ensure clarity.

Calculate the three-month rolling average for reseller sales

1. Open the MDX Query Editor to the MDX Step-by-Step database.

2. In the code pane, enter the following query to retrieve reseller sales for the three periods preceding and including January 2002:

```
SELECT
    {([Measures].[Reseller Sales Amount])} ON COLUMNS,
    {
        LastPeriods(
            3,
            [Date].[Calendar].[Month].[January 2002]
            )
        } ON ROWS
FROM [Step-by-Step]
```

3. Execute the query and review the results.

	Reseller Sales Amount
November 2001	$2,324,135.80
December 2001	$1,702,944.54
January 2002	$713,116.69

In this query, you use the *LastPeriods* function to retrieve the three-month period preceding and including January 2002. Analysis Services starts with the specified member, January 2002, and treats this as period 1. This leaves *n*-1 or 2 members to return in the set. Because *n* is a positive number, Analysis Services retrieves the January 2002 member's two preceding siblings to complete the set. (Notice that the November and December 2001 siblings were selected without regard for the change in the Calendar Year ancestor between them and the January 2002 member.)

This query demonstrates the basic functionality of the *LastPeriods* function, but your goal is to calculate a rolling average for reseller sales. Instead of using *LastPeriods* to define a set along an axis, you can use the function to define the set over which you will average values in a calculated member. As a starting point towards this goal, re-factor the query to return all months along the *ROWS* axis.

4. Alter the query to retrieve reseller sales for various months:

```
SELECT
    {([Measures].[Reseller Sales Amount])} ON COLUMNS,
    {[Date].[Calendar].[Month].Members} ON ROWS
FROM [Step-by-Step]
```

5. Execute the query and review the results.

	Reseller Sales Amount
July 2001	$489,328.58
August 2001	$1,538,408.31
September 2001	$1,165,897.08
October 2001	$844,721.00
November 2001	$2,324,135.80
December 2001	$1,702,944.54
January 2002	$713,116.69
February 2002	$1,900,788.93
March 2002	$1,455,280.41
April 2002	$882,899.94
May 2002	$2,269,116.71
June 2002	$1,001,803.77

Reseller sales vary considerably between various months. For example, take a look at the six-month period between October 2001 and March 2002. The wild swings between monthly sales make it difficult to determine any general upward or downward trends during this period. The same is true of the months between June 2002 and December 2002.

6. Alter the query to calculate a three-month rolling average for reseller sales:

```
WITH
MEMBER [Measures].[Three Month Avg Reseller Sales Amount] AS
    Avg(
        LastPeriods(
            3,
            [Date].[Calendar].CurrentMember
            ),
        ([Measures].[Reseller Sales Amount])
        )
SELECT
    {
        ([Measures].[Reseller Sales Amount]),
        ([Measures].[Three Month Avg Reseller Sales Amount])
        } ON COLUMNS,
    {[Date].[Calendar].[Month].Members} ON ROWS
FROM [Step-by-Step]
```

7. Execute the query and compare the monthly reseller sales values to the three-month rolling average values.

	Reseller Sales Amount	Three Month Avg Reseller Sales Amount
July 2001	$489,328.58	$489,328.58
August 2001	$1,538,408.31	$1,013,868.45
September 2001	$1,165,897.08	$1,064,544.66
October 2001	$844,721.00	$1,183,008.80
November 2001	$2,324,135.80	$1,444,917.96
December 2001	$1,702,944.54	$1,623,933.78
January 2002	$713,116.69	$1,580,065.68
February 2002	$1,900,788.93	$1,438,950.06
March 2002	$1,455,280.41	$1,356,395.35
April 2002	$882,899.94	$1,412,989.76
May 2002	$2,269,116.71	$1,535,765.69
June 2002	$1,001,803.77	$1,384,606.81

The three-month rolling average smoothes out some of the variability in the data, making general trends more easily observed. The period from October 2001 to March 2002 that reflected so much variability based on monthly sales totals now appears to be trending only slightly upward. The period from June 2002 and December 2002 that also displayed considerable variability appears to be trending more significantly upward. Without the smoothing effect of the rolling average, these trends would be harder to observe and differentiate.

Performing Period-over-Period Analysis

Historical values are frequently used in data analysis to provide perspective on current values. When comparing historical to current values, it is important you select values from time periods relatively similar to one another. Although no two time periods are exactly alike, analysts often compare values from what are referred to as *parallel periods* to minimize differences resulting from cyclical, time-dependent variations in the data.

To understand parallel periods, consider the month of April 2003. This month is the fourth month of the calendar year 2003. In a business heavily influenced by annual cycles, you might compare values for this month to those for the month of April in a prior year. In doing so, you might accurately (or inaccurately) assume that differences in current and historical values are due to factors other than the annual cyclical influence.

Should you compare values for April 2003 to those of January 2003 or October 2002? Your first response may be to say no. However, if your business is heavily influenced by quarterly cycles, this might be completely appropriate. April 2003 is the first month of a calendar quarter. January 2003 is the first month of the prior quarter and is therefore a parallel member based on quarter. October 2002 is also a parallel member except that it is from two quarters prior. What constitutes an appropriate parallel period for your analysis is highly dependent upon the time-based cycles influencing your business.

To assist you with the retrieval of parallel period members, Analysis Services provides the *ParallelPeriod* function:

```
ParallelPeriod( [Level [,n [, Member]]] )
```

The function's first argument identifies the level of the time hierarchy across which you wish to identify the parallel period member. If no level is identified, the parent level of the current time member is assumed.

The function's second argument identifies how far back along the identified level you wish to go to retrieve the parallel member. If no value is provided, a value of 1 is assumed, indicating the prior period.

The function's final argument identifies the member for which the parallel period is to be determined. The position of this member relative to its ancestor in the specified level determines the member retrieved from the historical period. If no member is identified, the current time member is assumed.

Calculate growth over prior period

1. Open the MDX Query Editor to the MDX Step-by-Step database.

2. In the code pane, enter the following query to retrieve reseller sales for the months of calendar year 2003:

```
SELECT
    {([Measures].[Reseller Sales Amount])} ON COLUMNS,
    {
        Descendants(
            [Date].[Calendar].[Calendar Year].[CY 2003],
            [Date].[Calendar].[Month],
            SELF
            )
        } ON ROWS
FROM [Step-by-Step]
```

3. Execute the query and review the results.

	Reseller Sales Amount
January 2003	$1,317,541.83
February 2003	$2,384,846.59
March 2003	$1,563,955.08
April 2003	$1,865,278.43
May 2003	$2,880,752.68
June 2003	$1,987,872.71
July 2003	$2,665,650.54
August 2003	$4,212,971.51
September 2003	$4,047,574.04
October 2003	$2,282,115.88
November 2003	$3,483,161.40
December 2003	$3,510,948.73

The query returns reseller sales for the months of calendar year 2003. To assess the strength of these numbers in a business influenced by annual sales cycles, you might compare them to sales in the prior year. To do this, start by identifying the prior period for each month.

4. Alter the query to identify the parallel period in the prior year for each month:

```
WITH
MEMBER [Measures].[x] AS
    ParallelPeriod(
        [Date].[Calendar].[Calendar Year],
        1,
        [Date].[Calendar].CurrentMember
        ).Name
SELECT
    {
        ([Measures].[Reseller Sales Amount]),
        ([Measures].[x])
        } ON COLUMNS,
    {
        Descendants(
            [Date].[Calendar].[Calendar Year].[CY 2003],
            [Date].[Calendar].[Month],
            SELF
            )
        } ON ROWS
FROM [Step-by-Step]
```

5. Execute the query and review the results.

	Reseller Sales Amount	x
January 2003	$1,317,541.83	January 2002
February 2003	$2,384,846.59	February 2002
March 2003	$1,563,955.08	March 2002
April 2003	$1,865,278.43	April 2002
May 2003	$2,880,752.68	May 2002
June 2003	$1,987,872.71	June 2002
July 2003	$2,665,650.54	July 2002
August 2003	$4,212,971.51	August 2002
September 2003	$4,047,574.04	September 2002
October 2003	$2,282,115.88	October 2002
November 2003	$3,483,161.40	November 2002
December 2003	$3,510,948.73	December 2002

In the preceding query, the *ParallelPeriod* function is used to identify the parallel period in the prior year for each month in calendar year 2003 along the *ROWS* axis. The *ParallelPeriod* function returns a member and the name of that member is returned with a new calculated member to verify that the appropriate member is being identified. Now that you are comfortable the correct member is being located, you can use the returned member to determine prior period sales.

6. Alter the query to calculate prior period sales:

```
WITH
MEMBER [Measures].[Prior Period Reseller Sales Amount] AS
    (
        ParallelPeriod(
            [Date].[Calendar].[Calendar Year],
            1,
            [Date].[Calendar].CurrentMember
            ),
        [Measures].[Reseller Sales Amount]
        )
    ,FORMAT="Currency"
SELECT
    {
        ([Measures].[Reseller Sales Amount]),
        ([Measures].[Prior Period Reseller Sales Amount])
        } ON COLUMNS,
    {
        Descendants(
            [Date].[Calendar].[Calendar Year].[CY 2003],
            [Date].[Calendar].[Month],
            SELF
            )
        } ON ROWS
FROM [Step-by-Step]
```

7. Execute the query and review the results.

	Reseller Sales Amount	Prior Period Reseller Sales Amount
January 2003	$1,317,541.83	$713,116.69
February 2003	$2,384,846.59	$1,900,788.93
March 2003	$1,563,955.08	$1,455,280.41
April 2003	$1,865,278.43	$882,899.94
May 2003	$2,880,752.68	$2,269,116.71
June 2003	$1,987,872.71	$1,001,803.77
July 2003	$2,665,650.54	$2,393,689.53
August 2003	$4,212,971.51	$3,601,190.71
September 2003	$4,047,574.04	$2,885,359.20
October 2003	$2,282,115.88	$1,802,154.21
November 2003	$3,483,161.40	$3,053,816.33
December 2003	$3,510,948.73	$2,185,213.21

Using the member returned by the *ParallelPeriod* function to assemble a tuple allows you to retrieve reseller sales for the prior period. This newly calculated measure is returned along the *COLUMNS* axis for comparison against sales in the months displayed across the rows. To facilitate comparison, you might wish to present the percent change in sales from the prior period.

8. Alter the query to calculate the percent change in sales (growth) between the current and prior periods:

```
WITH
MEMBER [Measures].[Prior Period Reseller Sales Amount] AS
    (
        ParallelPeriod(
            [Date].[Calendar].[Calendar Year],
            1,
            [Date].[Calendar].CurrentMember
            ),
        [Measures].[Reseller Sales Amount]
        )
    ,FORMAT="Currency"
MEMBER [Measures].[Prior Period Growth] AS
    (
        ([Measures].[Reseller Sales Amount])-
            ([Measures].[Prior Period Reseller Sales Amount])
        ) /
        ([Measures].[Prior Period Reseller Sales Amount])
    ,FORMAT="Percent"
SELECT
    {
        ([Measures].[Reseller Sales Amount]),
        ([Measures].[Prior Period Reseller Sales Amount]),
        ([Measures].[Prior Period Growth])
        } ON COLUMNS,
    {
        Descendants(
            [Date].[Calendar].[Calendar Year].[CY 2003],
            [Date].[Calendar].[Month],
            SELF
            )
        } ON ROWS
FROM [Step-by-Step]
```

9. Execute the query and review the results.

	Reseller Sales Amount	Prior Period Reseller Sales Amount	Prior Period Growth
January 2003	$1,317,541.83	$713,116.69	84.76%
February 2003	$2,384,846.59	$1,900,788.93	25.47%
March 2003	$1,563,955.08	$1,455,280.41	7.47%
April 2003	$1,865,278.43	$882,899.94	111.27%
May 2003	$2,880,752.68	$2,269,116.71	26.95%
June 2003	$1,987,872.71	$1,001,803.77	98.43%
July 2003	$2,665,650.54	$2,393,689.53	11.36%
August 2003	$4,212,971.51	$3,601,190.71	16.99%
September 2003	$4,047,574.04	$2,885,359.20	40.28%
October 2003	$2,282,115.88	$1,802,154.21	26.63%
November 2003	$3,483,161.40	$3,053,816.33	14.06%
December 2003	$3,510,948.73	$2,185,213.21	60.67%

The results show each month of calendar year 2003 experienced considerable growth in reseller sales from those of the month in the prior year.

A Word of Caution

As explained at the start of this chapter, the time-based MDX functions are not time-aware and simply employ basic navigation for their functionality. This is illustrated by rewriting the query in Step 4 of the previous exercise with the navigation functions *Cousin*, *Ancestor*, and *Lag*:

```
WITH
MEMBER [Measures].[x] AS
    Cousin(
        [Date].[Calendar].CurrentMember,
        Ancestor(
            [Date].[Calendar].CurrentMember,
            [Date].[Calendar].[Calendar Year]
            ).Lag(1)
        ).Name
SELECT
    {
        ([Measures].[Reseller Sales Amount]),
        ([Measures].[x])
        } ON COLUMNS,
    {
        Descendants(
            [Date].[Calendar].[Calendar Year].[CY 2003],
            [Date].[Calendar].[Month],
            SELF
            )
        } ON ROWS
FROM [Step-by-Step]
```

	Reseller Sales Amount	x
January 2003	$1,317,541.83	January 2002
February 2003	$2,384,846.59	February 2002
March 2003	$1,563,955.08	March 2002
April 2003	$1,865,278.43	April 2002
May 2003	$2,880,752.68	May 2002
June 2003	$1,987,872.71	June 2002
July 2003	$2,665,650.54	July 2002
August 2003	$4,212,971.51	August 2002
September 2003	$4,047,574.04	September 2002
October 2003	$2,282,115.88	October 2002
November 2003	$3,483,161.40	November 2002
December 2003	$3,510,948.73	December 2002

As previously mentioned, the use of basic navigation to provide time-based functionality imposes some constraints on your time dimension. One of these is that all members of a time period should be provided in the cube. Again, the query in Step 4 from the previous exercise provides a very clear demonstration of why this is important. Here is that query adjusted to present the months of calendar year 2002 along the *ROWS* axis:

```
WITH
MEMBER [Measures].[x] AS
    ParallelPeriod(
        [Date].[Calendar].[Calendar Year],
```

```
        1,
        [Date].[Calendar].CurrentMember
        ).Name
SELECT
    {
        ([Measures].[Reseller Sales Amount]),
        ([Measures].[x])
        } ON COLUMNS,
    {
        Descendants(
            [Date].[Calendar].[Calendar Year].[CY 2002],
            [Date].[Calendar].[Month],
            SELF
            )
        } ON ROWS
FROM [Step-by-Step]
```

	Reseller Sales Amount	x
January 2002	$713,116.69	July 2001
February 2002	$1,900,788.93	August 2001
March 2002	$1,455,280.41	September 2001
April 2002	$882,899.94	October 2001
May 2002	$2,269,116.71	November 2001
June 2002	$1,001,803.77	December 2001
July 2002	$2,393,689.53	(null)
August 2002	$3,601,190.71	(null)
September 2002	$2,885,359.20	(null)
October 2002	$1,802,154.21	(null)
November 2002	$3,053,816.33	(null)
December 2002	$2,185,213.21	(null)

Notice in the results of this query that the month of January 2002 has a parallel period of July 2001. January 2002 is the first month-level descendant of calendar year 2002. Its parallel period in the prior year is the first month-level descendant of calendar year 2001. Because the first month recorded in 2001 is July, July 2001 becomes the parallel period of January 2002 based on simple navigation. Apply this logic to July 2002, the seventh month-level descendant of calendar year 2002, and you see why it has no parallel period in 2001, a year in which only six months were recorded.

If all twelve months for calendar year 2001 had been recorded, this problem could have been avoided. However, this problem would now be deferred to the fiscal calendar whose years start prior to 2001. In other words, there is no way in this dimension to provide complete sets of members under each period.

So what's the solution to this problem? The short answer is there really isn't one. You as the query developer must be aware of boundary issues such as this when developing queries employing time-based functions. You might have data at the head and tail of the time dimension extended to cover periods for which no data is recorded to avoid misalignment as illustrated previously, but you still need to be aware that no data is recorded for those periods so that some forms of analysis, such as period-over-period growth, might not be appropriate.

Combining Time-Based Metrics

Throughout this chapter, you have explored the various time-based functions and how they can be used to enhance business analysis and solve business problems. Although each of these functions is valuable on its own, they are often used in combination to provide even greater insight and clarity into the analysis of business data. These may seem like very challenging metrics to assemble, but in reality they are no more complex than most other metrics calculated throughout this book. The trick is to remember tuple and expression basics.

Calculate year-to-date and prior period year-to-date sales

1. Open the MDX Query Editor to the MDX Step-by-Step database.

2. Enter the following query to retrieve reseller sales for the months of calendar year 2003:

```
SELECT
    {
        ([Measures].[Reseller Sales Amount])
        } ON COLUMNS,
    {
        Descendants(
            [Date].[Calendar].[CY 2003],
            [Date].[Calendar].[Month],
            SELF
            )
        } ON ROWS
FROM [Step-by-Step]
```

3. Execute the query and review the results.

	Reseller Sales Amount
January 2003	$1,317,541.83
February 2003	$2,384,846.59
March 2003	$1,563,955.08
April 2003	$1,865,278.43
May 2003	$2,880,752.68
June 2003	$1,987,872.71
July 2003	$2,665,650.54
August 2003	$4,212,971.51
September 2003	$4,047,574.04
October 2003	$2,282,115.88
November 2003	$3,483,161.40
December 2003	$3,510,948.73

The query returns reseller sales by month for calendar year 2003. Using the *PeriodsToDate* function, you can calculate year-to-date sales just like before.

4. Alter the query to calculate a year-to-date sales:

```
WITH
MEMBER [Measures].[Year to Date Reseller Sales] AS
    Aggregate(
        PeriodsToDate(
            [Date].[Calendar].[Calendar Year],
            [Date].[Calendar].CurrentMember
            ),
        ([Measures].[Reseller Sales Amount])
        )
    ,FORMAT="Currency"
SELECT
    {
        ([Measures].[Reseller Sales Amount]),
        ([Measures].[Year to Date Reseller Sales])
        } ON COLUMNS,
    {
        Descendants(
            [Date].[Calendar].[CY 2003],
            [Date].[Calendar].[Month],
            SELF
            )
        } ON ROWS
FROM [Step-by-Step]
```

5. Execute the query and review the results.

	Reseller Sales Amount	Year to Date Reseller Sales
January 2003	$1,317,541.83	$1,317,541.83
February 2003	$2,384,846.59	$3,702,388.42
March 2003	$1,563,955.08	$5,266,343.51
April 2003	$1,865,278.43	$7,131,621.94
May 2003	$2,880,752.68	$10,012,374.62
June 2003	$1,987,872.71	$12,000,247.33
July 2003	$2,665,650.54	$14,665,897.87
August 2003	$4,212,971.51	$18,878,869.38
September 2003	$4,047,574.04	$22,926,443.41
October 2003	$2,282,115.88	$25,208,559.29
November 2003	$3,483,161.40	$28,691,720.69
December 2003	$3,510,948.73	$32,202,669.43

Using the Year To Date Reseller Sales calculated member in a tuple, you can easily calculate year-to-date sales for the prior period.

6. Alter the query to calculate the prior period year-to-date sales:

```
WITH
MEMBER [Measures].[Prior Period Year to Date Reseller Sales] AS
    (
        ParallelPeriod(
            [Date].[Calendar].[Calendar Year],
            1,
            [Date].[Calendar].CurrentMember
            ),
        [Measures].[Year to Date Reseller Sales]
        )
    ,FORMAT="Currency"
```

```
MEMBER [Measures].[Year to Date Reseller Sales] AS
    Aggregate(
        PeriodsToDate(
            [Date].[Calendar].[Calendar Year],
            [Date].[Calendar].CurrentMember
            ),
        ([Measures].[Reseller Sales Amount])
        )
    ,FORMAT="Currency"
SELECT
    {
        ([Measures].[Reseller Sales Amount]),
        ([Measures].[Year to Date Reseller Sales]),
        ([Measures].[Prior Period Year to Date Reseller Sales])
        } ON COLUMNS,
    {
        Descendants(
            [Date].[Calendar].[CY 2003],
            [Date].[Calendar].[Month],
            SELF
            )
        } ON ROWS
FROM [Step-by-Step]
```

7. Execute the query and review the results.

	Reseller Sales Amount	Year to Date Reseller Sales	Prior Period Year to Date Reseller Sales
January 2003	$1,317,541.83	$1,317,541.83	$713,116.69
February 2003	$2,384,846.59	$3,702,388.42	$2,613,905.62
March 2003	$1,563,955.08	$5,266,343.51	$4,069,186.04
April 2003	$1,865,278.43	$7,131,621.94	$4,952,085.98
May 2003	$2,880,752.68	$10,012,374.62	$7,221,202.69
June 2003	$1,987,872.71	$12,000,247.33	$8,223,006.46
July 2003	$2,665,650.54	$14,665,897.87	$10,616,695.99
August 2003	$4,212,971.51	$18,878,869.38	$14,217,886.70
September 2003	$4,047,574.04	$22,926,443.41	$17,103,245.90
October 2003	$2,282,115.88	$25,208,559.29	$18,905,400.11
November 2003	$3,483,161.40	$28,691,720.69	$21,959,216.44
December 2003	$3,510,948.73	$32,202,669.43	$24,144,429.65

This exercise demonstrates a very simple approach to combining calculated members that use time-based functions. When formulating complex metrics, you can easily lose sight of the basic techniques allowing logic in one calculated member to be leveraged for another. As easily as you combined a period-to-date calculation with a prior period calculation, you could extend this query to include the difference, variance, or percent growth of the current year year-to-date values compared to the prior year year-to-date values or any flavors thereof.

The *OpeningPeriod* and *ClosingPeriod* Functions

We would be remiss if we did not mention the *OpeningPeriod* and *ClosingPeriod* functions. The introduction of expanded support for semi-additive measures in the 2005 release of

Analysis Services has diminished the role of these functions, which return the first and last members of a period:

```
OpeningPeriod( [Level [, Member]] )
ClosingPeriod( [Level [, Member]] )
```

The *OpeningPeriod* and *ClosingPeriod* functions return the first or last member, respectively, of the descendants from a given level and a specified member. If no level is specified, Analysis Services assumes the topmost level of the time hierarchy. If no member is specified, Analysis Services assumes the current time member. As with the other time-based functions, you are encouraged to supply both arguments to ensure clarity.

As previously mentioned, both the *OpeningPeriod* and *ClosingPeriod* functions have seen their use diminished with recent releases of Analysis Services. Historically, these functions have been used to calculate values now returned by the FirstChild, FirstNonEmpty, LastChild, and LastNonEmpty aggregate functions. These aggregate functions are frequently employed with finance facts, exchange rates, and other snapshot facts to identify period starting and ending values.

For example, the end-of-day exchange rate employs the LastNonEmpty aggregate function to provide access to the last available value within a given period. But what if you needed to determine the end-of-day exchange rate at the start of a period? The following query illustrates the use of the *OpeningPeriod* function to calculate this value:

```
WITH
MEMBER [Measures].[First Child Rate] AS
    (
        OpeningPeriod(
            [Date].[Calendar].[Date],
            [Date].[Calendar].CurrentMember
            ),
            [Measures].[End of Day Rate]
            )
        ,FORMAT="Standard"
SELECT
    {
        ([Measures].[First Child Rate]),
        ([Measures].[End of Day Rate])
        } ON COLUMNS,
    {[Date].[Calendar].Members} ON ROWS
FROM [Step-by-Step]
WHERE ([Destination Currency].[Destination Currency].[Euro])
```

	First Child Rate	End of Day Rate
All Periods	1,03	,97
CY 2001	1,03	,91
H2 CY 2001	1,03	,91
Q3 CY 2001	1,03	,99
July 2001	1,03	1,00
July 1, 2001	1,03	1,03
July 2, 2001	1,03	1,03
July 3, 2001	1,04	1,04
July 4, 2001	1,04	1,04
July 5, 2001	1,03	1,03
July 6, 2001	1,03	1,03
July 7, 2001	1,03	1,03

This query provides both the first and last available end-of-day exchange rates for the specified period. The former is provided through the MDX *OpeningPeriod* function; the latter is provided through a cube aggregate function. You could further extend the query to identify the difference or variance in exchange rates across the opening and closing of the period.

Chapter 9 Quick Reference

To	Do this
Retrieve the periods-to-date for any specified period	Use the *PeriodsToDate* function to return a set of sibling members from the same level as a given member, starting with the first sibling and ending with the given member, as constrained by a specified level of a calendar hierarchy. For example, the following query retrieves the periods-to-date over the calendar year for each of the Month members along the *ROWS* axis to calculate a year-to-date total for reseller sales:

```
WITH
MEMBER [Measures].[Year to Date Reseller Sales] AS
    Aggregate(
        PeriodsToDate(
            [Date].[Calendar].[Calendar Year],
            [Date].[Calendar].CurrentMember
            ),
        ([Measures].[Reseller Sales Amount])
        )
SELECT
    {
        ([Measures].[Reseller Sales Amount]),
        ([Measures].[Year to Date Reseller Sales])
        } ON COLUMNS,
    {[Date].[Calendar].[Month].Members} ON ROWS
FROM [Step-by-Step]
```

To	Do this

Retrieve the periods-to-date for a year	Use the *Ytd* function to return a set of sibling members from the same level as a given member, starting with the first sibling and ending with the given member, as constrained by the Year level of a calendar hierarchy. For example, the following query retrieves the year-to-date periods for each of the Month members along the *ROWS* axis to calculate a year-to-date total for reseller sales:
	
	``WITH
	MEMBER [Measures].[Year to Date Reseller Sales] AS
	    Aggregate(
	        Ytd([Date].[Calendar].CurrentMember),
	        ([Measures].[Reseller Sales Amount])
	        )
	SELECT
	    {
	        ([Measures].[Reseller Sales Amount]),
	        ([Measures].[Year to Date Reseller Sales])
	        } ON COLUMNS,
	    {[Date].[Calendar].[Month].Members} ON ROWS
	FROM [Step-by-Step]```
	
	For quarter-to-date, month-to-date, and week-to-date calculations, use the *Qtd*, *Mtd*, and *Wtd* functions, respectively, in a similar manner.

Retrieve a number of prior periods	Use the *LastPeriods* function to retrieve a set of members up to and including a specified member. For example, the following query retrieves the last three months for each of the Month members along the *ROWS* axis to calculate a rolling three-month average for reseller sales:
	
	``WITH
	MEMBER [Measures].[Three Month Avg Reseller Sales Amount] AS
	    Avg(
	        LastPeriods(
	            3,
	            [Date].[Calendar].CurrentMember
	            ),
	        ([Measures].[Reseller Sales Amount])
	        )
	SELECT
	    {
	        ([Measures].[Reseller Sales Amount]),
	        ([Measures].[Three Month Avg Reseller Sales Amount])
	        } ON COLUMNS,
	    {[Date].[Calendar].[Month].Members} ON ROWS
	FROM [Step-by-Step]```

To	Do this
Retrieve a parallel member	Use the *ParallelPeriod* function to identify a member from a prior period in the same relative position as a specified member. For example, the following query retrieves prior period reseller sales for each of the Month members along the *ROWS* axis:

```
WITH
MEMBER [Measures].[Prior Period Reseller Sales Amount] AS
    (
        ParallelPeriod(
            [Date].[Calendar].[Calendar Year],
            1,
            [Date].[Calendar].CurrentMember
            ),
        [Measures].[Reseller Sales Amount]
        )
    ,FORMAT="Currency"
SELECT
    {
        ([Measures].[Reseller Sales Amount]),
        ([Measures].[Prior Period Reseller Sales Amount])
        } ON COLUMNS,
    {
        Descendants(
            [Date].[Calendar].[Calendar Year].[CY 2003],
            [Date].[Calendar].[Month],
            SELF
            )
        } ON ROWS
FROM [Step-by-Step]
```

To	Do this
Retrieve the opening period or closing period	Use *OpeningPeriod* or *ClosingPeriod* functions, respectively. For example, the following query employs the *OpeningPeriod* function to retrieve the exchange rate for the first day in each period:

```
WITH
MEMBER [Measures].[First Child Rate] AS
    (
        OpeningPeriod(
            [Date].[Calendar].[Date],
            [Date].[Calendar].CurrentMember
            ),
            [Measures].[End of Day Rate]
        )
        ,FORMAT="Standard"
SELECT
    {
        ([Measures].[First Child Rate]),
        ([Measures].[End of Day Rate])
        } ON COLUMNS,
    {[Date].[Calendar].Members} ON ROWS
FROM [Step-by-Step]
WHERE ([Destination Currency].[Destination Currency].[Euro])
```

Part III
MDX Applications

Chapter 10
Enhancing the Cube

After completing this chapter, you will be able to:

- Construct cube-scoped calculated members

- Assemble cube-scoped named sets

In Part III of this book, you complete the transition from theory to application started in the previous section. These last three chapters go beyond simple query development to present you with a few practical applications of the MDX language.

Within these remaining chapters, you will notice some significant differences from material presented in previous chapters. First, the *SELECT* statement that has been so prominently featured is relegated to a role more consistent with how you will use it in typical, real-world scenarios. Second, exercises that have been non-cumulative in earlier chapters now consistently build on one another. Finally, you will be required to use some new tools, such as the Business Intelligence Development Studio (BIDS), to implement these applications. Instructions on the use of these tools will be provided, but narrowly focused on accomplishing your immediate goals.

In this chapter, you explore the enhancement of the cube through the MDX script. Through the MDX script, expressions defining sets and controlling how the values of particular cells are calculated are incorporated into the definition of the cube. Although named sets and calculated members can be defined within a query, embedding these in the cube allows them to be more consistently employed by cube users, especially those without access to query-development tools or the requisite knowledge of MDX.

Understanding the MDX Script

Each Analysis Services cube contains a single MDX script. The script consists of a series of statements instructing Analysis Services on how to determine the value of cells within the cube space.

The first statement in most MDX scripts is the *CALCULATE* statement. An MDX script consisting of nothing more than this one statement is referred to as a basic script. The *CALCULATE* statement instructs Analysis Services to determine the value of cells within the cube as defined by the cube's design.

> **Note** The *CALCULATE* statement is the first statement in most but not all MDX scripts. In some highly specialized circumstances, other statements may precede the *CALCULATE* statement. This very rarely occurs, and you should not move the *CALCULATE* statement from the topmost position in the MDX script without a clear understanding of the impact on your cube.

The basic MDX script is enhanced with the addition of *CREATE MEMBER*, *CREATE SET*, and scripting language statements. *CREATE MEMBER* statements define calculated members, much like the ones you have been creating in the WITH clauses of your queries. The *CREATE SET* statements define *named sets*, allowing sets to be referenced using an alias. The scripting statements are a class of statements providing you fine-grained control over cell-value assignments. Each of these types of statements is discussed in greater detail later in this chapter.

It is important to note that the MDX script is evaluated from top to bottom. Therefore the order of the statements within the script determine their solve order. Solve order issues, discussed in Chapter 5, "Working with Expressions," are resolved between statements in the script by altering their sequence.

> **Note** In relation to statements submitted against the cube, such as *SELECT* statements issued through the MDX Query Editor, the statements in the MDX script are evaluated first.

To view a cube's MDX script, you can launch the Analysis Services project associated with the cube's database using the Business Intelligence Development Studio (BIDS). BIDS is a series of Microsoft Visual Studio project types and designers installed with Microsoft SQL Server. These support the development of various SQL Server objects such as Integration Services packages, Reporting Services reports, and, relevant to this chapter, Analysis Services databases.

Once the Analysis Services project is launched, you can view the script by launching the Cube Designer for the appropriate cube and navigating to the designer's Calculations tab. Commands accessible through this tab allow you to make and save modifications. These modifications are isolated to the Analysis Services project until the project is deployed to an instance of Analysis Services.

Review the MDX script of the MDX Step-by-Step database

1. On the Microsoft Windows task bar, click the Start button.

2. On the Start Menu, select All Programs and then select Microsoft SQL Server 2008 to expose the SQL Server Business Intelligence Development Studio shortcut.

3. Click the SQL Server Business Intelligence Development Studio shortcut to launch the application.

   If this is the first time you have run BIDS, you will see a dialog box indicating that the application is being configured for its first use. This process may take a few minutes to complete before the application is fully launched.

   Once fully launched, BIDS presents you with the Start page as shown in the following screenshot. If you have previously used BIDS or Visual Studio 2008 on your system, the layout of BIDS on your screen may differ from what is shown here.

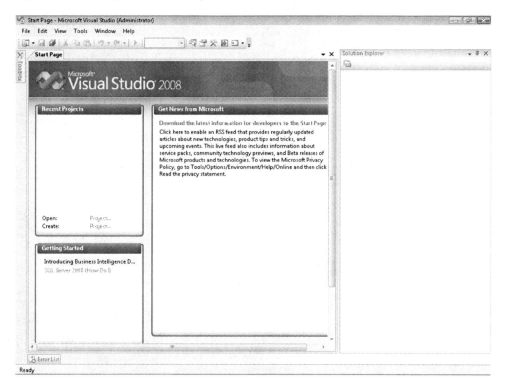

   If you have never run BIDS before, the first thing you might notice is that BIDS runs as part of Visual Studio. Visual Studio serves as the host for the BIDS projects and designers. If you do not have Visual Studio installed prior to installing BIDS, SQL Server installs a Visual Studio shell for you. On systems with prior installations of Visual Studio, possibly for C# or Visual Basic development, the BIDS components seamlessly integrate and show up as just another project type.

4. On the File menu, select Open and then select Project/Solution to launch the Open Project dialog box.

5. Use the Open Project dialog box to navigate to the Microsoft Press\MDX SBS\Setup\ Analysis Services folder installed as part of this book's samples. The MDX Step-by-Step solution file (MDX Step-by-Step.sln) is located here.

6. Select the MDX Step-by-Step solution file and click Open to open the solution.

After you open the solution, locate Solution Explorer, as illustrated in Figure 10-1. Solution Explorer is a browser-type window within which you can see the various components of the Analysis Services project, including the Step-by-Step cube.

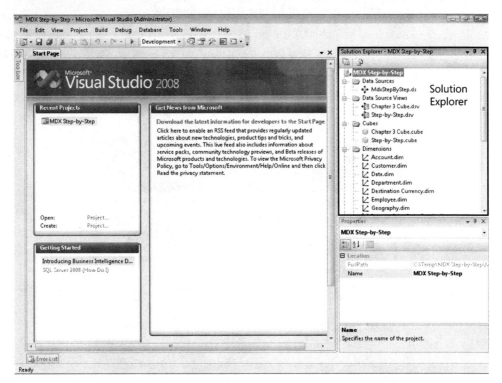

FIGURE 10-1 The Solution Explorer window for the MDX Step-by-Step project

7. In Solution Explorer, expand the Cubes folder to expose the Step-by-Step.cube object, if it is not already exposed. This object represents the Step-by-Step cube against which you have been submitting queries throughout much of this book.

8. Right-click the Step-by-Step.cube object and select View Designer.

Selecting View Designer launches the Cube Designer for the Step-by-Step cube, as shown in Figure 10-2. The Cube Designer provides a number of interfaces for viewing and editing various components of the cube. These interfaces are organized as a series of tabs along the top of the designer. The default is the Cube Structure tab. Two tabs to the right is the Calculations tab through which you can view the cube's MDX script.

9. Click the Calculations tab to expose the MDX script, as shown in Figure 10-3.

Calculations Tab

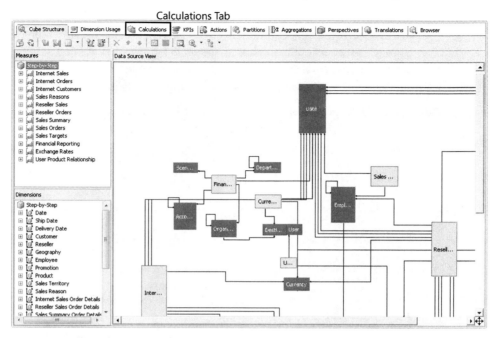

FIGURE 10-2 The Cube Designer for the Step-by-Step cube

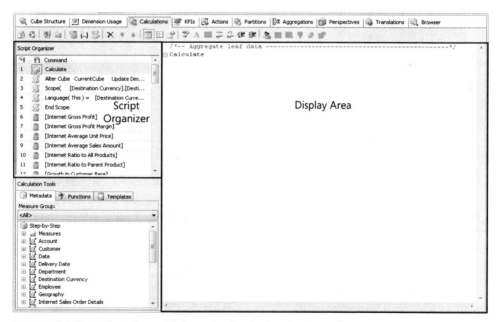

FIGURE 10-3 The Calculations tab's form view for the Step-by-Step cube

The Calculations tab opens to its default form view, as illustrated in Figure 10-3. In the form view, a Script Organizer is provided on the left-hand side of the tab. Here statements in the MDX script are presented as a series of individual items. A scroll bar on its right allows you to scroll through the complete list of statements in the script.

Selecting an item in the Script Organizer affects the form displayed in the Display Area to the right. Script statements, such as the *CALCULATE* statement, are presented through a formatted text editor as shown in Figure 10-3. Named sets and calculated members are presented through more structured forms. To view a particular statement and its associated form simply select the appropriate item in the Script Organizer.

10. In the Script Organizer, select the calculated member named Internet Gross Profit. Notice how the form to its right changes with its selection.

Selecting the calculated member causes the Display Area to present a form displaying the various components of the member's associated *CREATE MEMBER* statement. More information on these components is provided later in this chapter.

Notice the toolbar above the form and Script Organizer and just under the Calculations tab. Through this toolbar, a number of commands are made accessible. Those commands used in this chapter are illustrated in Figure 10-4.

FIGURE 10-4 The Calculations tab's toolbar

The New Calculated Member and New Named Set buttons allow you to add new statements to the script. New statements are placed just below the currently selected item in the Script Organizer. The Move Up and Move Down buttons allow you move a selected item in the Script Organizer up or down in the script's sequence. The Delete button allows you to remove a selected statement from the script.

11. With the Internet Gross Profit item selected, click the New Calculated Member button on the toolbar. Notice the addition of a calculated member named *Calculated Member* to the Script Organizer.

		Command	
1		Calculate	
2		Alter Cube CurrentCube Update Dim...	
3		Scope([Destination Currency].[Desti...	
4		Language(This) = [Destination Curre...	
5		End Scope	
6		[Internet Gross Profit]	
7		[Calculated Member]	
8		[Internet Gross Profit Margin]	
9		[Internet Average Unit Price]	
10		[Internet Average Sales Amount]	
11		[Internet Ratio to All Products]	
12		[Internet Ratio to Parent Product]	
13		[Growth in Customer Base]	
14		[Reseller Gross Profit]	
15		[Reseller Gross Profit Margin]	

Script Organizer

12. Using the Script Organizer, select the newly created member, Calculated Member.

13. Use the Move Up button to move the newly created member, Calculated Member, just above Internet Gross Profit.

14. With the newly created member, Calculated Member, selected, click the Delete button to remove it from the MDX script. Click OK when asked to confirm the deletion of this calculated member.

Using the form view, you can easily select and modify individual items in the MDX script. To view the script in its entirety, use the toolbar's Script View button to switch to the script view.

15. Use the Script View button to switch from the form view to the script view.

16. Use the scrollbar to the right of the script view to browse the structure of the MDX script.

17. When you are done browsing, click the Form View button to switch back to the form view.

18. Save the changes to the project by selecting Save All from the File menu.

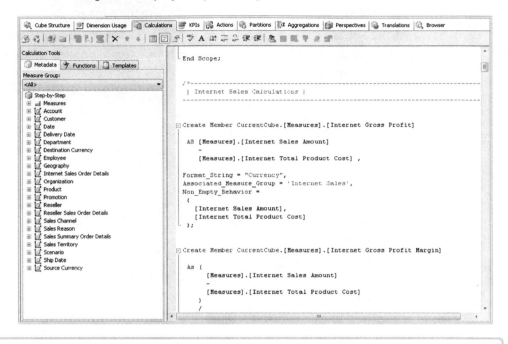

The Scripting Statements

The previous section of this chapter introduced you to the *CALCULATE* statement. This statement is one of the MDX script statements. The MDX script statements represent a subset of the MDX language only applicable within the MDX script. These statements provide Analysis Services with explicit instruction on how to determine the value of a cell.

The script statements are considered fairly advanced, so a detailed exploration of their use is outside the scope of this book. A brief description of three of the basic script statements is provided in Table 10-1. For more details and examples, it is recommended you review content provided through SQL Server Books Online.

TABLE 10-1 The Basic Scripting Statements

Statement	Description
SCOPE	The *SCOPE* statement block identifies a set of cells to which a value is to be assigned.
FREEZE	The *FREEZE* statement locks the current value of a set of cells. The *FREEZE* statement is used within a *SCOPE* statement block to exclude a subset of in-scope cells from a value assignment.
THIS	The *THIS* object identifies the cells within scope and is often the target of a value assignment.

Constructing Calculated Members

Throughout the chapters of this book, you have been assembling calculated members in the WITH clause of your *SELECT* statements. These calculated members are only accessible to the queries with which they are defined. As such, they are referred to as query-scoped calculated members.

Cube-scoped calculated members, on the other hand, are accessible to all users with access to a cube. These are defined within a cube's MDX script through *CREATE MEMBER* statements. Cube-scoped calculated members have access to a bit more functionality to provide greater consistency than their query-scoped counterparts. They are also essential when analytic applications do not support the ad hoc definition of calculated members.

> **Note** In addition to cube-scoped and query-scoped calculated members, Analysis Services provides support for *session-scoped* calculated members. Such members are accessible by multiple queries within a given user session. You can think of a session as roughly equivalent to a connection to Analysis Services. Session-scoped calculated members are often implemented by specialized applications supporting complex interactions with Analysis Services data.

Assembling a Basic Calculated Member

Calculated members are defined in the MDX script using the *CREATE MEMBER* statement. This statement employs a number of elements but the basic form is illustrated in the following statement definition:

```
CREATE MEMBER CURRENTCUBE.MemberName AS
    Expression
    [, Property=Value, ... n]
```

The two critical elements of the *CREATE MEMBER* statement are *MemberName* and *Expression*. The *MemberName* supplies the name of the calculated member and assigns it to a particular hierarchy. The *Expression* determines how the value associated with the cell is derived.

If you are comfortable with the definition of calculated members in the WITH clause of a *SELECT* statement, you should be relatively comfortable with the *CREATE MEMBER* statement. The cube-scoped calculated member's *MemberName* and *Expression* elements are the same as the name and expression you would assign to a query-scoped calculated member. In fact, it is recommended you first develop your cube-scoped calculated members as query-scoped calculated members, allowing you to test their evaluation before moving them into the MDX script.

When developing the expression to be used for a cube-scoped calculated member, it is important to keep in mind one key difference between the query-scoped and cube-scoped calculated members. With query-scoped calculated members, the calculated member is only employed within the logic of the query. In other words, how it is used is very predictable. With cube-scoped calculated members, the potential uses of the calculated member vary greatly.

Therefore, you must design cube-scoped calculated members in a manner providing consistent and appropriate evaluation across a variety of possible uses. This is often challenging without a solid understanding of the structure of your cube. Even with such an understanding, it is critical that you thoroughly test your cube-scoped calculated members.

The following four exercises walk you through the development, implementation, deployment, and verification of a basic calculated member. Each exercise builds on the one preceding it. Please follow them in sequence to build a basic calculated member.

Develop a basic query-scoped calculated member

1. Open the MDX Query Editor to the MDX Step-by-Step database.

2. In the code pane, enter the following query defining a simple, query-scoped calculated member:

```
WITH
MEMBER [Product].[Category].[All Products].[Bikes & Accessories] AS
    ([Product].[Category].[Bikes]) + ([Product].[Category].[Accessories])
SELECT
    {
        ([Measures].[Reseller Sales Amount]),
        ([Measures].[Reseller Order Count]),
        ([Measures].[Discount Percentage])
        } ON COLUMNS,
    {[Product].[Category].AllMembers} ON ROWS
FROM [Step-by-Step]
```

3. Execute the query and verify the values associated with the calculated member, Bikes & Accessories.

	Reseller Sales Amount	Reseller Order Count	Discount Percentage
All Products	$80,450,596.98	3,796	0.66%
Accessories	$571,297.93	1,315	1.17%
Bikes	$66,302,381.56	3,153	0.75%
Clothing	$1,777,840.84	2,410	1.18%
Components	$11,799,076.66	2,646	0.04%
Bikes & Accessori...	$66,873,679.48	4,468	1.92%

You may remember the Bikes & Accessories calculated member from an exercise in Chapter 5, "Working with Expressions." Within that exercise, the calculated member was used with the default Reseller Sales Amount measure. Reseller Sales Amount is an additive measure, so the simple addition of the values associated with these two categories produced an accurate result.

In this exercise, you are preparing to implement the Bikes & Accessories calculated member within the Step-by-Step cube's MDX script. As a result, you must test the calculated member against a variety of measures, some of which may not be additive. For example, adding Reseller Order Count values for Bikes and Accessories to one another leads to an invalid result because the measure is a distinct count and therefore non-additive. The same is true of calculated measures such as Discount Percentage. So instead of simple addition, you must employ a more flexible means of combining the two values.

4. Alter the expression to determine the value of the calculated member in a more robust and flexible manner:

```
WITH
MEMBER [Product].[Category].[All Products].[Bikes & Accessories] AS
    Aggregate(
        {
            ([Product].[Category].[Bikes]),
            ([Product].[Category].[Accessories])
            },
        [Measures].CurrentMember
        )
SELECT
    {
        ([Measures].[Reseller Sales Amount]),
        ([Measures].[Reseller Order Count]),
        ([Measures].[Discount Percentage])
        } ON COLUMNS,
    {[Product].[Category].AllMembers} ON ROWS
FROM [Step-by-Step]
```

5. Execute the query and verify the values associated with the calculated member, Bikes & Accessories.

	Reseller Sales Amount	Reseller Order Count	Discount Percentage
All Products	$80,450,596.98	3,796	0.66%
Accessories	$571,297.93	1,315	1.17%
Bikes	$66,302,381.56	3,153	0.75%
Clothing	$1,777,840.84	2,410	1.18%
Components	$11,799,076.66	2,646	0.04%
Bikes & Accessori...	$66,873,679.48	3,250	0.75%

The Bike & Accessories calculated member now employs the *Aggregate* function to ensure values associated with the Bike and Accessories members are combined in an appropriate manner across a variety of measures, as demonstrated by the query's results. The expression is now ready to be moved into the cube.

Note For more information on the *Aggregate* function, please refer back to Chapter 7, "Performing Aggregation."

For the next three exercises, leave the MDX Query Editor open with the query you just developed in place.

Implement a basic cube-scoped calculated member

1. If you have not already done so, open the MDX Step-by-Step solution in BIDS.

2. Open the Cube Designer for the Step-by-Step cube and move to its Calculations tab to access the cube's MDX script.

3. Verify you are in the form view. If you are not, click the Form View button on the toolbar to switch to it now.

4. Scroll to the bottom of the Script Organizer, select the last item, and click the New Calculated Member button to add a new calculated member to the script.

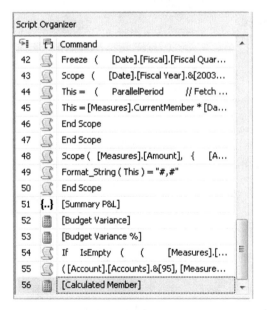

Clicking the New Calculated Member button adds a new *CREATE MEMBER* statement to the cube's MDX script. This statement defines a calculated member with the default name of Calculated Member.

The form view is now updated to present the newly added calculated member. Using this form, you can modify the *MemberName* and *Expression* elements of the underlying statement, defining the cube-scoped Bikes & Accessories member.

5. In the Name text box, replace the default name, [Calculated Member], with **[Bikes & Accessories]**. Be certain to include the brackets with the name.

6. In the section entitled Parent Properties, use the Parent Hierarchy drop-down list to select the Product dimension's Category attribute-hierarchy.

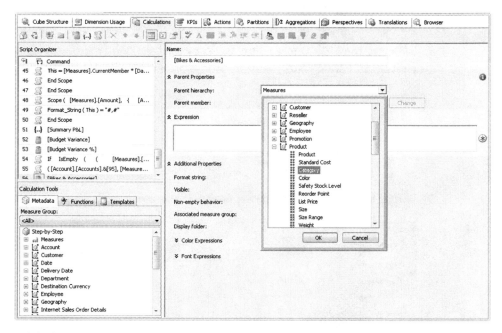

7. Click the Change button associated with the Parent Member field, select the All Products member from the resulting dialog box, and then click OK to confirm your selection and close the dialog box.

With these selections you have now assigned the *MemberName* element of the *CREATE MEMBER* statement the value *[Product].[Category].[All Products].[Bikes & Accessories]*. This is identical to the assignment used by the query-scoped calculated member in the previous *SELECT* statement. Now it's time to set the *Expression* element.

8. Switch to the MDX Query Editor and copy the calculated member's expression from your *SELECT* statement. The expression is presented here for clarity:

```
Aggregate(
    {
        ([Product].[Category].[Bikes]),
        ([Product].[Category].[Accessories])
        },
    [Measures].CurrentMember
    )
```

9. Return to BIDS and paste the expression in the form view's Expression text box.

Name:

    [Bikes & Accessories]

☆ Parent Properties   ⓘ

    Parent hierarchy: Product.Category

    Parent member: [All Products]   Change

☆ Expression

```
Aggregate(
    {
        ([Product].[Category].[Bikes]),
        ([Product].[Category].[Accessories])
        },
    [Measures].CurrentMember
    )
```

☆ Additional Properties

    Format string:

    Visible: True

    Non-empty behavior:

    Associated measure group: (Undefined)

    Display folder:

    ☆ Color Expressions

    ☆ Font Expressions

10. Click the Check Syntax button on the toolbar to verify that the expression and other elements of the calculated member are syntactically correct.

11. Click the Script View button to review the Bike & Accessories member's *CREATE MEMBER* statement as it exists within the MDX script.

```
    (
        [Scenario].[Scenario].[Budget Variance %]
    ) =
    "#;;Not Budgeted"
End If;


    // Assignment of constant for Statistical Accounts account member.
    // This will allow parent member to be visible by default.

    ( [Account].[Accounts].&[95], [Measures].[Amount] ) = "NA";

CREATE MEMBER CURRENTCUBE.[Product].[Category].[All Products].[Bikes & Accessories]
    AS Aggregate(
        (
            ([Product].[Category].[Bikes]),
            ([Product].[Category].[Accessories])
            ),
        [Measures].CurrentMember
        ),
    VISIBLE = 1  ;
```

12. Switch back to the form view.

13. Save the changes to the cube by selecting Save All from the File menu.

With the calculated member successfully defined, you must now deploy your changes to Analysis Services.

Deploy the cube-scoped calculated member

1. In Solution Explorer, right-click the MDX Step-by-Step database object and select Properties.

2. In the MDX Step-by-Step Property Pages dialog box, under Configuration Properties, select Deployment.

3. Verify that Processing Option is set to Default, Deployment Mode is set to Deploy Changes Only, and Server identifies the Analysis Services instance on which the MDX Step-by-Step sample database resides. The Server setting may differ from the one shown in the provided screenshot.

4. Make any required changes to these settings and click OK to update the project and close the dialog box.

5. Within the Solution Explorer, expand the Data Sources folder and right-click the MdxStepByStep.ds data source. Select View Designer from the shortcut menu.

6. On the General tab of the Data Source Designer, click the Edit button to open the Connection manager dialog box.

7. Update the Server Name text box with the name of the SQL Server instance to which you installed the SQL Server sample database. If you have installed this database on the local, default instance you do not need to modify the text box.

8. Click OK button to close the dialog box. Click OK again to close the Data Source designer.

9. Save any changes to the project by selecting Save All from the File menu.

Note In future deployments, you will not need to repeat these last five steps if configured correctly here.

10. From the Build menu, select Deploy MDX Step-by-Step to deploy changes to Analysis Services. Keep track of the Deployment Progress window that appears on your screen.

Note You may receive a message indicating the MDX Step-by-Step database already exists and asking whether you want to proceed with overwriting it. If you receive this message, click the Yes button to proceed with the deployment.

Once successfully deployed, the calculated member is now incorporated into the definition of the Step-by-Step cube.

Verify the cube-scoped calculated member

1. Return to the MDX Query Editor.

2. Alter the query in the code pane by removing the query-scoped calculated member Bikes & Accessories:

```
SELECT
    {
        ([Measures].[Reseller Sales Amount]),
        ([Measures].[Reseller Order Count]),
        ([Measures].[Discount Percentage])
        } ON COLUMNS,
    {[Product].[Category].AllMembers} ON ROWS
FROM [Step-by-Step]
```

3. Execute the query and verify that the cube-scoped calculated member, Bikes & Accessories, is presented in the results with the same values as before.

	Reseller Sales Amount	Reseller Order Count	Discount Percentage
All Products	$80,450,596.98	3,796	0.66%
Accessories	$571,297.93	1,315	1.17%
Bikes	$66,302,381.56	3,153	0.75%
Clothing	$1,777,840.84	2,410	1.18%
Components	$11,799,076.66	2,646	0.04%
Bikes & Accessori...	$66,873,679.48	3,250	0.75%

Key Performance Indicators

A key performance indicator (KPI) is a measurement gauging a critical aspect of a business. In Analysis Services, special KPI objects are implemented to incorporate these measurements into the definition of a cube.

Each KPI object has four parts:

- **Value**   The actual value of the measurement

- **Goal**   The target value against which the value is assessed

- **Status**   A value between –1 and 1 indicating how the value should be interpreted, with 1 representing a high (good) assessment, 0 representing a moderate (neutral) assessment, and –1 being a low (bad) assessment

> ■ **Trend** A value indicating the direction of the change in the value over time with a 1 indicating an increasing (positive) change in the measure, 0 indicating an unchanging measure, and –1 indicating a decreasing (negative) change in the measure
>
> Each of these four parts of a KPI object is implemented as an MDX expression. You could think of a KPI object as little more than a collection of four closely related calculated members and you wouldn't be too far off. Where KPIs differentiate themselves from calculated members is in the definition of KPI rollups to parent KPIs and in how some end-user applications access and display their values.
>
> When implementing KPIs, it is important to keep in mind that these are evaluated after the calculations in the MDX script. In some situations, this can lead to difficulties in accurately calculating the parts of a KPI. In these situations, you may resolve the problem by implementing the KPI's value, target, status, and trend parts as calculated members in the script and simply reference these members in the KPI. With this approach, you can tightly control the order in which the values of these parts are determined relative to items in the MDX script.

Setting Calculated Member Properties

Like their query-scoped counterparts, cube-scoped calculated members make available a number of standard properties. Some of these properties are listed in Table 10-2.

TABLE 10-2 Some Standard Properties of Cube-Scoped Calculated Members

Property	Description
FORMAT_STRING	This property contains the standard or custom format string instructing Analysis Services on how to translate the cell's value into its formatted value.
DISPLAY_FOLDER	This property identifies the folder within which a calculated member should be displayed.
ASSOCIATED_MEASURE_GROUP	This property identifies the measure group with which a calculated member associated with the Measures dimension will be displayed.
VISIBLE	This property indicates whether the calculated member is visible. A value of 0 indicates it is not visible.
NON_EMPTY_BEHAVIOR	This property identifies the set of measures to evaluate to determine whether the calculated member itself should be evaluated.

The *FORMAT_STRING* property works just as it does with query-scoped calculated members. It accepts a variety of standard and custom format string values, as described in Chapter 5, "Working with Expressions."

The *DISPLAY_FOLDER* and *ASSOCIATED_MEASURE_GROUP* properties provide metadata used by browser-type interfaces, such as the metadata pane of the MDX Query Editor, to affect how the calculated member is presented within the cube's structure. Although largely cosmetic, these two properties can affect whether some interfaces are capable of displaying the calculated member. Please refer to documentation associated with your specific application to determine what impact these two properties will have on the display of a calculated member.

The *VISIBLE* property is also largely cosmetic. However, it is very useful for hiding calculated members implemented for the purpose of assembling more complex calculated members. These hidden calculated members are loosely referred to as intermediate calculated members. Setting a calculated member's *VISIBLE* property to 0 (False in the form view), hides it from view in browser-type displays but still allows the member to be referenced.

Finally, the *NON_EMPTY_BEHAVIOR* property identifies a set of measures to be evaluated within the current context. If any measure in this set is empty, the calculated member's expression is bypassed and the calculated member is treated as empty. Effective use of the *NON_EMPTY_BEHAVIOR* property can boost query performance and in some situations help avoid errors which would otherwise occur if the expression is evaluated against empty measures.

In the following four exercises, you use these properties to implement a complex calculated member. As before, each of these exercises builds on each other.

Assemble a complex query-scoped calculated member

1. Review the following expression calculating a transaction-level standard deviation for reseller sales:

```
(
    (
        ([Measures].[Squared Reseller Sales Amount]) /
            (([Measures].[Reseller Transaction Count])-1)
    ) -
    (
        (
            ([Measures].[Reseller Sales Amount])/
                ([Measures].[Reseller Transaction Count])
                )^2
        )
    )^(0.5)
```

This expression calculates the standard deviation in a manner consistent with the calculation that might be performed in a relational database against non-aggregated fact records. In Chapter 7, "Performing Aggregation," this was referred to as the transaction-level standard deviation.

This expression is relatively complex. If you were to attempt to incorporate the expression as-is into a calculated member, you might struggle to implement it correctly and introduce errors along the way. Even if you were to implement it correctly, you might struggle to explain the expression to someone else or even interpret it yourself without heavy use of comments. In this situation, it makes sense to break down the expression into more easily understood, bite-sized units of logic. Recognizing the preceding expression calculates an average, derives variance using this average, and then calculates standard deviation as the square root of variance, the expression can be implemented as a series of three calculated members, each building on the one preceding it.

2. If you have not already done so, open the MDX Query Editor to the MDX Step-by-Step database.

3. In the code pane, enter the following query to calculate the transaction-level average, variance, and standard deviation for Reseller Sales Amount:

```
WITH
MEMBER [Measures].[Reseller Sales Amount Average] AS
    ([Measures].[Reseller Sales Amount])/
        ([Measures].[Reseller Transaction Count])
    ,FORMAT_STRING="Currency"
MEMBER [Measures].[Reseller Sales Amount Variance] AS
    (
        ([Measures].[Squared Reseller Sales Amount]) /
            (([Measures].[Reseller Transaction Count])-1)
        ) -
        (([Measures].[Reseller Sales Amount Average])^2)
    ,FORMAT_STRING="Currency"
MEMBER [Measures].[Reseller Sales Amount Std Dev] AS
    ([Measures].[Reseller Sales Amount Variance])^(0.5)
    ,FORMAT_STRING="Currency"
SELECT
    {
        ([Measures].[Reseller Sales Amount Average]),
        ([Measures].[Reseller Sales Amount Variance]),
        ([Measures].[Reseller Sales Amount Std Dev])
        } ON COLUMNS
FROM [Step-by-Step]
```

4. Execute the query and verify the results.

Reseller Sales Amount Average	Reseller Sales Amount Variance	Reseller Sales Amount Std Dev
$1,322.00	$4,512,397.78	$2,124.24

The expressions are still complex but a bit more manageable when the logic is distributed across three calculated members. The portion that represents an average is broken out into its own calculated member. That member is employed to calculate variance, which is then used to derive standard deviation. These three calculated members can now be moved from the query into the cube.

Implement a complex cube-scoped calculated member

1. If you have not already done so, open the MDX Step-by-Step solution in BIDS.

2. Open the Cube Designer for the Step-by-Step cube and move to the Calculations tab to access the cube's MDX script. Ensure the form view is accessible.

3. Implement the Reseller Sales Amount Average calculated member using the expression developed in the query. The expression is presented here for clarity:

```
([Measures].[Reseller Sales Amount])/
    ([Measures].[Reseller Transaction Count])
```

Name:

[Reseller Sales Amount Average]

≫ Parent Properties

| Parent hierarchy: | Measures |
| Parent member: | | Change |

≫ Expression

```
    ([Measures].[Reseller Sales Amount])/
        ([Measures].[Reseller Transaction Count])
```

≫ Additional Properties

Format string:	
Visible:	True
Non-empty behavior:	
Associated measure group:	(Undefined)
Display folder:	

≫ Color Expressions

≫ Font Expressions

4. The query-scoped calculated member employs a Currency format string. Use the Format String drop-down list to configure this cube-scoped calculated member similarly.

If you were to deploy this calculated member, where would it be presented to users when they browse the cube's structure? It is associated with the Measures dimension but it is not associated with any one measure group. Because the statistic relates to Reseller Sales Amount, it might make sense to display it within the Reseller Sales measure group.

5. Set the Associated Measure Group drop-down list to Reseller Sales.

6. Repeat steps 3 through 5 to implement the Reseller Sales Amount Variance calculated member using the expression developed in the query. Set its Format String to Currency and its Associated Measure Group to Reseller Sales. The expression for this calculated member is provided here for clarity:

```
(
    ([Measures].[Squared Reseller Sales Amount]) /
        ((([Measures].[Reseller Transaction Count])-1)
    ) -
((([Measures].[Reseller Sales Amount Average])^2)
```

7. Repeat steps 3 through 5 one last time to implement the Reseller Sales Amount Std Dev calculated member using the expression developed in the query. Set its Format String to Currency and its Associated Measure Group to Reseller Sales. The expression for this calculated member is provided here for clarity:

```
([Measures].[Reseller Sales Amount Variance])^(0.5)
```

8. Use the Move Up and Move Down buttons to ensure that Reseller Sales Amount Average precedes Reseller Sales Amount Variance and Reseller Sales Amount Variance precedes Reseller Sales Amount Std Dev in the Script Organizer.

The calculated members are now ready to deploy, but before doing so, think carefully about how these will be received by users. Most users are familiar with averages, so Reseller Sales Amount Average will be readily understood and adopted. Standard deviation is a bit more esoteric, but still many analysts are comfortable with this statistic. You can therefore expect Reseller Sales Amount Std Dev to be relatively well received.

What about Reseller Sales Amount Variance? If your users are like most, they will likely find the variance statistic a bit confusing. As a result, the Reseller Sales Amount Variance calculated member is not likely to be used or, even worse, used inappropriately. Still, you need Reseller Sales Amount Variance to calculate Reseller Sales Amount Std Dev, so you cannot simply remove it from the cube. Instead, you should configure the calculated member to be hidden.

9. In the Script Organizer, select the Reseller Sales Amount Variance calculated member you just implemented.

10. In this member's form view, set the Visible property to False.

11. Save the changes to your script.

12. Deploy the changes to Analysis Services.

   With the calculated members deployed, your last step is to verify the members through the MDX Query Editor.

Verify a complex cube-scoped calculated member

1. Reselect the MDX Step-by-Step database from the MDX Query Editor's Available Databases drop-down list.

2. Use the metadata pane to browse the measures of the Reseller Sales measure group. Verify that the Reseller Sales Amount Average and Reseller Sales Amount Std Dev measures are visible but Reseller Sales Amount Variance is not.

From the metadata pane, it appears the two calculated members are displayed as expected. Reseller Sales Amount Average and Reseller Sales Amount Std Dev are visible in the Reseller Sales measure group and Reseller Sales Amount Variance is hidden.

3. In the code pane, enter the following query to retrieve the three calculated members:

```
SELECT
    {
        ([Measures].[Reseller Sales Amount Average]),
        ([Measures].[Reseller Sales Amount Variance]),
        ([Measures].[Reseller Sales Amount Std Dev])
        } ON COLUMNS
FROM [Step-by-Step]
```

4. Execute the query and review the results.

Reseller Sales Amount Average	Reseller Sales Amount Variance	Reseller Sales Amount Std Dev
$1,322.00	$4,512,397.78	$2,124.24

The query confirms that all three calculated members are functioning properly. The Reseller Sales Amount Variance calculated member, from which Reseller Sales Amount Std Dev is derived, is present and still accessible even though it is not displayed in the metadata pane.

Apply the *NON_EMPTY_BEHAVIOR* property

1. In the MDX Query Editor's code pane, enter the following query to retrieve reseller sales along with transaction-level averages and standard deviations for the various product subcategories:

```
SELECT
    {
        ([Measures].[Reseller Sales Amount]),
        ([Measures].[Reseller Sales Amount Average]),
        ([Measures].[Reseller Sales Amount Std Dev])
        } ON COLUMNS,
    {[Product].[Subcategory].Members} ON ROWS
FROM [Step-by-Step]
```

2. Execute the query and review the results.

	Reseller Sales Amount	Reseller Sales Amount Average	Reseller Sales Amount Std Dev
All Products	$80,450,596.98	$1,322.00	$2,124.24
Bib-Shorts	$166,739.71	$220.56	$138.53
Bike Racks	$197,736.16	$422.51	$282.62
Bike Stands	(null)	(null)	$0.00
Bottles and Cages	$7,476.60	$16.84	$11.17
Bottom Brackets	$51,826.37	$140.83	$106.15
Brakes	$66,018.71	$174.19	$126.35
Caps	$31,541.35	$26.46	$18.99
Chains	$9,377.71	$37.51	$26.65
Cleaners	$11,188.37	$26.70	$17.75
Cranksets	$203,942.62	$482.13	$442.50
Derailleurs	$70,209.50	$174.65	$124.01
Fenders	(null)	(null)	$0.00
Forks	$77,931.69	$389.66	$283.40

The results present total reseller sales along with transaction-level averages and standard deviations for the various product subcategories. Some subcategories, such as Bike Stands, have no sales associated with them. For subcategories such as these, the calculation of an average and standard deviation represents wasted effort. Even worse, although the average reflects no sales with a Null value, the standard deviation returns a value of 0. Though subtle, there is a difference between saying sales for a particular subcategory are perfectly consistent and saying there is no variability because sales are non-existent. In the event of no sales, standard deviation should reflect the same Null value reflected by the average and the base measure. This is accomplished by appropriately setting the *NON_EMPTY_BEHAVIOR* property for the calculated member.

3. In BIDS, open the Cube Designer for the Step-by-Step cube and move to its Calculations tab to access the cube's MDX script. Ensure the form view is accessible.

4. In the Script Organizer, locate the Reseller Sales Amount Average calculated member.

5. From the Non-Empty Behavior drop-down list, select Reseller Sales Amount and click OK.

6. Set the non-empty behavior in the same manner for the Reseller Sales Amount Variance and Reseller Sales Amount Std Dev calculated members.

    By setting the non-empty behavior to Reseller Sales Amount for each of these three calculated members, you have stated that if the Reseller Sales Amount measure is empty for the current context whenever the calculated member is to be evaluated, the expression should not to be resolved. Instead, Analysis Services should simply return a Null value for the calculated member. This reduces the time spent resolving the calculated member and improves the consistency of your results.

7. Save the changes to the cube.

8. Deploy the changes to Analysis Services.

9. Return to the MDX Query Editor.

10. Re-execute the previous query and observe the change in the results for the Bike Stands subcategory.

Reseller Sales Amount	Reseller Sales Amount Average	Reseller Sales Amount Std Dev
All Products	$80,450,596.98	$1,322.00	$2,124.24
Bib-Shorts	$166,739.71	$220.56	$138.53
Bike Racks	$197,736.16	$422.51	$282.62
Bike Stands	(null)	(null)	(null)
Bottles and Cages	$7,476.60	$16.84	$11.17
Bottom Brackets	$51,826.37	$140.83	$106.15
Brakes	$66,018.71	$174.19	$126.35
Caps	$31,541.35	$26.46	$18.99
Chains	$9,377.71	$37.51	$26.65
Cleaners	$11,188.37	$26.70	$17.75
Cranksets	$203,942.62	$482.13	$442.50
Derailleurs	$70,209.50	$174.65	$124.01
Fenders	(null)	(null)	(null)
Forks	$77,931.69	$389.66	$283.40

The Bike Stands subcategory now presents the Null value for the Reseller Sales Amount Std Dev calculated measure. This provides consistency with the Reseller Sales Amount Average and accuracy given the Null Reseller Sales Amount value.

Assembling Named Sets

Throughout this book, you have been assembling sets along query axes and within complex expressions. Instead of assembling a set with each use, you can define a set and then reference it using an alias. Such sets are referred to as *named sets*.

Named sets encourage the reuse of sets based on a consistent definition. Like calculated members, named sets can be defined at the query, session, and cube levels. For the same reasons of consistency in definition and accessibility, you are encouraged to implement named sets as cube-scoped (for example, within the MDX script).

> **Note** As with session-scoped calculated members, session-scoped named sets are typically implemented by end-user applications supporting the definition of custom sets.

Named sets are defined in the MDX script using the *CREATE SET* statement. This statement employs a number of elements but the basic form is illustrated in the following statement definition:

```
CREATE [DYNAMIC] [HIDDEN] SET CURRENTCUBE.SetName AS
    Expression
    [, Property=Value, … n]
```

As with the *CREATE MEMBER* statement, the *CREATE SET* statement contains two critical elements: *SetName* and *Expression*. The *SetName* defines the alias by which this set is referenced. The *Expression* defines the set's members either explicitly or through a set-building expression.

Also like its *CREATE MEMBER* counterpart, the *CREATE SET* statement supports the assignment of values to various properties. Of the available properties, *DISPLAY_FOLDER* is the most useful. If your set consists of tuples referencing a single hierarchy, the named set is automatically associated with the dimension housing that hierarchy. The *DISPLAY_FOLDER* property instructs browser-type interfaces such as the MDX Query Editor's metadata pane to present the named set under the specified folder within that dimension. This helps organize the presentation of your cube's metadata.

Unlike the *CREATE MEMBER* statement, the *CREATE SET* statement does not have a *VISIBLE* property. Instead, you can employ the optional *HIDDEN* keyword to make the set non-visible in browser interfaces.

In the following three exercises, you define a frequently used set as a cube-scoped named set, allowing it to be consistently used across multiple applications.

Create a query-scoped named set

1. If you have not already done so, open the MDX Query Editor to the MDX Step-by-Step database.

2. In the code pane, enter the following query returning reseller sales for the top five products based on those same sales:

```
SELECT
    {([Measures].[Reseller Sales Amount])} ON COLUMNS,
    TopCount(
        [Product].[Product].[Product].Members,
        5,
        ([Measures].[Reseller Sales Amount])
        ) ON ROWS
FROM [Step-by-Step]
```

3. Execute the query and review the set along the *ROWS* axis.

	Reseller Sales Amount
Mountain-200 Black, 38	$1,634,647.94
Mountain-200 Black, 38	$1,471,078.72
Road-350-W Yellow, 48	$1,380,253.88
Touring-1000 Blue, 60	$1,370,784.22
Mountain-200 Black, 42	$1,360,828.02

The set of top five products based on reseller sales is a set you have returned to repeatedly within this book. Instead of assembling the expression with every query that employs the set, you might wish to implement the set one time as a cube-scoped named set, allowing its definition to be reused throughout multiple queries. The first step is to define the set as a query-scoped named set.

4. Alter the query to assemble the set of top five products as a query-scoped named set named Top 5 Products:

```
WITH
SET [Top 5 Products] AS
    TopCount(
        [Product].[Product].[Product].Members,
        5,
        ([Measures].[Reseller Sales Amount])
        )
SELECT
    {([Measures].[Reseller Sales Amount])} ON COLUMNS,
    {[Top 5 Products]} ON ROWS
FROM [Step-by-Step]
```

5. Execute the query and review the results.

	Reseller Sales Amount
Mountain-200 Black, 38	$1,634,647.94
Mountain-200 Black, 38	$1,471,078.72
Road-350-W Yellow, 48	$1,380,253.88
Touring-1000 Blue, 60	$1,370,784.22
Mountain-200 Black, 42	$1,360,828.02

The set of top five products is now organized as a named set. Much like calculated members, it's a very simple matter to translate the query-scoped named set to a cube-scoped named set.

Create a cube-scoped named set

1. If you have not already done so, open the MDX Step-by-Step solution in BIDS.

2. Open the Cube Designer for the Step-by-Step cube and move to the Calculations tab to access the cube's script. Ensure the form view is accessible.

3. In the Script Organizer, move to the bottom of the Script Organizer and click the New Named Set button.

Clicking the New Named Set button adds a *CREATE SET* statement to the MDX script. In the form view, the basic elements of the statement are presented in text boxes and drop-down lists, as shown in the preceding screenshot. You may now replace the default values in the form to define the named set.

4. In the Name text box, replace the default name, [Named Set], with **[Top 5 Products]**. Be certain to include the brackets with the name.

5. In the Expression text box, paste the set-building expression from the query. The expression is presented here for clarity:

```
TopCount(
    [Product].[Product].[Product].Members,
    5,
    ([Measures].[Reseller Sales Amount])
    )
```

6. In the Display Folder text box, type the name **Sets**.

7. Leave the drop-down list associated with Type set to Dynamic.

The named set Top 5 Products has now been defined within the cube's script. Now it's time to deploy it to Analysis Services.

8. Save the changes to the project.

9. Deploy the changes to Analysis Services.

With the changes deployed to Analysis Services, revisit your query to verify the cube-scoped named set.

Validate a cube-scoped named set

1. Return to the MDX Query Editor.

2. Reselect the MDX Step-by-Step database from the MDX Query Editor's Available Databases drop-down list.

3. Use the metadata pane to browse the Sets folder of the Product dimension. Verify the newly defined Top 5 Products named set is present.

4. In the code pane, alter the query by removing the WITH clause containing the query-scoped named set:

```
SELECT
    {([Measures].[Reseller Sales Amount])} ON COLUMNS,
    {[Top 5 Products]} ON ROWS
FROM [Step-by-Step]
```

5. Execute the query and review the results.

	Reseller Sales Amount
Mountain-200 Black, 38	$1,634,647.94
Mountain-200 Black, 38	$1,471,078.72
Road-350-W Yellow, 48	$1,380,253.88
Touring-1000 Blue, 60	$1,370,784.22
Mountain-200 Black, 42	$1,360,828.02

The results show the named set is now available as part of the definition of the Step-by-Step cube.

Understanding Context and Named Sets

Named sets are deceptively simple. Consider the expression in the named set assembled in the last exercise:

```
TopCount(
    [Product].[Product].[Product].Members,
    5,
    ([Measures].[Reseller Sales Amount])
    )
```

The *TopCount* function employs an expression, *([Measures].[Reseller Sales Amount])*, to evaluate each product before ordering them and then returning the top five. That expression, like all expressions, is evaluated within a context. That context includes the product being evaluated along with any other parts of the context associated with the query (or even the user's session). Depending on the context, the set returned can vary.

Historically, cube- (and session-) scoped named sets were static. That is, they were resolved the first time they were employed and cached for reuse within their associated scope. As context varied from use to use, the named set did not. It consistently reflected the set within the context of its first use until the cache was flushed or the named set was dropped. For sets sensitive to context, such as the one in the previous exercise, this was problematic.

The 2008 release of Analysis Services introduces dynamic named sets. In a dynamic named set, the set is not cached but instead is resolved within the query context with each use. This allows cube- (and session-) scoped named sets to be more responsive to context, just like their query-scoped counterparts. To configure a cube-scoped named set as dynamic within BIDS, leave the Type drop-down list set to its default value, Dynamic, as you did in the previous exercise. If you're altering the script directly, place the *DYNAMIC* keyword immediately after the *CREATE* keyword in the *CREATE SET* statement.

Chapter 10 Quick Reference

To	Do this
Define a cube-scoped calculated member	Edit the cube's script using the Calculations tab in the Business Intelligence Development Studio's Cube Designer interface. Click the New Member button to add the member to the script and modify the member's name, expression, and other properties using the form view before deploying the updated script to Analysis Services.
Hide a cube-scoped calculated member	Set the calculated member's *VISIBLE* property to False. In the Calculations tab form view, this property is set through the Visible drop-down list.
Format a cube-scoped calculated member	Set the calculated member's *FORMAT_STRING* property to an appropriate standard or custom format string value. In the Calculations tab form view, this property is set through the Format String drop-down list.
Associate a calculated measure with a measure group	Set the calculated member's *ASSOCIATED_MEASURE_GROUP* property to the name of the appropriate measure group. In the Calculations tab form view, this property is set through the Associated Measure Group drop-down list.
Prevent the evaluation of a calculated member when one or more component values is empty	Set the calculated member's *NON_EMPTY_BEHAVIOR* property to the set of measures each of which must be non-empty for the calculated member's expression to be evaluated. In the Calculations tab form view, this property is set through the Non-Empty Behavior drop-down list.
Create a cube-scoped named set	Edit the cube's script using the Calculations tab in the Business Intelligence Development Studio's Cube Designer interface. Click the New Set button to add the named set to the script and modify the set's name, expression, and other properties using the form view before deploying the updated script to Analysis Services.
Force a cube-scoped named set to be evaluated with each query	Employ the *DYNAMIC* keyword in the definition of the named set. In the Calculations tab form view, this keyword is set through the Type drop-down list.
Force a cube-scoped named set to be evaluated once and then cached for reuse	Do not employ the *DYNAMIC* keyword in the definition of the named set. In the Calculations tab form view, set the Type drop-down list to Static.

Chapter 11
Implementing Dynamic Security

After completing this chapter, you will be able to:

- Retrieve the current user's Windows identity using MDX
- Employ the current user's identity to restrict access to hierarchies
- Employ the current user's identity to restrict access to cell data

Membership in a database role determines an end user's access to Analysis Services data. Through a role, access to particular members of an attribute-hierarchy or even the individual cells of a cube may be controlled using MDX expressions. When an end user's identity is part of the logic of these expressions, a role is said to employ dynamic security.

The purpose of this chapter is to introduce you to the implementation of dynamic security. It is assumed you are familiar with the basics of the Analysis Services security model as well as design concepts such as implementing attribute-hierarchies, dimensions, measure groups, and measures. If you are unfamiliar with these topics, you are strongly encouraged to read *Microsoft SQL Server 2008 Analysis Services Step by Step* by Scott Cameron (Microsoft Press, 2009).

Understanding Dynamic Security

End-user access to data is provided through roles defined within an Analysis Services database. Database roles can be assigned a number of rights to various objects within the database. To provide data access, database roles are assigned access to one or more of the database's cubes.

If no restrictions are defined, assigning access to a cube provides members of the role complete access to data within the cube. For less sensitive data (or with a highly trusted group of users), defining a role in this manner provides sufficient control over data access.

For more sensitive data, access rights must be more narrowly defined. Attribute-level restrictions may be used to determine which members of an attribute-hierarchy the users in a role may access. Criteria may also be defined to determine whether the contents of a particular cell are viewable. Each of these may be defined using MDX expressions.

The use of MDX expressions in defining attribute- and cell-level restrictions affords you quite a bit of control over data access. Typically, these expressions are relatively simple and evaluate in a manner consistent for all members of a particular role. However, you can employ the user's identity within these expressions to implement user-specific logic.

The key to this is the ability to identify the current user within the MDX expression. All connections to Analysis Services are established using Windows authentication. In other words, each user is associated with a valid Windows user account. Regardless of whether membership within a database role is established through a Windows user account or through a Windows group of which the Windows user is a member, the user's Windows identity is part of the metadata of the Analysis Services connection. This identity is accessible through the MDX *UserName* function:

```
UserName()
```

The *UserName* function is very simple in that it takes no arguments or qualifiers and simply returns a string representing the identity of the user associated with the current connection. This string takes the form *Authority\Name* where *Name* is the name of the user account and *Authority* is the name of the local computer or the domain with which the account is associated.

The combination of authority and account name uniquely identifies a user. However, when only local user accounts or accounts from a single domain are employed, the string returned by the *UserName* function may be parsed to isolate just the Name portion. This is done using the VBA functions first mentioned in Chapter 5, "Working with Expressions." (The parsing of the string returned by the *UserName* function is unnecessary in most real-world applications but is required for these exercises to work on various readers' systems.)

> **Important** The exercises in this chapter assume you are logged into the local system hosting the MDX Step-by-Step database and have administrative rights to both the operating system and the Analysis Services instance. If you are not able to log in to the host system or do not have these rights, you need to adjust the instructions provided to work with your particular circumstances.

Create a local user account for testing

1. On the Microsoft Windows task bar, click the Start button.

2. On the Start Menu, right-click Computer and select Manage to launch the Computer Management console.

3. In the Computer Management console, locate the Local Users And Groups item and expand it to expose the Users folder.

4. Right-click the Users folder and select New User to launch the New User dialog box.

5. Enter **MdxUser** for the user name and then enter a valid password you can remember. If you are using Windows default security settings, you can use **MdxUser1** as a valid password.

6. Clear the User Must Change Password At Next Logon check box.

7. Click Create to create the new user account, and then click Close to close the New User dialog box. This returns you to the Computer Management console.

The MdxUser account is the test user account you will use to evaluate dynamic security in this chapter. Because membership in Analysis Services roles is often assigned to Windows groups and not individual Windows user accounts, you will create a local group named MdxUsers and make the MdxUser account a member of it. Upon completing the exercises in this chapter, be certain to remove both the group and the user account from your local system.

8. In the Computer Management console, right-click the Groups folder and select New Group to launch the New Group dialog box.

9. Enter **MdxUsers** for the group name.

10. Click the Add button. In the Select Users dialog box, enter **MdxUser** in the Enter The Object Names To Select text box.

Note On your system, the text associated with the From This Location label in the Select Users dialog box will vary from that in the preceding screenshot.

11. Click the OK button to add the user to the group and return to the New Group dialog box.

12. Click the Create button to create the MdxUsers group and then click Close to close the New Group dialog box.

13. Close the Computer Management console.

Create a basic database role

1. Launch SQL Server Management Studio and connect to your Analysis Services instance.

2. In Object Explorer, expand the instance's Databases folder to expose the MDX Step-by-Step database.

3. Expand the MDX Step-by-Step database and locate its Roles folder.

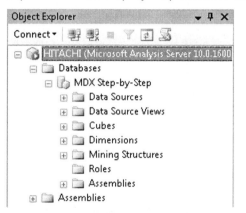

4. Right-click the Roles folder and select New Role to launch the Create Role dialog box.

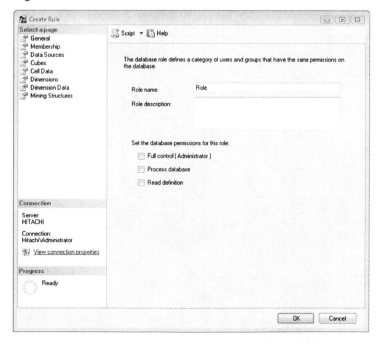

5. On the General page of the Create Role dialog box, enter **Mdx Users** in the Role Name text box.

6. Switch to the Membership page.

7. Click the Add button to launch the Select Users Or Groups dialog box.

8. Click the Object Types button to open the Object Types dialog box and then select the Groups object type.

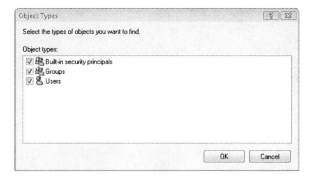

9. Click the OK button to close the Object Types dialog box and return to the Select Users Or Groups dialog box.

10. In the bottom text box of the Select Users Or Groups dialog box, enter **MdxUsers** to identify the local group created in the previous exercise.

11. Click the OK button to return to the Create Role dialog box.

12. Switch to the Cubes page and select an Access type of Read for the Step-by-Step cube.

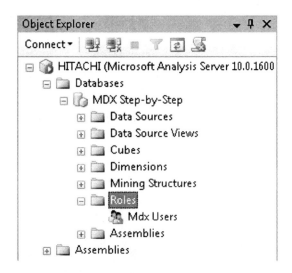

13. Click OK to create the role.

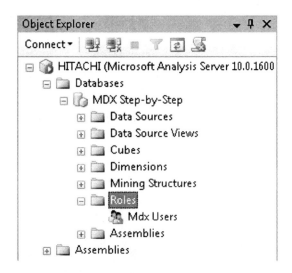

You have now created a database role, Mdx Users, assigning its members full read access to the data in the Step-by-Step cube in the MDX Step-by-Step database. The members of the local group, MdxUsers, of which the local user MdxUser is currently the only member, can now connect to this instance of Analysis Services and access this data.

> **Important**   As you perform exercises in other sections of this chapter, you will modify the
> Mdx Users role to demonstrate various forms of dynamic security. At the start of some of these
> exercises, you will be asked to re-create the Mdx Users role to ensure that it is in an appropriate
> state. Please do this using the steps just provided.

Evaluate the *UserName* function

1. On the Microsoft Windows task bar, click the Start button.

2. On the Start Menu, select All Programs and then select Accessories to expose the
   Command Prompt shortcut.

3. Select the Command Prompt shortcut to open the Command Prompt window.

4. In the Command Prompt window, enter **Set ComputerName** and press Enter to verify
   the name of your local system.

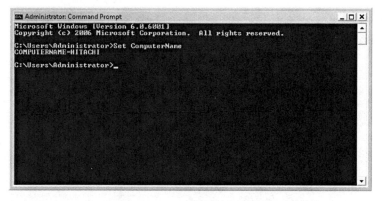

5. In the Command Prompt window, enter **RunAs /user:*computername*\MdxUser "ssms"**,
   substituting the name of your system in place of *computername*. Press Enter to submit
   the command.

6. When prompted, provide the password for the MdxUser account and press Enter.

The *ssms* portion of the command line is the name of the SQL Server Management Studio application. During installation of SQL Server, the operating system's environment path variable is set so that the SQL Server Management Studio application can be launched without specifying its folder location. If this is not properly set on your system, you will need to include the full path of the application's executable in the command line. This is typically "\Program Files\Microsoft SQL Server\100\Tools\Binn\VSShell\Common7\ IDE\Ssms.exe" on the drive on which the SQL Server components are installed.

Once the password is entered, the RunAs command launches SQL Server Management Studio under the credentials of the local MdxUser account. Using this command, you remain logged into the system as yourself with only the instance of SQL Server Management Studio launched through RunAs running under the alternate credentials.

Because this is the first time the MdxUser is running SQL Server Management Studio, the application may take a few minutes to configure. When this is completed, the application is fully launched as you have seen before.

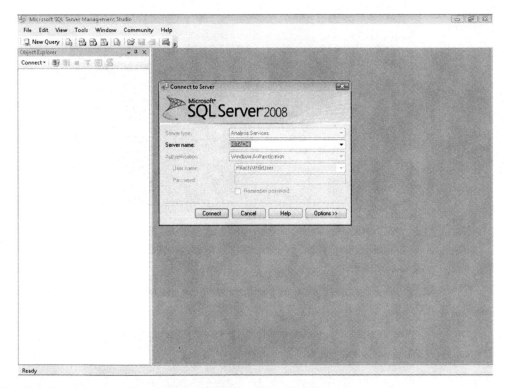

7. Click Connect to connect to your instance of Analysis Services.

8. On the toolbar, click the button labeled New Query to open a new instance of the MDX Query Editor.

Once connected, the current database should default to MDX Step-by-Step. If Object Explorer or the Properties window are open, you should hide them to recover space on your screen.

9. In the code pane, enter the following query employing the *UserName* function:

```
WITH
MEMBER [Measures].[Current User] AS
    UserName()
SELECT
    {[Measures].[Current User]} ON COLUMNS
FROM [Step-by-Step]
```

10. Execute the query and note the structure of the string returned.

The *UserName* function returns the name of the current user in the form *Authority\Name*. In this query, the authority is your local system so that the Authority portion of your results will vary from those in the preceding screenshot. However, the Name portion should be identical. This is critical for your success with the remaining exercises in this chapter.

To remove the Authority portion of the user name, you can use VBA functions to parse the returned string.

11. Alter the calculated member to return only the Name portion of the *UserName* string:

```
WITH
MEMBER [Measures].[Current User] AS
    VBAMDX!Right(
        UserName(),
        VBAMDX!Len(UserName()) -
            VBAMDX!Instr(UserName(),"\")
    )
SELECT
    {[Measures].[Current User]} ON COLUMNS
FROM [Step-by-Step]
```

12. Execute the query and note the change in the returned value.

The results displayed in the preceding screenshot should now exactly match those on your screen. Note the expression used to parse the *UserName* string; you will return to this expression repeatedly in this chapter.

The Empty Set

Throughout this chapter, the *SELECT* statement is used to develop and test the definition of sets. When developing sets, it is often easiest to assign the set of interest to the *ROWS* axis of your query, allowing you to scroll up and down the results pane to review the members in the returned set.

Assigning a set to the *ROWS* axis requires you to assign a set to the *COLUMNS* axis. Instead of assigning an arbitrary set, such as a set containing a single measure, you can simply assign the empty set to the *COLUMNS* axis.

The empty set is represented by a pair of open and closed braces: {}. The empty set contains nothing so that when assigned to the *COLUMNS* axis, nothing intersects with the members along the *ROWS* axis. As a result, the query returns no cells, just the members of the set along the *ROWS* axis as demonstrated in the following query:

```
SELECT
    {} ON COLUMNS,
    {[Product].[Product].[Product].Members} ON ROWS
FROM [Step-by-Step]
```

Messages	Results
All-Purpose Bike Stand	
AWC Logo Cap	
AWC Logo Cap	
AWC Logo Cap	
Bike Wash - Dissolver	
Cable Lock	
Chain	
Classic Vest, L	
Classic Vest, M	
Classic Vest, S	
Fender Set - Mountain	
Front Brakes	
Front Derailleur	
Full-Finger Gloves, L	
Full-Finger Gloves, M	

Implementing Attribute-Hierarchy Restrictions

Attribute-hierarchies are restricted through allowed and denied sets assigned to a database role. An allowed set identifies the members of an attribute-hierarchy the users in a role are permitted to access. A denied set identifies the members to which the users in a role are denied access. Both allowed and denied sets may be employed to fine-tune an attribute-hierarchy restriction but most database roles make use of just one or the other.

Note By restricting the members of an attribute-hierarchy, the other hierarchies in the dimension are restricted through auto-exists functionality.

In most implementations, allowed and denied sets are explicitly defined. When greater flexibility in the definition of a set is required, set-building MDX expressions are employed.

The logic in these expressions is typically such that all members of a given database role are assigned the same allowed or denied set. When the set is consistently defined, Analysis Services can cache and reuse data to resolve queries for different users in a given role.

However, in certain circumstances the definition of the allowed or denied set is so closely tied to the individual user that the establishment of fixed-set roles is not practical and offers little to no performance advantage. In these situations, instead of defining a large number of near user-specific roles, a smaller number of roles—often just one—can be defined with an allowed or denied set incorporating user-based logic.

In the sections that follow, two techniques are demonstrated for doing this. The first technique is frequently used with standard attribute-hierarchies. The other is more appropriate for use with parent-child hierarchies.

Restricting Standard Attribute-Hierarchies

To restrict a standard attribute-hierarchy using a user's identity, a relationship must be established between the user and the attribute-hierarchy on which you wish to define the allowed or denied set. This relationship is captured in a specialized measure group.

This measure group is very simple. It is based on a fact table containing two foreign keys, one referencing the attribute-hierarchy to be restricted and the other pointing to the User dimension. The User dimension is a simple dimension containing a single attribute-hierarchy that we will also call User. The members of the User attribute-hierarchy identify individual Windows users for whom dynamic security is to be defined.

The User dimension and the specialized measure group are implemented solely for the purpose of implementing dynamic security. As such, they should be made non-visible to end users. For the measure group, set the *Visible* property of its lone measure to *False* at design-time. For the User dimension, set the User attribute-hierarchy's *AttributeHierarchyVisible* property to *False* as well. With no visible measures in the measure group and no visible hierarchies in the User dimension, the measure group and User dimension are made non-visible to users.

With the attribute-hierarchy to be restricted now related to the User dimension through a measure group, expressions can now be defined to limit end-user access to data. The first defines the allowed set on the User attribute-hierarchy. This expression restricts user access to just those members of the User attribute-hierarchy with names matching the string returned by *UserName*. In other words, the user is restricted to just those User attribute-hierarchy members associated with his or her Windows user account.

The second expression is defined on the attribute-hierarchy related to the User dimension through the specialized measure group. This is defined as either an allowed or denied set depending on the logic you require. Using the *Exists* function, the set of members from this attribute-hierarchy related to the set of accessible members in the User attribute-hierarchy as recorded through the specialized measure group is retrieved. The allowed set on the User attribute-hierarchy limits the members of this attribute-hierarchy to just those tied to the current user.

In the exercises that follow, you implement a dynamic allowed set on the Product attribute-hierarchy of the Product dimension. A User dimension and a measure group named User Product Relationship relating users to products are employed as previously described. These items have been established in the Step-by-Step cube and are configured to be hidden from end users. If you wish to review the structure of these items, you may review the MDX Step-by-Step database definition using the MDX Step-by-Step solution used in the last chapter.

Design the allowed sets

> **Important** Before starting this exercise, if you have modified the Mdx Users database role, please drop and re-create it now.

1. Open the MDX Query Editor to the MDX Step-by-Step database using the MdxUser user account as described earlier in this chapter.

2. In the code pane, enter the following query to retrieve the members of the User hierarchy:

```
SELECT
    {} ON COLUMNS,
    {[User].[User].[User].Members} ON ROWS
FROM [Step-by-Step]
```

3. Execute the query and review the returned values.

Messages	Results
MdxOtherUser	
MdxUser	

The User dimension contains a single attribute-hierarchy, User, which is configured to be non-visible. Being non-visible prevents the User dimension and attribute-hierarchy from being displayed in the metadata pane and other browser interfaces but does not prevent you from accessing its members.

> **Note** The User attribute-hierarchy contains two members. The member named MdxOtherUser is presented so that you can verify that the set of members returned is properly restricted in the next step.

As described earlier, a critical part of the goal of restricting the Product attribute members is to define an allowed set on the User attribute-hierarchy limiting access to just those User members with names matching those of the current Windows user's account. For the local user MdxUser, this set is as follows:

```
{([User].[User].[User].[MdxUser])}
```

Using the *UserName* function, this set is assembled in a more dynamic manner:

```
"{([User].[User].[User].["+
    VBAMDX!Right(
        UserName(),
        VBAMDX!Len(UserName()) -
            VBAMDX!Instr(UserName(),"\")
        ) + "])}"
```

For the local user MdxUser, this expressions resolves to the string *"{([User].[User].[User].[MdxUser])}"*, which looks a lot like the previous set but is interpreted by Analysis Services as simply a string value. To convert the string-value to an actual set, the MDX *StrToSet* function is employed:

```
StrToSet(
    "{([User].[User].[User].[" +
        VBAMDX!Right(
            UserName(),
            VBAMDX!Len(UserName()) -
                VBAMDX!Instr(UserName(),"\")
            ) + "])}"
    )
```

 Note The *StrToSet* function is explained in Chapter 12, "Building Reports," along with the *StrToMember* and *StrToTuple* functions. For now, you should be aware that this function converts a string-based representation of a set into an actual set interpretable by Analysis Services.

4. Alter the query to define a set along the *ROWS* axis containing the User members with names matching those of the current user:

```
SELECT
    {} ON COLUMNS,
    StrToSet(
        "{([User].[User].[User].[" +
            VBAMDX!Right(
                UserName(),
                VBAMDX!Len(UserName()) -
                    VBAMDX!Instr(UserName(),"\")
                ) + "])}"
            ) ON ROWS
FROM [Step-by-Step]
```

5. Execute the query and verify that it returns the member associated with your user account.

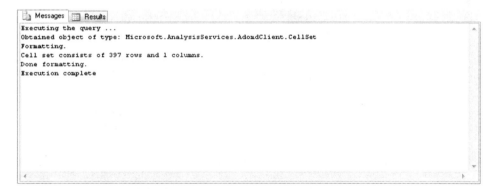

You have now assembled the set-building expression that you will use for the User attribute-hierarchy's allowed set. Next you need to assemble the allowed set for the Products attribute-hierarchy. Start by reviewing the unrestricted members of the Product attribute-hierarchy.

6. Enter the following query to return all products in the Product attribute-hierarchy:

```
SELECT
    {} ON COLUMNS,
    {[Product].[Product].[Product].Members} ON ROWS
FROM [Step-by-Step]
```

7. Execute the query, switch to the messages pane, and note the number of products returned.

```
Messages   Results
Executing the query ...
Obtained object of type: Microsoft.AnalysisServices.AdomdClient.CellSet
Formatting.
Cell set consists of 397 rows and 1 columns.
Done formatting.
Execution complete
```

The query returns a total of 397 members from the leaf-level of the Product attribute-hierarchy. This serves as a baseline for verifying the allowed set you are about to implement. The first step in assembling the allowed set is to construct its set-building expression.

8. Modify the query to retrieve those products associated with the user MdxUser as recorded through the User Product Relationship measure group:

```
SELECT
    {} ON COLUMNS,
    Exists(
        {[Product].[Product].[Product].Members},
        {[User].[User].[User].[MdxUser]},
        'User Product Relationship'
        ) ON ROWS
FROM [Step-by-Step]
```

9. Execute the query, switch to the messages pane, and note the number of members returned.

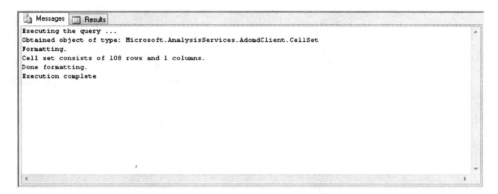

The results return those products associated with the MdxUser member of the User attribute-hierarchy as recorded in the User Product Relationship measure group. The number of products accessible, 108, is lower than the total number of products within the Product attribute-hierarchy, 397, indicating the MdxUser does not have complete access to the Products dimension.

The set-building expression employed along the *ROWS* axis is very similar to the one you need to employ for the allowed set with the Products attribute-hierarchy. In the query's expression, the name of the user, MdxUser, is hard-coded. Once the allowed set is defined on the User attribute-hierarchy of the User dimension, the hard-coded User member reference will be replaced with the more dynamic *Members* function.

Implement the allowed sets

1. Open SQL Server Management Studio as yourself, not MdxUser, and connect to your instance of Analysis Services.

2. In Object Explorer, locate the Mdx Users database role.

3. Right-click the Mdx Users role and select Properties to open the Edit Role dialog box.

4. In the Edit Role dialog box, navigate to the Dimension Data page.

5. From the Dimension drop-down list, select the User dimension located under the Step-by-Step cube. You need to scroll past the first series of dimensions until you encounter the dimensions under the Step-by-Step cube. Once selected, click OK.

6. On the Dimension Data page, click the Advanced tab.

7. From the Attribute drop-down list, verify that the User attribute-hierarchy is selected.

8. In the Allowed Member Set text box, paste the set-building expression from the *ROWS* axis of the query from step 4 in the previous exercise. The expression is presented here for clarity:

```
StrToSet(
    "{([User].[User].[User].[" +
        VBAMDX!Right(
            UserName(),
            VBAMDX!Len(UserName()) -
                VBAMDX!Instr(UserName(),"\")
            ) + "])}"
    )
```

9. Return to the Dimension drop-down list and select the Product dimension located under the Step-by-Step cube. As before, you need to scroll past the first series of dimensions until you encounter the dimensions under the Step-by-Step cube. Once selected, click OK.

10. On the Dimension Data page, verify that you are still on the Advanced tab.

11. From the Attribute drop-down list, select the Product attribute-hierarchy.

12. In the Allowed Member Set text box, paste the set-building expression from the *ROWS* axis of the query in step 8 of the previous exercise.

13. Alter the member reference to use the *Members* function instead of the hard-coded MdxUser member. The altered expression is presented here for clarity:

```
Exists(
    {[Product].[Product].[Product].Members},
    {[User].[User].[User].Members},
    'User Product Relationship'
    )
```

14. Click the OK button at the bottom of the Edit Role dialog box to save the changes to the role and close the dialog box.

Test the restrictions

1. If SQL Server Management Studio is open using the MdxUser user account, close it at this time.

2. Re-open the MDX Query Editor to the MDX Step-by-Step database using the MdxUser user account as described earlier in this chapter.

3. In the code pane, enter the following query to retrieve all available members of the Product attribute-hierarchy:

```
SELECT
    {} ON COLUMNS,
    {[Product].[Product].Members} ON ROWS
FROM [Step-by-Step]
```

4. Execute the query, switch to the messages pane, and review the number of products returned.

```
Messages   Results
Executing the query ...
Obtained object of type: Microsoft.AnalysisServices.AdomdClient.CellSet
Formatting.
Cell set consists of 109 rows and 1 columns.
Done formatting.
Execution complete
```

The results reveal that when logged in as the user MdxUser, you may now only access those members of the Product hierarchy associated with your account. As other members of the Mdx Users database role log in to the system, the allowed set is evaluated against their individual Windows user accounts to produce an allowed set tailored to them.

> **Note** You may notice that the number of products returned by this query is 109, whereas the number of products associated with the MdxUser according to the results of the earlier query is 108. The All Products member is not explicitly identified in the security measure group as related to the MdxUser or any other user. However, the allowed set always returns the (All) member, even though no explicit relationship between it and the user is defined in the measure group.

This restriction on the Product attribute-hierarchy is based on the allowed set defined against the User attribute-hierarchy. You can verify this allowed set by retrieving the set of available users from the User hierarchy.

5. Alter the query to retrieve all members of the User hierarchy:

```
SELECT
    {} ON COLUMNS,
    {[User].[User].[User].Members} ON ROWS
FROM [Step-by-Step]
```

6. Execute the query and review the results.

```
Messages   Results
MdxUser
```

The allowed set you defined on the User attribute-hierarchy limits you to the member named the same as your user account.

> **Note** As previously noted, the allowed set always returns the (All) member. You can verify this for the allowed set on the User attribute-hierarchy by removing the level specification in the previous query. The presence of the User attribute-hierarchy's (All) member in the allowed set has no impact on those Product members available to users.

Restricting Parent-Child Hierarchies

A parent-child hierarchy represents a self-referencing relationship within a dimension. Typical examples of parent-child hierarchies include Employees and Accounts. In the Employees parent-child hierarchy, individual Employee members report to supervisors who are themselves Employee members. In the Accounts parent-child hierarchy, individual Account members roll up into other Account members to form a business's chart of accounts.

In many cases, a hierarchy member and an individual Windows user have a one-to-one association. In the case of the Employees hierarchy, this association may tie an individual Employee member to an actual employee. In the case of the Accounts hierarchy, this association may tie an individual Account member to the person most directly responsible for its management.

Where this one-to-one relationships exists, the Windows account of the user related to a hierarchy attribute member may be recorded as a related attribute-hierarchy or property within the same dimension as the parent-child hierarchy. This negates the need for a separate User dimension and a related measure group to implement dynamic security.

With a parent-child hierarchy, dynamic security is typically implemented to limit users to those members with which they are directly associated as well as the ancestors and descendents of these members. Defining an allowed set on the embedded User attribute seems like the most intuitive way to implement this restriction. However, the recursive nature of the relationships within the parent-child hierarchy undermines this approach. Instead, you must employ a different technique to appropriately limit the parent-child hierarchy.

With this alternative approach, the User attribute's *AttributeHierarchyEnabled* property is set to *False* at design time. This configures the attribute as a dimension property. This property is then used to filter the members of the parent-child hierarchy, limiting the allowed set to those parent-child hierarchy members with a *User* property matching the name of the current Windows user. Relationships between these members and their ancestors and descendents provide the required access to dimension data.

> **Note** You could implement the User attribute as an attribute-hierarchy instead of a dimension property. However, if the User attribute is included in the dimension for no other purpose than the implementation of dynamic security, it is recommended you configure the attribute as a property to reduce the complexity of your cube space.

In the following exercises, you define an allowed set on the Employees parent-child hierarchy of the Employee dimension. A User property has been defined within the dimension to house the Name portion of the employee's Windows account. The employee, Stephen Y. Jiang, is identified in the dimension as the employee associated with the MdxUser Windows user account.

Stephen reports to Brian S. Welcker, who in turn reports to Ken J. Sanchez. Stephen is also a supervisor with a number of reporting employees of his own. Ken, Brian, Stephen himself, and his reports represent those employees in this hierarchy to which Stephen should have access.

Design the allowed set

> **Important** Before starting this exercise, if you have modified the Mdx Users database role, please drop and re-create it now.

1. Open the MDX Query Editor to the MDX Step-by-Step database using the MdxUser user account, as described earlier in this chapter.

2. In the code pane, enter the following query to reveal the members of the Employees parent-child hierarchy:

```
SELECT
    {} ON COLUMNS,
    {[Employee].[Employees].Members} ON ROWS
FROM [Step-by-Step]
```

3. Execute the query, switch to the messages pane, and review the number of rows returned.

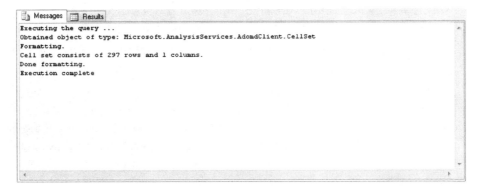

For each of these 297 employees, you can retrieve the associated Windows user account by accessing the dimension's User property.

4. Alter the query to retrieve the User property for each employee:

```
WITH
MEMBER [Measures].[User] AS
    [Employee].[Employees].CurrentMember.Properties("User")
SELECT
    {([Measures].[User])} ON COLUMNS,
    {[Employee].[Employees].Members} ON ROWS
FROM [Step-by-Step]
```

5. Execute the query and observe the Windows user account associated with Stephen Y. Jiang.

	User
All Employees	(null)
Ken J. Sánchez	ken0
Brian S. Welcker	brian3
Amy E. Alberts	amy0
Jae B. Pak	jae0
Rachel B. Valdez	rachel0
Ranjit R. Varkey Chudukatil	ranjit0
Stephen Y. Jiang	MdxUser
David R. Campbell	david8
Garrett R. Vargas	garrett1
Jillian Carson	jillian0
José Edvaldo. Saraiva	josé1
Linda C. Mitchell	linda3

The *User* property reveals the Windows user account associated with each employee. Using the *UserName* function you can filter the set of employees to just those associated with your user account, MdxUser.

6. Alter the query to restrict the set along the *ROWS* axis to only those members associated with the current user:

```
WITH
MEMBER [Measures].[User] AS
    [Employee].[Employees].CurrentMember.Properties("User")
SELECT
    {([Measures].[User])} ON COLUMNS,
    Filter(
        {[Employee].[Employees].Members},
        [Employee].[Employees].CurrentMember.Properties("User")=
            VBAMDX!Right(
                UserName(),
                VBAMDX!Len(UserName()) -
                    VBAMDX!Instr(UserName(),"\")
            )
        ) ON ROWS
FROM [Step-by-Step]
```

7. Execute the query and observe the restricted set along the *ROWS* axis.

```
Messages    Results
                        User
Stephen Y. Jiang     MdxUser
```

The query now returns a set with the one member associated with the MdxUser user account. This expression will be used to define the allowed set on the Employees hierarchy.

So how do you identify the ascendants and descendants of this account? For the purposes of defining an allowed set on a parent-child hierarchy, you don't. Instead, you rely on relationships and auto-exists functionality to handle the rest.

Implement the allowed set

1. Open SQL Server Management Studio as yourself, not MdxUser, and connect to your instance of Analysis Services.

2. In Object Explorer, locate the Mdx Users database role.

3. Right-click the Mdx Users role and select Properties to open the Edit Role dialog box.

4. In the Edit Role dialog box, navigate to the Dimension Data page.

5. From the Dimension drop-down list, select the Employee dimension located under the Step-by-Step cube. You need to scroll past the first series of dimensions until you encounter the Step-by-Step cube. Once selected, click OK.

6. On the Dimension Data page, click the Advanced tab.

7. From the Attribute drop-down list, select Employees.

8. In the Allowed Member Set text box, paste the Filter statement from step 6 of the preceding exercise. This expression is repeated here for clarity:

```
Filter(
    {[Employee].[Employees].Members},
    [Employee].[Employees].CurrentMember.Properties("User")=
        VBAMDX!Right(
            UserName(),
```

```
VBAMDX!Len(UserName()) -
    VBAMDX!Instr(UserName(),"\")
)
)
```

9. Click OK to save the changes to the role and close the Edit Role dialog box.

Test the restriction

1. If SQL Server Management Studio is open using the MdxUser user account, close it at this time.

2. Reopen the MDX Query Editor to the MDX Step-by-Step database using the MdxUser user account, as described earlier in this chapter.

3. In the code pane, enter the following query to retrieve all available members of the Employees parent-child hierarchy:

```
SELECT
    {} ON COLUMNS,
    {[Employee].[Employees].Members} ON ROWS
FROM [Step-by-Step]
```

4. Execute the query and review the results.

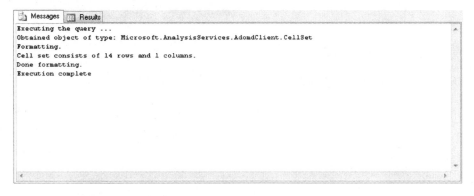

5. Switch to the messages pane and review the number of employees returned.

The results reveal that when logged in as the MdxUser, you may only access those 14 members of the hierarchy associated, directly or indirectly, with your account. These members include ancestors such as Brian S. Welcker, Ken J. Sanchez, and the hierarchy's (All) member, Stephen Y. Jiang himself, and his 10 reports. As other members of the Mdx Users database role log in to the system, the allowed set will be evaluated per their Windows user account to make available a set of members from the hierarchy appropriate for them.

> **Important** If you are proceeding to the exercises in the next section of this chapter, please do not drop the Mdx Users role at this time.

Implementing Cell-Level Restrictions

Cell-level restrictions can be implemented to determine whether a user can read or write the data of a given cell. A logical MDX expression evaluates to *True* or *False*, determining whether a particular permission is granted.

Three cell-level permissions are supported within Analysis Services: Read, Read Contingent, and Read/Write. If the logical expression associated with the Read permission evaluates to *True*, the user is permitted to read the current cell's data. If the logical expression associated with the Read Contingent evaluates to *True* and all cells from which the current cell are derived are readable, the user is permitted to read the current cell's data. If the logical expression associated with the Read/Write permission evaluates to *True*, the user is permitted to read the current cell's data and write data to the current cell if Read/Write access has been granted at the cube level. If a logical expression evaluates to *False*, the user may retrieve the current cell but its data is replaced with an alternate value, typically *#N/A*.

> **Note** For more information on the three cell-level permissions (Read, Read Contingent, and Read/Write), please refer to SQL Server Books Online. If no cell-level permissions are defined, all cells accessible given other restrictions are readable to users.

As with attribute-hierarchies, the *UserName* function can be employed with cell-level security to dynamically control data access. Quite frequently, dynamic cell-level restrictions are implemented in combination with dynamic restrictions on attributes to fine-tune data access for the individual user. The attribute-hierarchy restrictions limit the accessible cube space whereas cell-level restrictions limit the accessible cells within that space.

This combination of dynamic attribute and cell-level security is often employed with parent-child hierarchies to limit a user to the line of members associated with him or her and to then restrict access to sensitive data associated with higher-level members in the hierarchy.

In the following exercise, you implement such a combination of attribute and cell-level security on the Mdx Users database role. A logical expression is implemented to determine the user's Read permissions on the current cell. This expression determines whether the Windows user is associated with the Employees member tied to the cell or is an ancestor of this employee. If this is *True*, the cell is readable. If this is *False*, the cell's data is masked.

> **Important** It is assumed the Mdx Users database role is configured with an allowed set on the Employees parent-child hierarchy, as described in the series of exercises associated with the section titled "Restricting Parent-Child Hierarchies." If the Mdx Users database role is not currently configured in this manner, complete that set of exercises before proceeding.

Design the logical expression

1. Open the MDX Query Editor to the MDX Step-by-Step database using the MdxUser user account, as described earlier in this chapter.

2. In the code pane, enter the following query to reveal the members of the Employees parent-child hierarchy to which you have access:

```
SELECT
    {([Measures].[Reseller Sales Amount])} ON COLUMNS,
    {[Employee].[Employees].Members} ON ROWS
FROM [Step-by-Step]
```

3. Execute the query and review the members returned.

	Reseller Sales Amount
All Employees	$80,450,596.98
Ken J. Sánchez	$80,450,596.98
Brian S. Welcker	$80,450,596.98
Stephen Y. Jiang	$63,320,315.35
David R. Campbell	$3,729,945.35
Garrett R. Vargas	$3,609,447.22
Jillian Carson	$10,065,803.54
José Edvaldo. Saraiva	$5,926,418.36
Linda C. Mitchell	$10,367,007.43
Michael G. Blythe	$9,293,903.01
Pamela O. Ansman-Wolfe	$3,325,102.60
Shu K. Ito	$6,427,005.56
Tete A. Mensa-Annan	$2,312,545.69

The MdxUsers Windows account through which you are accessing the cube is associated with the member Stephen Y. Jiang. Stephen reports to Brian S. Welcker, who in turn reports to Ken J. Sanchez. Stephen is also a supervisor with a number of reporting employees of his own. Cell-level restrictions should limit Stephen to viewing his data and that of his descendants.

4. Alter the query to provide a calculated member returning *True* or *False* depending on whether the current user should have access to a particular cell:

```
WITH
MEMBER [Measures].[Is Accessible] AS
    Count(
        Intersect(
            Ascendants([Employee].[Employees].CurrentMember),
            Filter(
                {[Employee].[Employees].Members},
                [Employee].[Employees].CurrentMember.Properties("User")=
                    VBAMDX!Right(
                        UserName(),
                        VBAMDX!Len(UserName()) -
                            VBAMDX!Instr(UserName(),"\")
                    )
            )
        )
    ) > 0
```

```
SELECT
    {
        ([Measures].[Reseller Sales Amount]),
        ([Measures].[Is Accessible])
        } ON COLUMNS,
    {[Employee].[Employees].Members} ON ROWS
FROM [Step-by-Step]
```

5. Execute the query and observe the Is Accessible value.

	Reseller Sales Amount	Is Accessible
All Employees	$80,450,596.98	False
Ken J. Sánchez	$80,450,596.98	False
Brian S. Welcker	$80,450,596.98	False
Stephen Y. Jiang	$63,320,315.35	True
David R. Campbell	$3,729,945.35	True
Garrett R. Vargas	$3,609,447.22	True
Jillian Carson	$10,065,803.54	True
José Edvaldo. Saraiva	$5,926,418.36	True
Linda C. Mitchell	$10,367,007.43	True
Michael G. Blythe	$9,293,903.01	True
Pamela O. Ansman-Wolfe	$3,325,102.60	True
Shu K. Ito	$6,427,005.56	True
Tete A. Mensa-Annan	$2,312,545.69	True

The *Filter* expression identifies the set of employees with which the current Windows user is immediately associated. This is the same expression used for the allowed set in the previous exercise.

The *Ascendants* expression is used with the Employees member associated with the current cell to identify that member and its ancestors. If the set of the Employees member associated with the current cell and its ancestors overlaps with the Employees member associated with the current Windows user, the condition for read access has been met. In other words, the current Windows user is the employee associated with the current cell or one of its ancestors.

Any overlap between the two sets is revealed through an intersection of the sets and a count of the members in the intersection. If the count is greater than 0, a value of *True* is returned, indicating that the cell is readable.

Implement the cell-level restrictions

1. Open SQL Server Management Studio as yourself, not MdxUser, and connect to your instance of Analysis Services.

2. In Object Explorer, locate the Mdx Users database role.

3. Right-click the Mdx Users role and select Properties to open the Edit Role dialog box.

4. In the Edit Role dialog box, navigate to the Cell Data page.

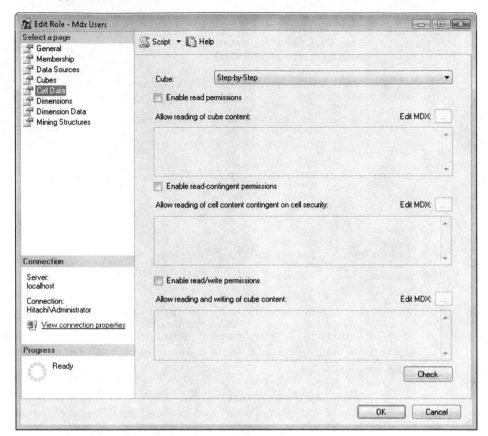

5. Verify that the Cube drop-down list shows the Step-by-Step cube selected.

6. Select the Enable Read Permissions check box.

7. In the text box under the Enable Read Permissions check box, enter the calculated member's expression from the query in step 4 of the preceding exercise. This expression is repeated here for clarity:

```
Count(
    Intersect(
        Ascendants([Employee].[Employees].CurrentMember),
        Filter(
            {[Employee].[Employees].Members},
            [Employee].[Employees].CurrentMember.Properties("User")=
                VBAMDX!Right(
                    UserName(),
                    VBAMDX!Len(UserName()) -
                        VBAMDX!Instr(UserName(),"\")
                )
        )
    )
) > 0
```

8. Click OK to save the changes to the role and close the Edit Role dialog box.

> **Note** Some readers have reported a warning message regarding the loading of a file or assembly with the previous step. This message does not appear to affect the results of the security as described in this exercise.

Test the cell-level restrictions

1. If SQL Server Management Studio is open using the MdxUser user account, close it at this time.

2. Reopen the MDX Query Editor to the MDX Step-by-Step database using the MdxUser user account, as described earlier in this chapter.

3. In the code pane, enter the following query to retrieve all available members of the Employees parent-child hierarchy:

```
SELECT
    {[Measures].[Reseller Sales Amount]} ON COLUMNS,
    {[Employee].[Employees].Members} ON ROWS
FROM [Step-by-Step]
```

4. Execute the query and review the results.

	Reseller Sales Amount
All Employees	#N/A
Ken J. Sánchez	#N/A
Brian S. Welcker	#N/A
Stephen Y. Jiang	$63,320,315.35
David R. Campbell	$3,729,945.35
Garrett R. Vargas	$3,609,447.22
Jillian Carson	$10,065,803.54
José Edvaldo. Saraiva	$5,926,418.36
Linda C. Mitchell	$10,367,007.43
Michael G. Blythe	$9,293,903.01
Pamela O. Ansman-Wolfe	$3,325,102.60
Shu K. Ito	$6,427,005.56
Tete A. Mensa-Annan	$2,312,545.69

As previously described, the MdxUsers Windows account through which you are accessing the cube is associated with the member Stephen Y. Jiang. Attribute-hierarchy restrictions limit your access to those members forming Stephen's lineage within the hierarchy. Cell-level restrictions then dictate that you may read cells associated with Stephen and his reporting employees but not those of employees above him in the Employees hierarchy.

Some Final Thoughts on Dynamic Security

The techniques demonstrated in this chapter do not address all the possible ways dynamic security can be implemented within Analysis Services. Instead, we have focused on a few selective examples from which you can learn the basic techniques. For real-world implementations, you need to tailor your approach to the specifics of your model and your business requirements. The key to successfully implementing dynamic security is to develop your set and logical expressions in a methodical manner with your specific model and requirements in mind and to test your results thoroughly.

Also, please be aware that dynamic security introduces quite a bit of overhead to your user's interactions with a cube. You should avoid using dynamic security when possible, reserving these techniques for those situations where standard approaches are not practical.

 Important Be certain to remove the MdxUsers group and MdxUser account from your local system upon completion of this chapter's exercises.

Chapter 11 Quick Reference

To	Do this
Identify the current user	Use the *UserName* function to return the qualified name of the current user's Windows account. The following query demonstrates the use of this function:

```
WITH
MEMBER [Measures].[Current User] AS
  UserName()
SELECT
  {[Measures].[Current User]} ON COLUMNS
FROM [Step-by-Step]
```

You can use the VBA functions to parse the string value returned by the function, isolating its authority or name parts.

Implement dynamic security on a standard attribute-hierarchy	Consider employing a User dimension and relating this dimension to the attribute-hierarchy to be restricted through a measure group. An allowed set on the User attribute of the User dimension can be defined using the following expression:

```
StrToSet(
  "{([User].[User].[User].[" +
    UserName() + "])}"
  )
```

The attribute to be restricted can then be limited using an allowed or denied set exploiting this relationship. The following expression demonstrates the definition of an allowed set on the Product attribute-hierarchy exploiting the relationship between the Product and User dimensions as defined by the User Product Relationship measure group:

```
Exists(
  {[Product].[Product].[Product].Members},
  {[User].[User].[User].Members},
  'User Product Relationship'
  )
```

Implement dynamic security on a parent-child hierarchy	Consider employing a *User* property with a relationship to the attribute forming the parent-child hierarchy. Filtering the members of the parent-child hierarchy with a *User* property matching the value of the current user defines an allowed set with a single member. Because of the recursive relationship in the parent-child hierarchy, all members in this member's lineage are available. The following expression demonstrates an allowed set defined in this manner:

```
Filter(
  {[Employee].[Employees].Members},
  [Employee].[Employees].CurrentMember.Properties("User")=
    UserName()
  )
```

To	Do this
Implement dynamic cell-level security	Consider employing a logical test based on the current user's identity in relation to the identity associated with an attribute associated with the current cell. The following expression demonstrates one such logical test limiting cell availability to cells associated with a given employee and his or her descendants:

```
Count(
  Intersect(
    Ascendants([Employee].[Employees].CurrentMember),
    Filter(
      {[Employee].[Employees].Members},
      [Employee].[Employees].CurrentMember.Properties("User")=
      UserName()
    )
  )
) > 0
```

Chapter 12
Building Reports

After completing this chapter, you will be able to:

- Assemble an MDX query to retrieve data for a Reporting Services report

- Employ report parameters to limit data returned from Analysis Services

- Apply proper formatting and aggregation to data within a report

Reporting Services, Microsoft's enterprise reporting solution, is distributed as part of the Microsoft SQL Server product suite along with Analysis Services. Because of the close affiliation between these products, many developers are first exposed to the MDX language during the development of reports.

Reporting Services reports provide an effective means of presenting Analysis Services data to business users. Although the tools provided make development of reports against an Analysis Services database as easy as possible, you still need to be aware of some challenges. In this chapter, you explore some of these while developing a simple Reporting Services report.

Getting Started

Figure 12-1 illustrates the report you assemble in this chapter. The report presents the Reseller Sales Amount and Reseller Order Count measures along with a ratio of these two values for various products. A single parameter allows you to select one or more product categories or subcategories, limiting the data presented in the report. All products associated with your parameter selection are displayed in the results whether or not they are empty for the presented measures. At the top of the table, a total row displays aggregate values for the data in the report.

This report is rather simple by design. Reporting Services provides a much wider range of presentation options than those explored here. However, this simple report affords you the opportunity to explore a number of items related to working with an Analysis Services data source in this particular environment. The techniques you learn here can be applied to more complex report development efforts. For more information on the full range of features available to you through Reporting Services, you are strongly encouraged to review *Microsoft SQL Server 2008 Reporting Services Step by Step* by Stacia Misner (Microsoft Press, 2009).

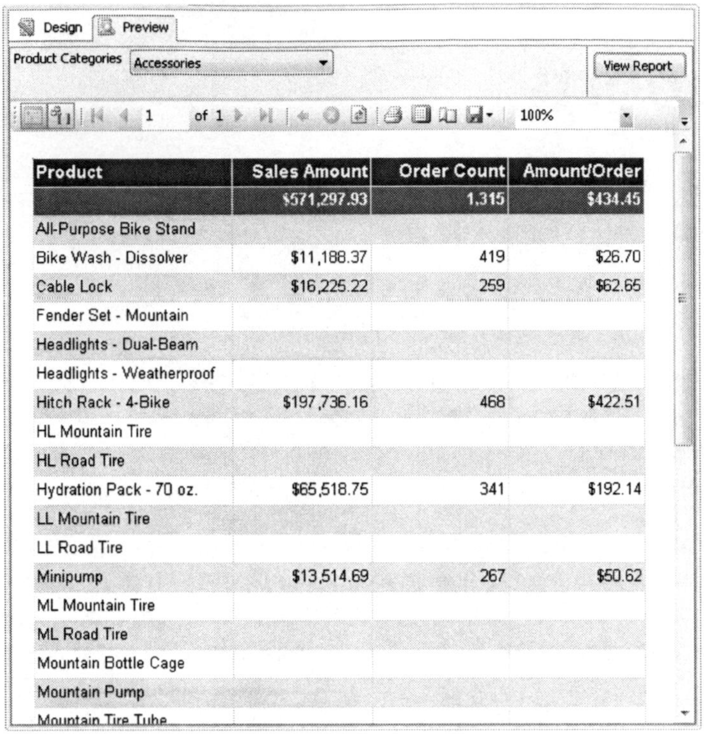

Product	Sales Amount	Order Count	Amount/Order
	$571,297.93	1,315	$434.45
All-Purpose Bike Stand			
Bike Wash - Dissolver	$11,188.37	419	$26.70
Cable Lock	$16,225.22	259	$62.65
Fender Set - Mountain			
Headlights - Dual-Beam			
Headlights - Weatherproof			
Hitch Rack - 4-Bike	$197,736.16	468	$422.51
HL Mountain Tire			
HL Road Tire			
Hydration Pack - 70 oz.	$65,518.75	341	$192.14
LL Mountain Tire			
LL Road Tire			
Minipump	$13,514.69	267	$50.62
ML Mountain Tire			
ML Road Tire			
Mountain Bottle Cage			
Mountain Pump			
Mountain Tire Tube			

FIGURE 12-1 The report assembled in this chapter

Create a new Report Server project

1. On the Microsoft Windows task bar, click the Start button.
2. On the Start Menu, select All Programs and then select Microsoft SQL Server 2008 to expose the SQL Server Business Intelligence Development Studio shortcut.
3. Click the SQL Server Business Intelligence Development Studio shortcut to launch the application.

   These are the same steps for launching Business Intelligence Development Studio (BIDS) presented in Chapter 10, "Enhancing the Cube." If you skipped Chapter 10 and are running BIDS for the first time, you may see a dialog box indicating the application is being configured for first-time use. This process may take a few minutes to complete before the application is fully launched.

   Once fully launched, BIDS presents you with the Start page, as shown in the following screenshot. If you have previously used BIDS or Visual Studio 2008 on your system, the application's layout on your screen may differ from what is shown here.

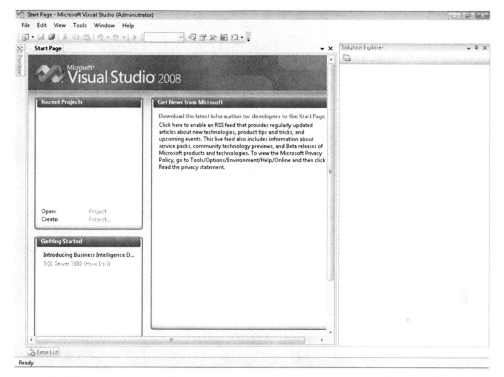

4. From the File menu, select New and then Project to open the New Project dialog box.

5. Verify Business Intelligence Projects is selected under Project Types on the far left side of the dialog box and then select Report Server Project under Templates on the right.

6. Toward the bottom of the dialog box, enter **MdxReports** in the (project) Name text box. Do not modify the solution name. You may use the Browse button to select an alternate location for the project if required.

7. Click OK to create the project.

With the creation of the new project, the BIDS interface is populated as shown in Figure 12-2. Notice that the Solution Explorer window is populated with items appropriate to the Report Server project and the Properties window is now present just below it.

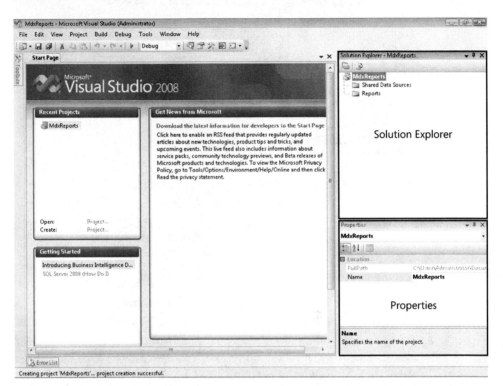

FIGURE 12-2 The BIDS interface following the creation of the MdxReports Report Server project

8. Locate the Reports folder within Solution Explorer. Right-click it, select Add, and then New Item to open the Add New Item dialog box.

9. In the Add New Item dialog box, select Report and give the report the name **MdxReport.rdl**.

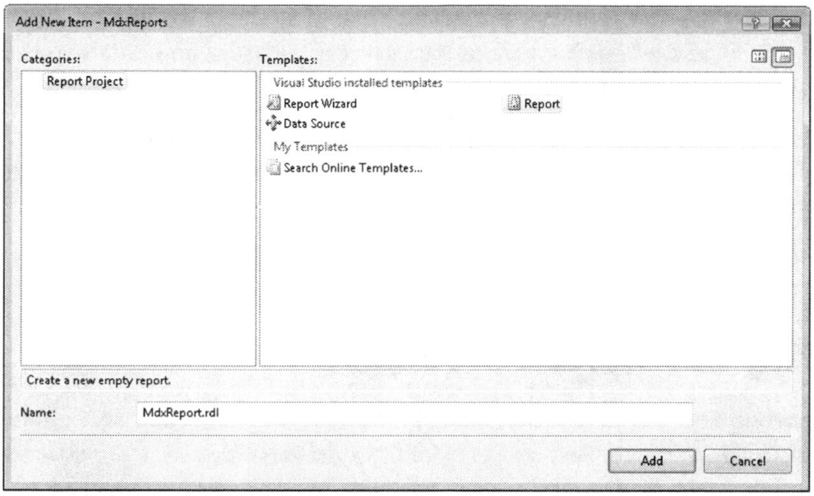

10. Click Add to add the new report to the project. The report is now displayed under the Reports folder in Solution Explorer.

When the MdxReport report is added to your project, the Report Designer window should be displayed as illustrated in Figure 12-3. If it is not, you can open the designer by right-clicking the MdxReport.rdl object in Solution Explorer and selecting View Designer.

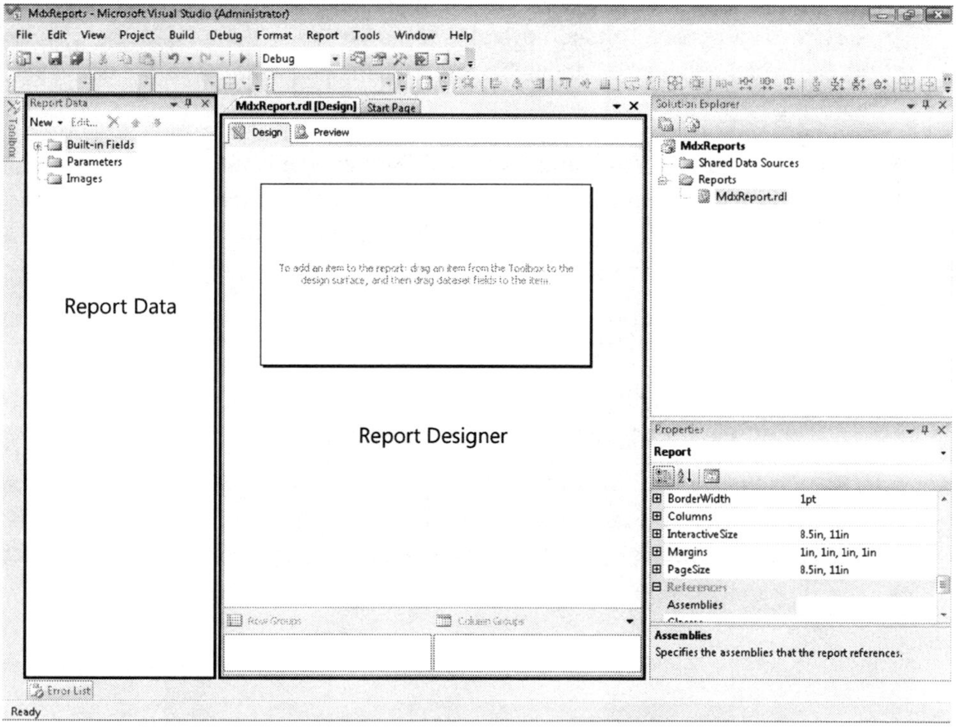

FIGURE 12-3 The Report Designer for the MdxReport report item.

Adding the report to your project also makes available the Report Data window. Within this window, you define various data sources, datasets, and parameters to be used in your report. These items are discussed in later sections of this chapter.

Your report server project is now prepared for the remaining exercises in this chapter. Before going forward, it's a good idea to save the changes you've made to your project.

11. On the File menu, select Save All to save the changes to the project.

Connecting to Analysis Services

In Reporting Services, data sources are items instructing Reporting Services how to connect to a particular resource. Data sources identify a provider (driver), a provider-specific connection string, and how to present the user's identity when connecting to the resource.

A Reporting Services data source may exist independent of a report, enabling its reuse across multiple reports. This is referred to as a *shared data source*.

A Reporting Services data source may also be defined for use within a specific report. This is referred to as an *embedded data source*.

Embedded data sources allow a data source's connection string to be handled as a Reporting Services expression. Although useful in some scenarios, this advantage is typically outweighed by the additional administrative burden of managing report-specific data sources in an enterprise environment.

For the purposes of this chapter, you make use of an embedded data source. This allows us to introduce you to the use of Reporting Services expressions with connection strings in the upcoming sidebar, "The Connection String as an Expression." However, our general recommendation is to use shared data sources whenever possible.

Create an embedded data source

1. On the toolbar of the Report Data window, click New and then click Data Source to open the Data Source Properties dialog box.

2. On the General page of the Data Source Properties dialog box, enter the name **MdxDataSource** for the data source item. Select the Embedded Connection option and then select Microsoft SQL Server Analysis Services from the Type drop-down list.

3. Click the Edit button to open the Connection Properties dialog box.

4. In the Connection Properties dialog box, enter the name of your Analysis Services instance in the Server Name text box. Use the drop-down list in the section labeled Connect To A Database to select the MDX Step-by-Step database.

5. Click OK to close the Connection Properties dialog box. Notice that the Connection String text box of the Data Source Properties dialog box now contains a connection string that reflects your previous entries.

6. In the Data Source Properties dialog box, switch to the Credentials page and verify that the Use Windows Authentication (Integrated Security) option is selected.

7. Click OK to close the Data Source Properties dialog box. Notice that a data source named MdxDataSource is now presented within the Report Data window.

8. Save the changes to your project.

The data source is now defined in your report. If you need to make changes to it, you can right-click the data source item in the Report Data window and select Data Source Properties to return to the dialog boxes described in the preceding steps.

The Connection String as an Expression

The connection string used with the Microsoft SQL Server Analysis Services provider employs a number of parameter-value pairs. The most basic of these are the Data Source and Initial Catalog parameters set through the steps described in the previous exercise, but many others are available. Through these other parameters you can fine-tune the connection established between Reporting Services and Analysis Services.

To view parameters available with the Analysis Services provider, click the Edit button next to the Connection String text box on the General page of the Data Source Properties dialog box. (If you need guidance on launching the Data Source Properties dialog box, please review the preceding exercise.) In the resulting Connection Properties dialog box, click the Advanced button to display a list of advanced properties as shown in the following screenshot. Use the scrollbar on the right-hand side of the list to review the available parameters.

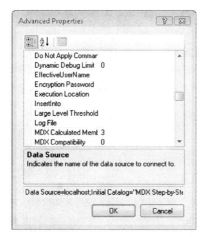

Whether you use an embedded or a shared data source, these parameters are available to you. However, it's only with embedded data sources that you can assemble a connection string using a Reporting Services expression, allowing values for these parameters to be dynamically set.

To access the expression builder for the connection string of an embedded data source, click the function button, labeled *fx*, next to the Connection String text box on the

General Page of the Data Source Properties dialog box. From the expression builder, you can develop fairly sophisticated expressions employing a variety of functions and predefined parameters.

For more information on Reporting Services expressions, review *Microsoft SQL Server 2008 Reporting Services Step by Step* by Stacia Misner (Microsoft Press, 2009). For information on the various parameters available within an Analysis Services connection string, please refer to SQL Server Books Online.

Designing the Dataset

With the connection to a data source defined, Reporting Services can now retrieve data for use in a report. In Reporting Services, the linking of a query to a particular data source and metadata about the data returned is referred to as a dataset.

Regardless of the data source employed, all Reporting Services datasets utilize a standardized structure for making data available within a report. The process of translating an Analysis Services cell set into this standard dataset structure is loosely referred to as *data flattening*.

The mechanics of data flattening are not as important as the constraints this process imposes on your MDX queries. For data flattening to work, MDX queries must employ either one or two axes. The first of these axes, the *COLUMNS* axis, is reserved exclusively for measures. Although not too terribly imposing, these rules do constrain how you write your MDX queries.

Thankfully, these constraints are not much of a concern for most report developers. Analysis Services provides a Query Designer with a rich, graphical (Design mode) interface allowing you to assemble your data set through drag-and-drop functionality. Behind the scenes, the designer takes care of the details of assembling the MDX query in a manner consistent with the previously described constraints. Switching to the designer's Query mode interface, you can further adjust the logic of your query, should you not be able to assemble the dataset you require with drag-and-drop functionality alone. Within the following exercises, you design the primary dataset used within your report using both the Design and Query mode interfaces of the Query Designer.

Assemble a basic MDX query

1. On the toolbar of the Report Data window, click New and then select Dataset to open the Dataset Properties dialog box.

2. Verify that you are on the Dataset Properties dialog box's Query page.

3. Enter **ResellerSalesByProduct** for the dataset's name and select MdxDataSource as the data source.

4. Click the Query Designer button, towards the bottom of the page, to launch the Query Designer.

The Query Designer starts in Design mode, as presented in Figure 12-4. In this mode, the metadata pane, very much like the one in the MDX Query Editor, is presented on the left side of the designer. Just below the metadata pane is the calculated members pane, within which query-scoped calculated members are accessed.

FIGURE 12-4 The Design mode interface of the Query Designer

The filter and data panes are to the right of the metadata pane. Items are dropped from the metadata and calculated members panes into the filter and data panes to assemble the MDX query. The data pane contains those members available to the report through the dataset. The filter pane contains those members used to restrict the data returned.

At the top of the window is the Query Designer toolbar. The toolbar provides access to various commands, as identified in Figure 12-5.

FIGURE 12-5 The Query Designer toolbar

5. At the top of the metadata pane, click the button to the right of Chapter 3 Cube to open the Cube Selection dialog box and select the Step-by-Step cube.

6. Click OK to return to the Cube Designer.

7. From the metadata pane, drag the Reseller Sales Amount measure from the Reseller Sales measure group to the data pane.

8. Now drag the Reseller Order Count measure from the Reseller Orders measure group to the data pane. As you prepare to drop the measure, notice the blue vertical bar that appears to the left or right of the Reseller Sales Amount measure from the previous step. This indicates whether the Reseller Order Count measure precedes or follows the Reseller Sales Amount measure in the dataset. Drop Reseller Order Count to the right of Reseller Sales Amount.

9. From the Product dimension, drag the Product attribute-hierarchy to the data pane. Notice that the data pane only allows you to drop the hierarchy to the left of the measures. As previously mentioned, only measures may appear on the *COLUMNS* axis. By forcing you to drop Products to the left of the measures, the designer enforces this constraint.

The query is now defined using measures and attributes available in the cube. Using the Query Designer, you can also add query-scoped calculated members to the dataset.

Add a calculated member to the MDX query

1. On the Query Designer toolbar, click the Add Calculated Member button to open the Calculated Member Builder dialog box.

2. Enter **Reseller Sales Per Order** for the member's name and verify that the parent hierarchy is set to Measures.

3. In the Expression text box, enter the following MDX expression to calculate the ratio of Reseller Sales Amount to Reseller Order Count. Alternatively, you can assemble this expression by dragging elements from the Step-by-Step cube in the metadata list provided at the bottom of the Calculated Member Builder dialog box.

```
([Measures].[Reseller Sales Amount]) / ([Measures].[Reseller Order Count])
```

4. Click Check to validate the expression and address any issues identified.

5. Click OK to create the calculated member Reseller Sales Per Order. Notice that it is now displayed in the Query Designer's calculated members pane.

6. Drag the query-scoped calculated member Reseller Sales Per Order to the right of Reseller Order Count in the data pane and execute the query.

The basic query is nearly complete. The last thing you need to do before moving on is verify the logic within the query and make one modification per the report requirements.

Modify the MDX query

1. On the Query Designer toolbar, click the Design button to switch to Query mode.

Notice the query assembled by the Query Designer now displayed at the top of the Query mode interface. The query lacks formatting, making it difficult to read. You could adjust its formatting, but any adjustments or modifications would be lost when you return to Design mode. The formatted version of the query is presented here simply for readability:

```
WITH
MEMBER [Measures].[Reseller Sales Per Order] AS
    ([Measures].[Reseller Sales Amount]) / ([Measures].[Reseller Order Count])
SELECT
    NON EMPTY {
        [Measures].[Reseller Order Count],
        [Measures].[Reseller Sales Per Order],
        [Measures].[Reseller Sales Amount]
        } ON COLUMNS,
    NON EMPTY { ( [Product].[Product].[Product].ALLMEMBERS ) }
        DIMENSION PROPERTIES
            MEMBER_CAPTION, MEMBER_UNIQUE_NAME
                ON ROWS
FROM [Step-by-Step]
    CELL PROPERTIES
        VALUE, BACK_COLOR, FORE_COLOR, FORMATTED_VALUE,
        FORMAT_STRING, FONT_NAME, FONT_SIZE, FONT_FLAGS
```

Reviewing the query, you should notice that the Query Designer has placed the *NON EMPTY* keyword along both the *COLUMNS* and *ROWS* axes. This is the default behavior of the Query Designer and, as explained in Chapter 4, "Working with Sets," may not always be appropriate. To remove the *NON EMPTY* keywords from the query, return to Design mode.

2. Click the Design button to switch back to Design mode.

3. On the toolbar, click the Show Empty Cells button.

4. Return to the Query mode interface and verify the removal of the *NON EMPTY* keywords from the query. The updated query reads as follows (shown with formatting for readability):

```
WITH
MEMBER [Measures].[Reseller Sales Per Order] AS
    ([Measures].[Reseller Sales Amount]) / ([Measures].[Reseller Order Count])
SELECT
    {
        [Measures].[Reseller Order Count],
        [Measures].[Reseller Sales Per Order],
        [Measures].[Reseller Sales Amount]
        } ON COLUMNS,
    { ( [Product].[Product].[Product].ALLMEMBERS ) }
        DIMENSION PROPERTIES
            MEMBER_CAPTION, MEMBER_UNIQUE_NAME
                ON ROWS
FROM [Step-by-Step]
    CELL PROPERTIES
        VALUE, BACK_COLOR, FORE_COLOR, FORMATTED_VALUE,
        FORMAT_STRING, FONT_NAME, FONT_SIZE, FONT_FLAGS
```

Reviewing the query further, you can see a few other items of interest. First, attribute-hierarchy members are retrieved from the leaf-level only. Furthermore, the *AllMembers* function is employed to retrieve not only stored but also any calculated members. Depending on your needs, you may wish to modify this logic. To do so, you would need to make the changes directly within the query using the Query mode interface.

> **Important** For the purpose of this and the following exercise, do not modify the query in the Query Designer's Query mode.

Second, you should notice the inclusion of the *CELL PROPERTIES* and *DIMENSION PROPERTIES* keywords in the query. These keywords and their associated properties are discussed in Chapter 3, "Understanding Tuples," and Chapter 5, "Working with Expressions."

Reporting Services presents the properties returned with these keywords as either properties of the fields within the dataset or assigns their values to new dataset fields. You should not remove the default properties requested by the Query Designer, but you may specify additional properties if needed.

5. Switch back to Design mode.

6. Click OK to close the Query Designer and return to the Dataset Properties dialog box. Notice that the query is now presented in the Query text box.

7. Click OK to close the Dataset Properties dialog box. Notice that the ResellerSalesByProduct dataset is now present in the Report Data window with four associated fields.

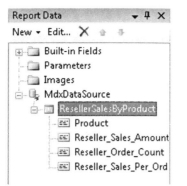

8. Save the changes to your project.

Adding Parameters to the Dataset

A dataset is now assembled with which you can populate your report. Although useful, quite a bit of data is returned making it difficult for users to focus on just those items of interest. Incorporating a parameter provides a means by which the dataset can be restricted based on user input.

Reporting Services provides a number of ways for you to design a parameter for use with a dataset based on an MDX query. The most basic (and reliable) technique is to simply allow the Query Designer to design it for you. This approach makes the incorporation of parameters into your MDX queries very easy but often requires minor adjustments. In the following exercises, you assemble a simple parameter using this technique, explore its implementation, and make some common modifications to tailor the parameter to your needs.

Add a parameter to the MDX query

1. In the Report Data window, right-click the ResellerSalesByProduct dataset and select Dataset Properties to reopen the Dataset Properties dialog box.

2. On the Dataset Properties dialog box's Query page, click Query Designer to start the Query Designer.

3. From the metadata pane, drag the Product Categories user-hierarchy to the filter pane.

   Dragging the Product Categories user-hierarchy to the filter pane creates a filter on the dataset. This filter limits the data retrieved from Analysis Services.

   The filter has several fields; the first four Dimension, Hierarchy, Operator and Filter Expression, define the basic filter. Dropping the user-hierarchy in the filter pane automatically populates the Dimension and Hierarchy fields with the appropriate information. The Operator field identifies how the restriction is applied to the data. By default this is set to Equal, indicating that the Product Categories hierarchy should be limited to the members of the set defined in the Filter Expression field. Other operators are available and discussed in the sidebar "The Filter Operators." For the purposes of this exercise, the Equal operator should be employed.

4. Click the Filter Expression field to open a drop-down list.

5. In the drop-down list, expand the All Products member and then expand the Bikes category member to select the Mountain Bikes subcategory member.

6. Click the OK button to close the drop-down list. Notice that the Filter Expression field now contains an explicit set.

As mentioned earlier, the data retrieved from Analysis Services (per the *Equal* operator) is to be restricted by the set in the Filter Expression field. To see how this is implemented, switch the Query Designer to Query mode.

7. Click the Design command to switch to Query mode. Once again, the formatted version of the query is presented here for readability, with the modified portions used to support the filter operation indicated in bold:

```
WITH
MEMBER [Measures].[Reseller Sales Per Order] AS
    ([Measures].[Reseller Sales Amount]) / ([Measures].[Reseller Order Count])
SELECT
    {
        [Measures].[Reseller Order Count],
        [Measures].[Reseller Sales Per Order],
        [Measures].[Reseller Sales Amount]
        } ON COLUMNS,
    { ([Product].[Product].[Product].ALLMEMBERS ) }
    DIMENSION PROPERTIES
        MEMBER_CAPTION, MEMBER_UNIQUE_NAME
            ON ROWS
FROM (
    SELECT
        ( { [Product].[Product Categories].[Subcategory].&[1] } ) ON COLUMNS
    FROM [Step-by-Step]
    )
WHERE ( [Product].[Product Categories].[Subcategory].&[1] )
    CELL PROPERTIES
        VALUE, BACK_COLOR, FORE_COLOR, FORMATTED_VALUE,
        FORMAT_STRING, FONT_NAME, FONT_SIZE, FONT_FLAGS
```

Notice the filter is implemented as a *SELECT* statement, nested in the *FROM* clause of the outermost *SELECT* statement. This is known as a nested sub-*SELECT* statement and has the impact of restricting the accessible cube space by the set defined along its axes. In this case, that set consists of the Mountain Bikes Subcategory member, identified by its member key.

Notice that the filter is also implemented in the *WHERE* clause of the outer *SELECT* statement. In many statements this is redundant and simply an artifact of how the Query Designer auto-generates its MDX statements. However, some scenarios require this outermost restriction. As a recommended best practice, we suggest you leave the filter as-is to avoid unforeseen consequences.

Leaving the filter in this form limits the data to a hard-coded set consisting of Mountain Bikes. Instead of hard-coding this specific constraint, it might be more interesting to employ a parameter, allowing users to determine how the data in the report is filtered.

8. Switch back to Design mode.

9. Locate the Parameter field to the far right of the Product Categories filter. Depending on your screen resolution, you may need to scroll the filter pane to the right using the scroll-bar located towards the bottom of the pane.

10. Select the Parameter check box.

11. To see the effect of setting the filter as a parameter, switch back to Query mode. The formatted query is as follows, with the altered portions indicated in bold:

```
WITH
MEMBER [Measures].[Reseller Sales Per Order] AS
    ([Measures].[Reseller Sales Amount]) / ([Measures].[Reseller Order Count])
SELECT
    {
        [Measures].[Reseller Order Count],
        [Measures].[Reseller Sales Per Order],
        [Measures].[Reseller Sales Amount]
        } ON COLUMNS,
    { ([Product].[Product].[Product].ALLMEMBERS ) }
    DIMENSION PROPERTIES
        MEMBER_CAPTION, MEMBER_UNIQUE_NAME
            ON ROWS
FROM (
    SELECT
        ( STRTOSET(@ProductProductCategories, CONSTRAINED) ) ON COLUMNS
    FROM [Step-by-Step]
    )
WHERE
    ( IIF(
        STRTOSET(@ProductProductCategories, CONSTRAINED).Count = 1,
```

```
      STRTOSET(@ProductProductCategories, CONSTRAINED),
      [Product].[Product Categories].currentmember
           )
      )
CELL PROPERTIES
      VALUE, BACK_COLOR, FORE_COLOR, FORMATTED_VALUE,
      FORMAT_STRING, FONT_NAME, FONT_SIZE, FONT_FLAGS
```

By selecting the check box in the Parameter field, the hard-coded set containing the Mountain Bikes member is now gone. In its place, the parameter *@ProductProductCategories* is now employed. The *@ProductProductCategories* parameter is a placeholder for a string Reporting Services submits with the query. To interpret the string as a set, the MDX function *StrToSet* is employed, as explained in the sidebar "The String Conversion Functions."

Reporting Services assembles the *WHERE* clause differently for single-member and multi-member sets. Because the number of members in the set is not known until run time, the *WHERE* clause now employs the *IIF* function to determine how the constraint in this portion of the query is enforced. Again, although you might find your query doesn't require this potentially redundant logic in the *WHERE* clause, we strongly recommend leaving it alone to avoid unexpected consequences.

12. Switch back to Design mode and click OK to close the Query Designer.

13. Click OK to close the Dataset Properties dialog box.

14. Save the changes to your project.

A parameter has now been incorporated into your query with just a few short steps. Using Report Designer capabilities you can modify the parameter, tailoring it to the needs of your report.

Modify the parameter

1. Return to the Report Data window and expand the Parameters folder. Notice that a parameter named *@ProductProductCategories* is now present following the changes in the last exercise.

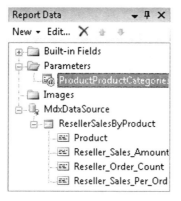

2. Right-click the @*ProductProductCategories* parameter and select Parameter Properties to open the Report Parameter Properties dialog box.

The Report Parameter Properties dialog box displays the default configuration of the parameter you established in the last exercise. Through this dialog box you can change many of the parameter's properties, although for this exercise you want to leave most of them as-is.

The one property you need to change is the parameter's default value. It is currently set to *[Product].[Product Categories].[Subcategory].&[1]*, the key value for the Product Categories Mountain Bikes member by which you originally filtered your data.

3. On the Report Parameter Properties dialog box, move to the Default Values page.

4. Select the No Default Value option to remove the default.

Before moving on, it is important to take a look at how the parameter's set of available values is being populated. This is exposed through the Available Values page.

5. Move to the Available Values page and notice option selections and the value in the Dataset drop-down list.

The *@ProductProductCategories* parameter is currently configured to obtain available values from a query. According to the Dataset drop-down list, that query is part of the ProductProductCategories dataset.

In the previous steps you did not explicitly define a dataset named ProductProductCategories, but when the filter on the Product Categories user-hierarchy was converted to a parameter, this dataset was automatically created. By default, the ProductProductCategories dataset is defined as a hidden dataset, making it not visible in the Report Data window. To see this dataset, you must reconfigure the Report Data window to display hidden datasets.

6. Click OK to close the Report Parameter Properties dialog box and return to the Report Data window.

7. Right-click the background of the Report Data window and select Show All Hidden Datasets from the short-cut menu. The ProductProductCategories dataset is now visible.

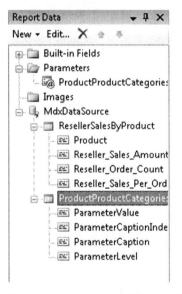

8. To review the ProductProductCategories dataset, right-click it and select Dataset Properties to open the Dataset Properties dialog box.

9. Click the Query Designer button and notice that the designer opens in Query mode. The dataset's query, presented here, is formatted for readability:

```
WITH
MEMBER [Measures].[ParameterCaption] AS
    [Product].[Product Categories].CURRENTMEMBER.MEMBER_CAPTION
MEMBER [Measures].[ParameterValue] AS
    [Product].[Product Categories].CURRENTMEMBER.UNIQUENAME
MEMBER [Measures].[ParameterLevel] AS
    [Product].[Product Categories].CURRENTMEMBER.LEVEL.ORDINAL
```

```
SELECT
    {
        [Measures].[ParameterCaption],
        [Measures].[ParameterValue],
        [Measures].[ParameterLevel]
    } ON COLUMNS,
    [Product].[Product Categories].ALLMEMBERS ON ROWS
FROM [Step-by-Step]
```

The query associated with this dataset is fairly straightforward. The members of the user-hierarchy available for selection in the parameter are presented along the *ROWS* axis. In keeping with the rules for data flattening, several properties of the Product Categories members are made available as calculated members associated with the Measures dimension and presented along the *COLUMNS* axis.

For the purpose of this exercise, you need to limit the parameter to those Product Categories members from the Subcategory level and above. This is easily done by modifying the set along the query's *ROWS* axis.

10. Modify the set along the *ROWS* axis to limit the parameter to members of the Subcategory level and above:

```
WITH
MEMBER [Measures].[ParameterCaption] AS
    [Product].[Product Categories].CURRENTMEMBER.MEMBER_CAPTION
MEMBER [Measures].[ParameterValue] AS
    [Product].[Product Categories].CURRENTMEMBER.UNIQUENAME
MEMBER [Measures].[ParameterLevel] AS
    [Product].[Product Categories].CURRENTMEMBER.LEVEL.ORDINAL
SELECT
    {
        [Measures].[ParameterCaption],
        [Measures].[ParameterValue],
        [Measures].[ParameterLevel]
    } ON COLUMNS,
    {
        Descendants(
            [Product].[Product Categories].[All Products],
            [Product].[Product Categories].[Subcategory],
            SELF_AND_BEFORE
            )
    } ON ROWS
FROM [Step-by-Step]
```

11. Execute the query and note the lack of members below the Subcategory level.

> **Important** The parameter as it exists now supports the selection of multiple members. With multi-valued parameters, Reporting Services introduces a *Select All* option at the top of the parameter list. When selected by a user, every member available in the parameter's data set is selected and submitted with the query through the parameter. If the parameter's dataset includes an (All) member (for example, All Products, this member becomes yet another member in the set when the *Select All* option is selected). Carefully consider the inclusion of (All) members in your parameters' datasets, especially with multi-valued parameters, to ensure that you are providing users with appropriate options.

12. Click OK to close the Query Designer.

13. Click OK to close the Dataset Properties dialog box.

14. Save the changes to your project.

The Filter Operators

The Query Designer's Design mode filter pane supports the use of a number of operators with MDX queries, identified in Table 12-1.

TABLE 12-1 Filter Operators Supported by the Query Designer

Name	Description
Equal	Limits the data to those values associated with a given set.
Not Equal	Limits the data to those values not associated with a given set.

TABLE 12-1 Filter Operators Supported by the Query Designer

Name	Description
In	Limits the data to those values associated with a given named set. The In operator does not support parameterization.
Not In	Limits the data to those values not associated with a given named set. The Not In operator does not support parameterization.
Contains	Limits the data to those values associated with a set whose members' captions contain a given string.
Begins With	Limits the data to those values associated with a set whose members' captions start with a given string.
Range (Inclusive)	Limits the data to those values associated with a set defined using a range operator.
Range (Exclusive)	Limits the data to those values associated with a set defined using a range operator but excluding the starting and ending members in that range.
MDX	Limits the data to those values associated with a set defined using set-building MDX expression. The MDX operator does not support parameterization.

Each of these operators is used to define a set which then constrains the cube space accessible by the query, similar to what was observed in the previous exercise. As you noticed in the last exercise, the operator is implemented through set logic. Some of this logic, such as the logic associated with the Equal operator, can easily be adjusted to support parameters. The logic associated with other operators, such as the In operator, does not support parameters.

The String Conversion Functions

Analysis Services converts string representations to internally recognized objects using a series of *string-to* functions, including *StrToSet*, *StrToMember*, and *StrToTuple*:

```
StrToSet( String [, CONSTRAINED] )
StrToMember( String [, CONSTRAINED] )
StrToTuple( String [, CONSTRAINED] )
```

Each of these functions accepts a string and attempts to convert it into a set, member, or tuple, depending on the function employed. The string must adhere to the basic form of the item to which it is being converted, whereas the optional *CONSTRAINED* flag requires the strings to adhere to even stricter criteria.

With the *StrToTuple* and *StrToMember* functions, the *CONSTRAINED* flag requires explicit member references to be employed, as opposed to an MDX expression resolving to a tuple or member, respectively. With the *StrToSet* function, the string must not only adhere to this rule but also be enclosed in braces if the *CONSTRAINED* flag is employed. The *CONSTRAINED* flag minimizes the risk of an injection-type attack when a string is introduced into a query.

Presenting the Data in the Report

With the primary dataset assembled, you can now turn your attention to presenting data in the report. Reporting Services makes available a number of report items for just this purpose, including tables, matrices, charts, and gauges. In this report, you use one of the more basic and most frequently employed report items, the table.

The table is ideal for the presentation of detailed data. Fields from a dataset are tied to the columns of the table with individual values presented along the table rows. Groups defined within the table allow these records to be aggregated, supporting the interpretation of what can be large volumes of data.

The presentation and aggregation of data originating from Analysis Services in a Reporting Services table presents several challenges. With careful implementation, these challenges can be effectively addressed, as demonstrated in the following exercises.

Assemble the table

1. From the View menu, select Toolbox. Click the pin icon in the toolbox's upper-right corner to lock it into position.

The toolbox provides access to a number of report items that you can incorporate into your report. Pinning it in place locks the toolbox into the position previously held by the Report Data window. To toggle between the toolbox and the Report Data window, use the tab at the bottom of the toolbox.

2. On the toolbox, locate the Table item and drag it onto the upper-left corner of the report presented in the center of your screen. You can reposition the table on the report if needed.

Notice the table is divided into two rows. The row labeled *Header* is the header row and is used to present the names of the various fields in the table. The row labeled *Data* is the data row. Fields from the dataset are placed on the data row, allowing individual values in the dataset to populate the table.

3. Using the tab at the bottom of the toolbox, switch to the Report Data window.

4. Locate the ResellerSalesByProduct dataset and make sure it is expanded to expose its four fields.

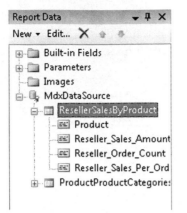

5. Drag the Product field from the ResellerSalesByProduct dataset to the leftmost column of the table's data row.

Product	Header	
[Product]	Data	

Notice that the header row is auto-populated with the name of the field you deposited in the data row. Dragging other fields to the remaining columns of the table produces a similar effect.

6. Drag the Reseller_Sales_Amount and Reseller_Order_Count fields from the dataset to the data row of the second and third columns of the table, respectively.

   To add the Reseller_Sales_Per_Order field to the table, a fourth column is required. You can add this manually or allow the Report Designer to handle this for you.

7. Drag (but don't drop) the Reseller_Sales_Per_Order field just over and to the right of the data row's last column. Observe how the side of the cell becomes highlighted in blue. Drop the field, allowing the Report Designer to add the field to an automatically created fourth column.

Product	Reseller Sales	Reseller Order	Reseller Sales
[Product]	[Reseller_Sales	[Reseller_Order	[Reseller_Sales

You have now established the basic table for your report. Switching to the designer's Preview mode allows you to see the report fully rendered with data.

8. Click the Preview tab along the top of the Report Designer to switch to Preview mode.

9. On the toolbar presented at the top of the report, use the Product Categories drop-down list to select the Accessories category.

10. Click the View Report button on the right-hand side of the toolbar and observe the report rendered below it.

The rendered report displays the products associated with the selected Accessories category along with three measures. From an aesthetic standpoint, the report is a little lacking. We'll address this after adding a total to the table.

11. Click the Design tab along the top of the Report Designer to switch the report back to Design mode.

12. Save the changes to the report.

Add report totals

1. In Design mode, notice the Row Groups pane towards the bottom of the Report Designer.

The Row Groups pane displays groups of data within the table. The subject of groups in Reporting Services tables and matrices is an important topic and one we cannot fully address in the scope of this book. That said, the Report Designer automatically assigns the detail data in the table to a group named (Details) and this provides the means by which you can add a total.

2. Click the drop-down arrow to the right of the (Details) group in the Row Groups pane.

3. Select Add Total and then Before from the drop-down list to add a total to the top of the table. Notice that a new row is added to the table between the header and data rows.

> **Note** If the report appears unchanged following the previous modifications, try clicking the Refresh button located in the toolbar above the report. This button is just to the left of the Print button.

This new row represents a total for the detail data in the report. By default, this total is calculated by Reporting Services using a summation function. This is not always appropriate with semi-additive and non-additive measures such as Reseller Order Count and Reseller Sales Per Order, presented in the table's third and fourth columns.

4. Preview the report by switching the report to Preview mode, selecting the Accessories category for the parameter value, and then clicking View Report. Review the totals for the various measures.

From past exercises, you may recognize these values as incorrect. The Reseller Order Count column is based on the Reseller Order Count measure, which employs a distinct count aggregate function. The Reseller Sales Per Order column is based on the Reseller Sales Per Order calculated member, which is a ratio. Simply summing these detail level values across the dataset within the report produces invalid totals.

Instead of relying on Reporting Services to perform aggregation, you should allow Analysis Services to handle this for you. To turn control of the aggregation back to Analysis Services, use the Reporting Services *Aggregate* function in place of the Reporting Services *Sum* function.

5. Return to Design mode.

6. Right-click the third cell of the totals row, the cell just below the header value *Reseller Order Count*, and select Expression to open the Expression dialog box.

7. Alter the expression to employ the *Aggregate* function as follows:

```
=Aggregate(Fields!Reseller_Order_Count.Value)
```

8. Click OK to close the Expression dialog box.

9. Repeat steps 6 through 8 for the fourth cell of the totals row, the cell just below the header value *Reseller Sales Per Order*, replacing the Reporting Services *Sum* function with *Aggregate*:

```
=Aggregate(Fields!Reseller_Sales_Per_Order.Value)
```

10. Preview the report and observe the change in the totals. Again, select the Accessories category for the parameter value before rendering the report.

The totals for the Reseller Order Count and Reseller Sales Per Order columns now employ the Reporting Services *Aggregate* function. The effect of using this function is that the Product hierarchy's (All) member, All Products, is added to the set along the *ROWS* axis of the dataset's underlying query. In other words, Reporting Services defers the calculation of the total to Analysis Services to better ensure that it is properly calculated.

11. Return to Design mode and save the changes to the report.

Format the table

1. In Design mode, click on any cell of the table and notice the gray bars presented on the top and left of the table.

2. Select the gray bar to the left of the header row. Notice the header row is now highlighted.

3. From the designer's toolbar, click the bold button. If you have worked with other Microsoft Office products you will immediately recognize this button.

4. Select the header row cell of the second column. This cell contains the text Reseller Sales Amount. Replace this text with **Sales Amount**.

5. Repeat this for the next two cells, replacing Reseller Order Count with **Order Count** and Reseller Sales Per Order with **Amount/Order**.

6. Click the gray bar above each of these cells and click the align-right button from the designer's toolbar. Again, if you are familiar with the Microsoft Office products, you will recognize this button. Depending on the resolution of your screen, the button may be in a drop-down list to the right of the bold button.

7. Switch to Preview mode and review the report.

Product	Sales Amount	Order Count	Amount/Order
	571297.9278	1315	434.447093384 03
All-Purpose Bike Stand			
Bike Wash - Dissolver	11188.3725	419	26.7025596658 711
Cable Lock	16225.22	259	62.6456370656 371
Fender Set - Mountain			
Headlights - Dual-Beam			
Headlights - Weatherproof			

The layout of the table is a little better now. The text in the headers has been pared down a bit and bolded to stand out from the detail data, and all but the first column have been right-justified, which is traditional with numeric values.

> **Note** The column names have been shortened to prevent text wrapping in the header. If you are still experiencing this, you may expand the individual columns a bit as you would in Microsoft Office Excel. This is purely a cosmetic issue and has no impact on future steps.

One thing you will notice about the numeric values in the data rows is that they are not formatted. For each cell accessed, Analysis Services, per the instruction in the MDX query, returns the *VALUE* and *FORMATTED_VALUE* properties. Each of these cell properties has been mapped by Reporting Services to the dataset fields' *Value* and *FormattedValue* properties, respectively. By default, each field's *Value* property is presented in the table, but you can change this to use *FormattedValue*.

8. Switch the report to Design mode.

9. Right-click the data row cell for the second column, the bottommost cell under the Reseller Sales heading. Select Expression from the shortcut menu to open the Expression dialog box.

10. In the Expression dialog box, replace the *Value* property of the field with the *FormattedValue* property so that the expression reads as follows:

```
=Fields!Reseller_Sales_Amount.FormattedValue
```

11. Click OK to close the Expression dialog box.

12. Repeat steps 9 through 11 for the third and fourth cells of the data row, using the *FormattedValue* property in place of the *Value* property.

13. Switch to the Preview mode and review the change in the data rows. As before, be sure to select the Accessories category for the value of your parameter before rendering the report.

The numeric values for the data rows under Sales Amount and Order Count now reflect formatting consistent with the formatting instructions in Analysis Services. The data rows for the last field, Amount/Order, are unchanged because they are retrieved through a query-scoped calculated member with which *FORMAT_STRING* property has not been set. To format this value, you could modify the MDX query, but you could just as easily use Reporting Service's *Format* function to accomplish the same goal.

14. Switch the report to Design mode.

15. Right-click the data row cell of the table's fourth column and select Expression to open the Expression dialog box as before.

16. Alter the expression to format the value using the *Format* function as follows:

```
=Format(Fields!Reseller_Sales_Per_Order.Value, "Currency")
```

17. Click OK to close the Expression dialog box.

18. Switch the report to Preview mode, select the Accessories category for the parameter value, and click View Report. Observe the change to the format of the data row values in the last column.

Product	Sales Amount	Order Count	Amount/Order
	571297.9278	1315	434.447093384 03
All-Purpose Bike Stand			
Bike Wash - Dissolver	$11,188.37	419	$26.70
Cable Lock	$16,225.22	259	$62.65
Fender Set - Mountain			
Headlights - Dual-Beam			
Headlights - Weatherproof			
Hitch Rack - 4	$107,736.16	468	$422.51

Design | Preview

Product Categories: Accessories — View Report

1 of 1

The detail data in the last column now employs appropriate formatting. This formatting is applied by Reporting Services and not Analysis Services but accomplishes the same goal. This same approach must be taken with the values in the totals row.

19. Switch the report to Design mode.

20. Use the *Format* function to format the values in each of the totals cells. For the total under Sales Amount and Amount/Order use a format of *Currency*. For the total under Order Count, use a format of ###,###.

> **Note** To learn more about the formats supported by the Reporting Services *Format* function, please refer to SQL Server Books Online.

21. Switch the report to Preview mode and observe the change in the format of the totals.

22. Switch back to Design mode and save the changes to the report.

The Finishing Touches

The look and feel of your report is critical for drawing users in and guiding them through the data. To put it nicely, the report developed in this chapter as it stands right now is not a model for what your reports should look like if you want to win over your users. Because the focus of this chapter is working with MDX and Analysis Services data in Reporting Services, the step-by-step details of how the current report can be transformed into the report shown previously in Figure 12-1 are well out of scope. However, we will share the general changes required.

To make your report look like the one presented in Figure 12-1, adjust the width of the first column to 1.75 inches and the width of each of the three other columns to 1.2 inches. Modify the font style for the header row to Arial 11pt with a bold typeface; apply a font color of white and a background color of #4e0000 (this is the hexadecimal value for the Red, Blue, and Green components of the background color). Modify the font style for the totals row to Arial 10pt with a bold typeface; apply a font color of white and a background color of #b6122d.

The final step is to add the alternating background color to the data row. Unlike the background color for the header and total rows, which use a fixed color, the background color for the data row uses an expression to alternate the color on odd rows. The following expression is used to achieve this effect:

```
=Iif(RowNumber("ResellerSalesByProduct") Mod 2 = 1, "Gainsboro", "White")
```

This expression is applied to the *BackgroundColor* property of the table row. If the current row number is an odd number, the background color is set to *Gainsboro* (a light gray); otherwise, the background color is set to *White*.

Once again, for more complete coverage of Reporting Services, you are encouraged to review *Microsoft SQL Server 2008 Reporting Services Step by Step* by Stacia Misner (Microsoft Press, 2009).

Chapter 12 Quick Reference

To	Do this
Start a Reporting Services project	Start the Business Intelligence Development Studio application. On the File menu, select New and then select Project. In the New Project dialog box, select Business Intelligence Projects under Project types and then select Report Server Project under Templates. Enter an appropriate name and location for the project and click OK to create the project.
Add a report to your project	In Solution Explorer, right-click the Reports folder and select Add and then select New Item. In the Add New Item dialog box, select the Report item and enter an appropriate name for it, preserving the .rdl extension. Click Add to add the report to your project.
Create an embedded data source connected to Analysis Services	In the Report Data window, click New and then click Data Source. On the General Page of the Data Source Properties dialog box, enter an appropriate name for the data source and select the Embedded Data Source option. In the Type drop-down list, select Microsoft SQL Server Analysis Services. Click the Edit button, enter the name of the Analysis Services instance, and select the appropriate database from the drop-down list. Click OK to return to the Data Source Properties dialog box. Verify that Use Windows Authentication is selected on the Credentials page and click OK to create the data source.
Define a dataset against a cube	In the Report Data window, click New and then click Dataset. On the Query page of the Dataset Properties dialog box, enter a name for the dataset and select the appropriate data source. Click the Query Designer button to start the Query Designer. Above the metadata pane, select the appropriate cube. Drag measures and attributes from the metadata pane to the detail and filter panes to define the query. Click OK to close the Query Designer and click OK again to add the dataset to your project.
Add a query-scoped calculated member to a dataset	In the Query Designer, click the Add Calculated Member button. In the Calculated Member Builder dialog box, enter a name for the calculated member and set its parent hierarchy. Enter an expression for the calculated member and click OK to add the member to the query. Drag the newly created calculated member from the calculated member pane to the data pane to make it available in the dataset.

To	Do this
Add a parameter to a dataset	In the Query Designer, add a filter to your query employing either the Equals, Not Equals, Contains, Begins With, Range (Inclusive), or Range (Exclusive) operators. Select the Parameter check box for the filter.
Present formatted data in a report	Use the field's *FormattedValue* property instead of its default *Value* property. The *FormattedValue* property is mapped to the *FORMATTED_VALUE* cell property. If a format string has not been assigned, the *FormattedValue* property will be the same as the *Value* property. In this situation, use the Reporting Services *Format* function to format the value within the report.
Aggregate data using Analysis Services aggregation logic	Use the Reporting Services *Aggregate* function instead of the default *Sum* function to force an (All) member into the MDX query, allowing Analysis Services to handle aggregations.

Index

Symbols and Numbers

Bryan C. Smith

Bryan is a manager of specialized services with Hitachi Consulting's Microsoft Database Technologies team. As a member of this team, he designs and implements business intelligence solutions for clients in a variety of industries using the products in the Microsoft SQL Server suite. Bryan has degrees from Texas A&M and Duke Universities, holds a number of Microsoft certifications, and has more than 10 years of experience developing solutions supporting data analysis. Bryan lives in the Dallas area with his (amazing) wife, Haruka, and their two (equally amazing) children, Aki and Umi.

C. Ryan Clay

C. Ryan Clay is a senior architect with Hitachi Consulting, specializing in business intelligence, data management, portal and collaboration, and SAP integration/interoperability solutions employing Microsoft technologies. Ryan has implemented Microsoft Business Intelligence solutions using Analysis Services and MDX for a variety of Fortune 500 clients in the retail, construction, finance, and consumer goods industries. Ryan holds degrees in computer science as well as a number of Microsoft certifications and is active in the Microsoft community through speaking engagements and presentations at regional and national events. He lives in the Dallas area with his wife and daughter.

Hitachi Consulting

As the global consulting company of Hitachi Ltd. (NYSE: HIT), Hitachi Consulting is a recognized leader in delivering proven business and IT solutions to Global 2000 companies across many industries. We leverage decades of business process, vertical industry, and leading-edge technology experience to understand each company's unique business needs. From business strategy development through application deployment, our consultants are committed to helping clients quickly realize measurable business value and achieve sustainable return on investment. For more information, visit *www.hitachiconsulting.com*. Hitachi Consulting – Inspiring your next success®.

What do you think of this book?

We want to hear from you!

Do you have a few minutes to participate in a brief online survey?

Microsoft is interested in hearing your feedback so we can continually improve our books and learning resources for you.

To participate in our survey, please visit:

www.microsoft.com/learning/booksurvey/

...and enter this book's ISBN-10 or ISBN-13 number (located above barcode on back cover*). As a thank-you to survey participants in the United States and Canada, each month we'll randomly select five respondents to win one of five $100 gift certificates from a leading online merchant. At the conclusion of the survey, you can enter the drawing by providing your e-mail address, which will be used for prize notification only.

Thanks in advance for your input. Your opinion counts!

* Where to find the ISBN on back cover

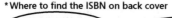
ISBN-13: 000-0-0000-0000-0
ISBN-10: 0-0000-0000-0

0 000000 000000   00000

Example only. Each book has unique ISBN.